THE WISDOM *of*
the LOTUS SUTRA

THE WISDOM OF THE

LOTUS SUTRA

A DISCUSSION

VOLUME v

EXAMINING CHAPTERS 17–22:

DISTINCTIONS IN BENEFITS · THE BENEFITS
OF RESPONDING WITH JOY · BENEFITS OF THE TEACHER OF
THE LAW · THE BODHISATTVA NEVER DISPARAGING
SUPERNATURAL POWERS OF THE THUS COME ONE
ENTRUSTMENT

Daisaku Ikeda
Katsuji Saito · Takanori Endo · Haruo Suda

World Tribune
Press

Published by
World Tribune Press
606 Wilshire Blvd.
Santa Monica, CA 90401

ISBN 978-0-915678-73-0

Design by Gopa & Ted2, Inc.
Cover image © Photodisc

10 9 8 7 6 5

Library of Congress Cataloging-in-Publication Data

The Wisdom of the Lotus Sutra : a discussion : /
Daisaku Ikeda. . . [et al].
    p. cm.
    Includes index.
    ISBN: 0-915678-70-5 (v. 2 : alk.paper)
    1. Tripitaka. Sutrapitaka.
Saddharmapundarikasutra — Criticism.
interpretation, etc. I. Ikeda, Daisaku.

BQ2057.W57 2000
294.3'85—dc21
                        00-011670

Table of Contents

Editor's Note

This book comprises a series of discussions among SGI President Daisaku Ikeda, Soka Gakkai Study Department Chief Katsuji Saito and vice chiefs Takanori Endo and Haruo Suda. It was first serialized in English starting with the April 1995 issue of *Seikyo Times* (now *Living Buddhism*).

The following abbreviations appear in some citations:

+ GZ refers to *Nichiren Daishonin gosho zenshu* [The Complete Writings of Nichiren Daishonin; the Japanese-language compilation of letters, treatises, essays and oral teachings of Nichiren Daishonin] (Tokyo: Soka Gakkai, 1952).

+ LSOC refers to *The Lotus Sutra and Its Opening and Closing Sutras*, translated by Burton Watson (Tokyo: Soka Gakkai, 2009).

+ OTT refers to *The Record of the Orally Transmitted Teachings*, translated by Burton Watson (Tokyo: Soka Gakkai, 2004).

+ WND refers to *The Writings of Nichiren Daishonin*, volume 1 [WND-1] (Tokyo: Soka Gakkai, 1999) and volume 2 [WND-2] (Tokyo: Soka Gakkai, 2006).

PART I

"Distinctions in Benefits" Chapter

1 Those Who Spread the Mystic Law Accumulate Great Life Force

The Buddha preaches a rarely encountered Law,
one never heard from times past.
The world-honored one possesses great powers
and his life span cannot be measured.
The countless sons of the Buddha,
hearing the world-honored one make distinctions
and describe the benefits of the Law they will gain,
find their whole bodies filled with joy. (LSOC, 276)

Ikeda: We now come to three chapters that all contain the word *benefit* in their titles: "Distinctions in Benefits," the seventeenth; "The Benefits of Responding with Joy," the eighteenth; and "Benefits of the Teacher of the Law," the nineteenth. Each provides an explanation of the benefit of the Mystic Law. In particular, they describe the great benefit of spreading that Law, and the change and growth that one devoted to working for kosen-rufu experiences. In that sense, it is SGI members who are truly living the teachings of these chapters. Let us proceed with that conviction.

To start with, what is the meaning of *benefit*?

Suda: Basically, the term means "gain." It also implies the Buddhist concept of the beneficial power to produce good fortune and merit. Beneficial power is action that creates happiness and good, while good fortune and merit are the effects produced by this power. Positive action, or making good causes, has intrinsic virtue that brings good fortune and merit. In some cases, the term *benefit* is used to refer to this innate virtue of positive action.

WE ACCUMULATE BENEFIT THROUGH ACTION

Ikeda: That's a pretty complicated explanation! The bottom line is, positive action has inherent benefit. Benefit is definitely not something that comes to us from the outside; rather, it wells forth from within our lives, manifested through our own actions. It gushes out like water rising from a spring. That's what benefit is.

Endo: In other words, it has nothing to do with relying on some external power to grant one's wishes, like awaiting a windfall.

Ikeda: Nichiren Daishonin says that benefit arises through purifying the six sense organs. The purification of the senses—sight, sound, smell, taste and touch as well as the mind—is itself the purification of one's life. In other words, *benefit* means doing our human revolution and transforming our destiny.

The section of *The Record of the Orally Transmitted Teachings* dealing with the "Benefits of the Teacher of the Law" chapter says, "The word 'benefits' (*kudoku*) means the reward that is represented by the purification of the six sense organs. . . . Thus the word *kudoku* means to attain Buddhahood in one's present form. It also means the purification of the six sense organs" (OTT, 147–48).

Attaining Buddhahood, that is to say, doing one's human revolution, is the supreme benefit. All the so-called worldly benefits manifest as concrete proof of happiness to the extent that we have purified our lives; this is in accord with the principle of the oneness of life and environment.

Saito: So, elevating our state of life is the foundation of all benefit.

Ikeda: Yes. When we change, we can, as Nichiren says, "gather fortune from ten thousand miles away" (WND-1, 1137).

President Toda often said, "Supposing the benefit I have received is comparable in size to this auditorium, then what you call benefit is only about the size of the tip of your little finger." Mr. Toda received enormous benefit as the result of his actions for the sake of the Law, enduring great persecution alongside his mentor, Tsunesaburo Makiguchi, the founding president of the Soka Gakkai, and willingly accompanying him to prison in the struggle to promote kosen-rufu.

Nichiren Daishonin says, "The element *ku* in the word *kudo-ku* means good fortune or happiness. It also refers to the merit achieved by wiping out evil, while the element *toku* or *doku* refers to the virtue one acquires by bringing about good" (OTT, 148). Benefit in Nichiren Buddhism means getting rid of evil in one's life and bringing forth goodness. To manifest benefit we need to carry out the practice of propagating Nichiren's teaching. Doing so means refuting the mistaken beliefs that cause people to suffer and enabling them instead to live based on the Mystic Law.

Saito: Propagation is the action we take to eliminate evil and produce good. By carrying out this practice for others, we also manifest the same effect in our own lives.

Ikeda: On the other hand, Nichiren says, "Both teacher and followers will surely fall into the hell of incessant suffering if they see enemies of the Lotus Sutra but disregard them and fail to reproach them" (WND-1, 747). Sharing Buddhism with others is all-important.

The next three chapters that we will study mark the start of the transmission section[1] of the Lotus Sutra. *Transmission,* as the word implies, means "propagation." In other words, the chapters after "Life Span"[2] explain the benefit of propagating the teaching. We can only become happy inasmuch as we strive to help others become happy through faith in the Mystic Law. This is the concept of benefit in Buddhism.

Endo: In terms of the mentor-disciple relationship, transmission is the work of the disciples. Therefore, from this chapter forward the focus will be on the efforts of the Buddha's disciples.

A LIVING PHILOSOPHY MUST ADDRESS THE REALITY OF LIFE

Suda: Some mistakenly interpret the teaching of benefit as indicating a preoccupation with material gain and on that account look upon Buddhism as an inferior religion. But the Buddhist doctrine of benefit has to do primarily with purifying and revolutionizing one's life.

Ikeda: Perhaps it would be more accurate to look at benefit in terms of value, or value creation. There are three kinds of value: beauty, gain and good.[3] The opposites of these could be termed *antivalues.* Don't all people aim to create value in their lives?

Suda: Working, eating, reading books, trying to cure disease— all are attempts to acquire or create some kind of value.

Ikeda: Everyone seeks happiness, just as plants and trees instinctively grow toward the sun. We always strive for a better life. This is only natural. To ignore or lose such drive is like being dead.

Saito: Consciously or not, all people seek happiness, value and benefit. It seems to me that this is indisputable. It is from the standpoint of this truth that all theory and explanation must begin. Any philosophy not based on this premise is dead theory with no bearing on reality.

Endo: Never in the history of Buddhism has the idea of gain been rejected. All along, Buddhism has urged that people accumulate benefit.

The Buddhist term *benefit* is written in Japanese with two Chinese characters. The first can be interpreted as meaning happiness and the second as meaning gain.[4]

Suda: Of course, benefit in Buddhism does not refer only to the kind of gain visible to the eye. If Buddhism were to reject such gain altogether, however, it would be merely abstract doctrine divorced from actual life, an enervated religion lacking the power to help people realize concrete improvement in their lives.

EVEN ILLUSION BECOMES BENEFIT

Ikeda: Many people certainly hold the biased view that religion pertains merely to the subjective realm of life. But Buddhism is the law of life; it is a teaching for daily life.

Viewed subjectively, life is a matter of self—of how we experience our own existence. Viewed objectively, from the outside, it is a matter of how we live—our daily activities. It's neither entirely one nor the other. Partiality to the subjective view leads to an emphasis on the spiritual, while partiality to the objective view leads to an emphasis on the material.

Buddhism rejects bias toward either of these extremes, enabling us to purify and strengthen our inner being while improving our daily lives. Put another way, through realizing improvement in daily life, we elevate our being.

For example, Buddhism speaks of attaining a state in which all our wishes are fulfilled. Wishes relate to the objective world. Being fulfilled means a sense of satisfaction experienced in the subjective realm. When these two are fused harmoniously, we attain the state of "fulfillment of all wishes"; this is a condition of happiness. That is how President Toda framed the issue.

Suda: This suggests that even a person with few wishes can readily find fulfillment.

Ikeda: I think it was Socrates who said that having few desires is the path to happiness.

Saito: It seems to me that practitioners of Hinayana Buddhism seek to attain happiness through the elimination of desire. In contrast, Mahayana Buddhism, and the Lotus Sutra in particular, teaches the principle that "earthly desires are enlightenment." It imparts the wisdom that enables us to channel the life-energy of earthly desires in the direction of good rather than something destructive.

Ikeda: The Lotus Sutra teaches that we can make our entire being blaze with the strong desire to attain a great objective. It teaches not that we should suppress anger, for instance, but that anger has a role to play in fueling our efforts to battle iniquity.

The Record of the Orally Transmitted Teachings reads, "As to the benefits, the distinction is here made clear that earthly desires associated with the three poisons of greed, anger, and foolishness that are a part of each and every one of the living beings of the Ten Worlds will now, just as they are, become the benefits of the Wonderful Law" (OTT, 234).

To urge people to discard the three poisons—greed, anger and foolishness—from their lives would only breed hypocrisy. Moreover, people who suppress their true feelings, who are content with being docile, powerless and merely swept along by outside influences, are perfect candidates to be exploited and used by the negative forces rampant in the Latter Day of the Law.

Nichiren Daishonin, however, urges that we challenge evil with great indignation and passion. When we base ourselves on the Mystic Law, everything becomes a source of value creation. This is the philosophy of the Lotus Sutra.

Benefit, or gain, and loss are not exclusive to the realm of religion. All people's lives are, in a way, a succession of gains and losses, value and antivalue. In business, selling is gain or value. But if the goods are sold at too low a price, the business takes a loss. When a painter realizes his or her subjective desire to paint a wonderful masterpiece (i.e., create the value of beauty), a fusion of subject and object occurs, filling the person with a sense of happiness. And when the painting is purchased, gain is realized.

When we create value, we feel happy. The purpose of the Lotus Sutra is to enable us to develop in our inner, or subjective, world the great life force to create value no matter what circumstances we may encounter in our outer, or objective, world. This is the process called human revolution.

Suda: That is true benefit.

Ikeda: Taking faith in Nichiren Buddhism does not mean that all difficulties will disappear. Being alive means that we will have problems of one kind or another. But no matter what happens, it's important that we remain firm in our hearts. The Mystic Law is the teaching of "earthly desires are enlightenment" and "the sufferings of birth and death are nirvana."

As long as we have the spirit of faith to dedicate our lives to advancing kosen-rufu, everything that happens to us will become our benefit without fail. Though we may not realize it while it's happening, gradually our lives enter a path where all wishes are fulfilled and we can honestly say, "Everything that I've gone through has really been for the best." This said, let's begin our study of these three chapters, starting with "Distinctions in Benefits."

The "Benefit of the 'Life Span' Verse Section"

Endo: This chapter describes how those who had heard the preaching of the preceding "Life Span" chapter received benefit of different kinds according to their states of life. This benefit is distinguished into twelve different levels. That is why the chapter is called "Distinctions in Benefits."

Saito: Nichiren calls this benefit collectively the "benefit of the verse section of the 'Life Span' chapter." In "Letter to Horen" he says:

> But it is not for me to describe the blessings deriving from the verse section of the "Life Span" chapter. Rather I refer to the subsequent "Distinctions in Benefits" chapter, which elaborates on them. It says that those people who became Buddhas after hearing the above verse section are equal in number to the particles of dust in a minor world system or a major world system. (WND-1, 516)

Ikeda: We could discuss this from many angles. But from the standpoint of Nichiren Buddhism, listening to the preaching of the verse section and thus becoming a Buddha is the benefit of worshiping the "Nam-myoho-renge-kyo Thus Come One." This is the great benefit of revering the Gohonzon. It is the great benefit of believing and understanding that since the remote past our lives have been one and inseparable with the life of the "Buddha of time without beginning."

Suda: The "Distinctions in Benefits" chapter begins as follows: "At that time, when the great assembly heard the Buddha describe how his life span lasted such a very long number of kalpas, immeasurable, boundless asamkhyas of living beings gained a great many rich benefits" (LSOC, 274).

Endo: It explains the content of these "great many rich benefits" as follows:

> *Some abide in the stage of no regression,*
> *some have acquired dharanis,*
> *some can speak pleasingly and without hindrance*
> *or retain ten thousand, a million repetitions of the teachings.*
> *Some bodhisattvas numerous as the dust particles*
> *of a major world system*
> *are all able to turn*
> *the unregressing wheel of the Law.*
> *Some bodhisattvas numerous as the dust particles*
> *of an intermediate world system*
> *are all able to turn*
> *the pure wheel of the Law. . . .*
> *Thus when living beings*
> *hear of the great length of the Buddha's life,*
> *they gain pure fruits and rewards*
> *that are immeasurable and free of outflows.* (LSOC, 276)

Ikeda: In this passage, Bodhisattva Maitreya is summarizing and restating the benefit that Shakyamuni has described.

Endo: Regarding the first of these benefits, that of abiding in the stage of non-regression, *non-regression* means "not backsliding." In other words, it is to attain the state in which one can advance eternally, always realizing growth and improvement.

Ikeda: That's right. It has often been said that to not advance or struggle is to retreat. A person who attains the stage of non-regression is already a winner.

Saito: To "acquire dharanis" means gaining the ability "to retain all that they hear" (LSOC, 274).

Ikeda: Nichiren Daishonin says, "When great obstacles arise, just as they were told would happen, few remember it and bear it firmly in mind" (WND-I, 471). And "Foolish men are likely to forget the promises they have made when the crucial moment comes" (WND-I, 283). Essentially, taking faith in this sutra means attaining a state of life where we do not forget our promises. It means correctly remembering and putting into practice the teachings of the mentor.

THE MORE WE SPEAK, THE MORE POWERFUL OUR "VOICE"

Suda: To "speak pleasingly and without hindrance" is also expressed elsewhere as gaining "the eloquence that allows them to speak pleasingly and without hindrance" (LSOC, 274). This is referring to the ability to freely explain the Law without impediment and in a manner that brings joy to listeners.

Ikeda: Nichiren says, "The voice carries out the work of the Buddha" (OTT, 4). We have to use our voices. This means we must speak eloquently and intelligently. There may also be times when having the gift of gab is useful!

Of course, eloquence does not mean simply being long-winded. Sometimes just a few well-chosen words can deftly refute a misconception. Also, using the voice to do the Buddha's work means correctly responding to whatever others want to know in the depths of their hearts. If you do not know the answer, you can invite the person to join you in going to talk with someone who does. Sometimes that's the best course to take.

What is important is to know how to move people's hearts and to empathize with them. In short, this is what it means to freely employ one's voice for kosen-rufu.

THE SPIRIT NEVER RESTS

Suda: Next, the sutra says the bodhisattvas gain "dharanis that allow them to retain hundreds, thousands, ten thousands, millions, immeasurable repetitions of the teachings" (LSOC, 274). The Chinese character used in this expression meaning "repetition" is often used to describe the function of a centrifuge, separating matter according to weight through centrifugal force. This seems to indicate the spiritual power to separate out and sublimate earthly desires by "rotating" them at a tremendous speed, thereby revealing the greatness of the Buddha. The Sanskrit term *dharani* denotes the spiritual power to promote good and thwart evil.

Ikeda: As this passage implies by its description of things rotating at high velocity, to live a truly peaceful existence requires diligently and vigorously challenging the negative forces that aim to cause suffering. The benefits enumerated next also contain the idea of rotation.

Suda: Yes, the fifth kind of benefit is the ability to "turn the unregressing wheel of the Law." And the sixth is the ability to "turn the pure wheel of the Law" (LSOC, 274). The "wheel of the Law" comes from the fact that the Buddha, in expounding the Law, is metaphorically said to turn the wheel of teaching. I think these passages express an unceasing and dynamic faith—a faith dedicated to conveying the Buddha's pure teaching to others and spreading it far and wide.

Endo: The passage continues by saying that many bodhisattvas "gained assurance that they would attain supreme perfect enlightenment after eight rebirths"(LSOC, 274–75). It further states that after four, three, two or one more rebirths, many bodhisattvas will attain the perfect and unsurpassed enlightenment.

The passage concludes, "Living beings numerous as the dust particles of eight worlds were all moved to set their minds upon supreme perfect enlightenment" (LSOC, 275).

Saito: The Great Teacher T'ien-t'ai of China categorizes these benefits according to the fifty-two stages of bodhisattva practice.[5] The sutra describes various benefits that bodhisattvas receive. At first, it may seem to suggest that people can only receive benefit according to their specific level of attainment. To the contrary, I think it actually reveals the great power of the "Life Span" chapter to benefit any and all people.

Ikeda: All benefit that can be attained through bodhisattva practice comes from faith in the "Life Span" chapter. That's because those bodhisattvas who reach the stage of enlightenment almost equivalent to the Buddha's when they hear the "Life Span" chapter simultaneously awaken to the Mystic Law of time without beginning. At that moment, they make the transition from the stage of common mortals who have simply embraced the Lotus Sutra to that of the Buddha.

It is as though they are steadily climbing a mountain with their sights set on reaching the state of enlightenment, the life state of the Buddha. But when they arrive at the top, at the summit of the "Life Span" chapter, what scene unfolds before them? They perceive that the true Buddha enlightened from time without beginning is constantly and tirelessly carrying out activities in the world to lead all beings to enlightenment. They understand that they once received his instruction. And they realize that they were originally united in a relationship of mentor and disciple with the Buddha who is one with the universe.

In other words, they recollect the truth of their own lives, remembering where they came from and where they are going, and they envision their true identity. They recall their mission to work together ceaselessly with the eternal and fundamental Buddha to lead others to enlightenment.

Essentially, those bodhisattvas awaken to the truth that Buddhahood, or enlightenment, is certainly not a static goal. Embracing the Lotus Sutra itself is the way to enlightenment for ordinary people. To live with the original cause of Buddhahood as the center of one's life and never stop progressing is to embody the life of the Buddha.

This is the conclusion of this sutra.

Saito: This is not clearly stated on the surface of the "Life Span" chapter. But the teaching that the Buddha attained enlightenment in the extremely remote past provides us with a clue that enables us to understand this.

Suda: Shakyamuni explains that he attained enlightenment in the remote past. Those in the assembly who hear this and consequently reach the stage of enlightenment almost equal to the Buddha understand that the Mystic Law from time without beginning, the teaching by which Shakyamuni became enlightened, is itself the true cause for attaining Buddhahood.

Endo: I think therefore that the fundamental teaching of the sutra is that the common mortals who embrace it instantly arrive at a state of enlightenment equal to that of Shakyamuni.

CELESTIAL BODIES EXHIBIT A WIDE RANGE OF ASPECTS UPON DEATH

Ikeda: Those people return to the very core of their own lives. They understand that they are one with the single great living entity that is the entire universe.

This might seem like a digression, but I recently saw several photos of dying stars released by NASA.[6] These were taken by the Hubble Space Telescope. Interestingly, the stars exhibited a variety of shapes: sphere-shaped, balloon-shaped, sprinkler-shaped, butterfly-shaped, rocket engine exhaust-shaped and pinwheel-shaped.

Endo: Stars also go through the cycle of birth and death.

Ikeda: It seems that stars exhibit different kinds of death depending on their mass. Many stars of approximately the same mass as our sun burn out completely in the final stage and, while slowly emitting gas, eventually become dim stars known as white dwarfs.

Saito: Among people, too, there are those who completely burn out and quietly fade away.

Ikeda: On the other hand, a star with several times the mass of the sun will produce a brilliant explosion called a supernova upon its death.

In his *Meigetsuki* (Bright Moon Diary), Japanese literary figure Fujiwara no Teika discusses the great supernova that created what today we call the Crab Nebula. On the Western calendar, that was in the year 1054, during the latter half of Japan's Heian period.

Endo: That's just two years after 1052, the year traditionally marking the start of the Latter Day of the Law.

Suda: The luminosity of a supernova suddenly increases by millions of times the normal brightness of the original star. Some are so brilliant that they can be seen with the naked eye even in daylight. They grow dim in time.

Ikeda: The supernova that appeared in 1054 was recorded by astronomers in China and Arabia. Line drawings were found in caves in North America that seem to record the same event.

Endo: The Crab Nebula is about 7,200 light years away. For the death of a star so remote to have caused such a stir on Earth means it must have been an exhibition of enormous energy—a truly remarkable event.

Suda: No doubt there are people who aspire to go out in such a blaze of glory!

Saito: From the photos recently released, I was intrigued to see that stars in the same class as our sun seem to undergo many kinds of death.

Ikeda: Everything in the universe is alive. Everything is an entity of life and death, an entity of the Mystic Law.

Even if we look only at the material aspect, matter that is scattered throughout the universe as a result of the death of a star will be used in the birth of new stars and in the bodies of biological organisms. The atoms making up our bodies, too, were once shining as part of a star somewhere.

Human beings are children of the stars, of the universe. Our lives are one with the great life of the universe. The benefit of Nam-myoho-renge-kyo is literally the benefit of the entire universe. It is inexhaustible. Limitless.

The "Distinctions in Benefits" chapter says, "He will gain immeasurable merits, boundless as the open air" (LSOC, 284–85), and "Their virtue will be uppermost, immeasurable and boundless as the open sky, east, west, north and south, in the four intermediate directions, and up and down, is immeasurable and boundless. The blessings of such persons will be as immeasurable and boundless as this" (LSOC, 282).

Attaining a State of Life in Which All Wishes Are Fulfilled

Ikeda: The benefit of the Gohonzon is infinite and boundless. Therefore, it is impossible to explain thoroughly.

In his commentary on Nichiren Daishonin's "The True Object of Worship," Nichikan, the twenty-sixth high priest, says: "[If you have faith in this Gohonzon and chant Nam-myoho-renge-kyo even for a short while,] no prayer will go unanswered, no offense unexpiated, no good fortune unbestowed, and all righteousness proven."[7] Such absolute conviction contains all the benefits of the four stages of faith and five stages of practice[8] described in the "Distinctions in Benefits" chapter.

As long as we have faith, there is no difficulty we cannot overcome. The great life force of the lion king wells up in our lives, Nichiren's boundless spirit comes pouring out. The "Distinctions in Benefits" chapter describes the practitioners of the sutra as roaring "like a lion" (LSOC, 280) in the same manner as the Buddha.

Saito: Those who hear of and believe in the unfathomable life span of the Buddha state the following pledge upon accepting the Lotus Sutra:

> *Our wish is that in future ages*
> *we may use our long lives to save living beings.*
> *Just as today the world-honored one,*
> *king of the Shakyas,*
> *roars like a lion in the place of enlightenment,*
> *preaching the Law without fear,*
> *so may we too in ages to come,*
> *honored and revered by all,*
> *when we sit in the place of enlightenment*
> *describe our life spans in the same manner.* (LSOC, 280)

Ikeda: "Long lives" here means living with the unsurpassed life of the Mystic Law. The Chinese term for *lion* comprises two elements: the first means "teacher" or "mentor," and the second, "disciple." "Roars like a lion" refers to the oneness of mentor and disciple where mentor and disciple roar together. This is the true meaning of propagation.

Early in my practice, I made the determination: "President Toda is the mentor of propagation in the Latter Day, and I am his disciple. Therefore, it is impossible for me not to propagate Nichiren Daishonin's teaching." With that resolve, I accomplished propagation of the Daishonin's teaching second to none.

The chapter says that the disciples are "without fear." We should never be afraid. We need not be fearful or complain or lament our situation. Rather, we must have bright, vital faith. Then the limitless beneficial power of the Mystic Law will flow through our lives.

All along, I have continued to spread the Daishonin's teaching and protect the Soka Gakkai while enduring all manner of persecution and overcoming all kinds of obstacles. As a result, I have received truly immense benefit from my practice to the Gohonzon.

Although we are all chanting to the same Gohonzon, if our faith is weak, we will not savor the truly great joy of faith pouring out of our lives. The benefit we receive differs depending on our faith. Each person's benefit is unique and different. This is the meaning of "distinctions in benefits."

Again, while the manner in which benefit manifests differs for each person depending on his or her faith, life condition and karma, as long as we persevere in faith, in the end we are sure to attain the state in which all wishes are fulfilled. This is the profound meaning of "distinctions in benefits."

For example, while we should of course exercise care to avoid accidents, Nichiren teaches that even if we should die in an unfortunate accident, as long as we have embraced strong faith, then "without a moment's delay" (WND-2, 859) we will return to the ranks of those working for kosen-rufu.

A passage from the Nirvana Sutra cited in his writings says: "Even if you are killed by a mad elephant, you will not fall into the three evil paths. But if you are killed by an evil friend, you are certain to fall into them" (WND-1, 620). In modern terms, to be "killed by a mad elephant" would be comparable to dying in a traffic accident.

Those who die in the course of carrying out activities for kosen-rufu cannot fail to receive great effects from their faith. Nichiren makes this clear in such writings as "Lessening One's Karmic Retribution." This sort of death literally exemplifies the principle of giving one's life for the sake of the Law. This is the noblest way to die.

A Sense of Calm and Security at the Moment of Death

Saito: A little earlier it was mentioned that dying stars exhibit a variety of aspects. The same is true of people's deaths.

Akiko Kojima, the secretary of the Soka Gakkai nurses group, expressed to me her belief that the view of life and death that we hold while alive is a very important factor in determining our final moments. But if it is only a matter of theory and knowledge, she says, it will count for absolutely nothing when that moment comes. Ms. Kojima further said that under the assault of the three poisons that spew forth at the time of death, unless you feel true calm and security in the depths of your heart, you cannot weather the ordeal.

Naturally, status and wealth are irrelevant; nor do leadership positions in the organization count for anything at the time of death. Ms. Kojima says that, even if leaders go to extreme lengths to conceal their pain out of a sense of responsibility, they cannot hide their suffering at the moment of death.

Endo: There was a member who until the moment he died never ceased encouraging those who came to visit him. As the end approached, his wife, who had looked after him throughout his illness, began crying. Noticing this, he turned to her and said, "There's no need to cry," adding, "I think that this is the end. Please convey my thanks to all of the nurses for their hard work." He died encouraging his wife to the very end.

Suda: I also heard the story of a member whom the nurses would later compare to a marshmallow. The reason was that each nurse who attended her felt as though gently embraced in a soft marshmallow. The woman possessed abundant warmth and concern for others. To the very last, she continued to bring joy to those around her with her magnanimous spirit.

Ikeda: That is the life of a bodhisattva. No, of a Buddha. Not only do such people strive to revolutionize their own state of life, but to the very end they make constant efforts to elevate those around them.

Saito: The "Distinctions in Benefits" chapter describes the benefit that accrues to those who understand the importance of the long duration of the Buddha's life span, that is to say, the benefit of awakening to the eternity of life. This probably manifests in their appearance at the time of death.

Ikeda: Yes. This is not mere theorizing divorced from reality. We must live earnestly, always moving forward energetically, proud to experience complete fulfillment in both life and death. Buddhism was expounded to enable us to manifest such magnificent life force.

The "Distinctions in Benefits" chapter in one place speaks of people who are "diligent and courageous, mastering all the good doctrines, keen in faculties and wisdom, good at answering difficult questions" (LSOC, 283). Diligent and courageous—doesn't this describe SGI members?

A Life of Struggle to the Finish

Suda: Ms. Kojima also told me that one patient impressed her more than any other. That patient, a member, died of cancer. But no matter how dire his situation became in the course of his illness, he maintained a fighting spirit to the very last.

Even when he was receiving treatment, and even when he was experiencing the most pain, his will to fight never abated. He would tell his doctors and nurses exactly how he felt and discuss methods of treatment with them, all the while challenging his situation with every ounce of his energy.

Ms. Kojima says that his eyes left the strongest impression on her. She describes them as the eyes of a master swordsman. At one point in his treatment he recovered somewhat and was discharged from the hospital, only to be hospitalized again when the cancer recurred. But even then, she reports, his swordsman's eyes glowed with the same unshakable determination. She also relates feeling that, even though his body was being devoured by cancer, his life itself continued to burn as strongly as ever.

Ikeda: To live vigorously through every ordeal is proof that someone understands the eternity of life. Eternal life cannot be verified with our eyes, but it is something that we can believe in.

Saito: The Lotus Sutra repeatedly emphasizes the importance of belief.

Ikeda: Belief means basing one's entire life on the Law. It is the state where our actions themselves manifest faith. This occurs when we carry out propagation and encourage our friends. By struggling to communicate an understanding of the Mystic Law to someone, we polish our own lives. And a life that has been thoroughly polished can soar freely throughout past, present and future.

Without our even realizing it, we attain a state of eternal freedom. Like a rocket that can traverse the universe, our lives store up an inexhaustible supply of energy. We develop the great life force of a lion king. That is the benefit of the "Life Span of the Thus Come One" chapter.

Saito: I am reminded of the benefit described in "Distinctions in Benefits" of gaining the "truth of birthlessness" (LSOC, 274). Similar to the benefit of "abiding in the stage of non-regression" that we talked about earlier, this indicates a state of confidence that there is neither birth nor death, that, in other words, life is eternal. It basically affirms that all phenomena are free from birth and death.

Ikeda: Our lives are one with the eternal Buddha. The Buddha is none other than our own lives. When we have this great confidence, we will never become deadlocked. We can advance limitlessly, overcoming all suffering, all sadness, all inertia. We attain a calm state of non-regression.

Endo: That is a life imbued with the optimism of Buddhism.

Ikeda: Buddhist optimism is not the escapist optimism of those who throw up their hands and say, "Somehow or other things will work out." Rather it means clearly recognizing evil as evil and suffering as suffering and resolutely fighting to overcome it. It means believing in one's ability and strength to struggle against any evil or any obstacle. It is to possess a fighting optimism.

Speaking of optimism, I remember the smiling face of Dr. Norman Cousins, who was known as the "conscience of America." Although he did not practice Buddhism, in his belief in the power of the human being he was no different from a Buddhist. Dr. Cousins once wrote:

> No one need fear death. We need fear only that we may die without having known our greatest power—the power of his free will to give his life for others. If something comes to life in others because of us, then we have made an approach to immortality.[9]

When we devote ourselves to the happiness of others, when, of our own free will, we undertake the struggle of a bodhisattva, the immense force of life without beginning or end wells up in our being. The eternal life of the Buddha permeates our being like a rising tide. Then, there is no way that we cannot dramatically change our lives for the better.

In that sense, chanting Nam-myoho-renge-kyo, spreading Nichiren Buddhism and working for kosen-rufu in themselves are the greatest benefits. Nichiren states, "There is no true happiness for human beings other than chanting Nam-myoho-renge-kyo" (WND-1, 681). This plainly indicates that a life dedicated to kosen-rufu is most noble and lofty. The "Distinctions in Benefits" chapter imparts the wisdom to recognize this.

NOTES

1. Transmission section: One of the three divisions of a sutra, together with preparation and revelation. The preparation section explains the reason a sutra is being expounded. The revelation section constitutes the main body of the teaching. And the transmission section is the concluding part where the benefit of the sutra is set forth and its transmission to future generations is urged.

2. Strictly speaking, the first half of the "Distinctions in Benefits" chapter belongs to the "revelation" section of the essential teaching, along with the latter half of "Emerging from the Earth," the

fifteenth chapter, and the "Life Span" chapter in its entirety. This portion of the sutra is referred to collectively as the "one chapter and two halves."

3. Beauty, gain and good: In his theory of value, the first Soka Gakkai president, Tsunesaburo Makiguchi, argued that these constitute the core values, in contrast to the traditional values of truth, good and beauty.

4. *The Record of the Orally Transmitted Teachings* says, "The element *ku* in the word *kudoku* means good fortune or happiness" (OTT, 148). The *Shoman Hokutsu* says, "'*toku* (*doku*)' means 'gain.'" (*Shoman Hokutsu*: A commentary on the Shrimala Sutra by Chi-tsang [Jpn Kichizo, 549–623], a priest of the San-lun [Jpn Sanron] school of China.)

5. Fifty-two stages of bodhisattva practice: Progressive stages through which a bodhisattva is said to advance, from the time of first resolve until finally attaining Buddhahood. They consist of ten stages of faith, ten stages of security, ten stages of practice, ten stages of devotion, ten stages of development, a stage almost equal to enlightenment (*togaku*) and enlightenment (*myogaku*).

6. NASA press release, December 17, 1997.

7. *Fujishugaku yoshu* (Essential Writings of the Fuji School), ed. Hori Nichiko (Tokyo: Seikyo Shimbunsha, 1978), vol. 4, p. 213.

8. The four stages of faith are: 1) to believe in and understand the sutra even for a moment, 2) to generally understand the import of the words of the sutra, 3) to expound the teaching of the sutra widely for others, and 4) to realize with deep faith the truth expounded by the Buddha. The five stages of practice are: 1) to rejoice on hearing the Lotus Sutra, 2) to read and recite the sutra, 3) to expound the sutra to others, 4) to embrace the sutra and practice the six paramitas, and 5) to perfect one's practice of the six paramitas.

9. Norman Cousins, *Human Options* (New York: W.W. Norton and Company, 1981), p. 45.

PART II

"The Benefits of Responding with Joy" Chapter

2 Joyfully Spreading the Mystic Law

Saito: The "Benefits of Responding with Joy" chapter will be the theme of this chapter.

Ikeda: When we respond with joy, we receive benefit—that, in essence, is the meaning of the title. In other words, we receive great benefit to the extent that we joyfully exert ourselves in faith. Here, again, we see that the heart is the all-important factor. If you're going to practice Buddhism anyway, you might as well enjoy it rather than complain about it!

When you're faced with a challenge, do you sigh deeply and say, "Oh no, not again"? Or do you confront it head on, determined to use the situation to accumulate still more good fortune? This slight distinction in attitude makes a world of difference in the end.

The "Benefits of Responding with Joy" chapter clarifies the great benefit that accrues from courageously encouraging others to practice Nichiren Buddhism.

Endo: We entered the transmission section[1] of the Lotus Sutra with "Distinctions in Benefits," the seventeenth chapter, which we discussed in chapter 1.

Suda: Transmission, meaning to cause or allow to spread, plainly refers to propagation.

THE DESIRE TO ACCOMPLISH KOSEN-RUFU

[After the Buddha has entered extinction, suppose there are people who, hearing this sutra, respond with joy and] put forth effort in preaching and expounding for the sake of their parents and relatives, their good friends and acquaintances. These persons, after hearing, respond with joy and they too set about spreading the teachings. One person, having heard, responds with joy and spreads the teachings, and the teachings in this way continue to be handed along from one to another until they reach a fiftieth person.

Ajita,[2] the benefits received by this fiftieth good man or good woman who responds with joy I will now describe to you—you must listen carefully. . . .

Or suppose there is a person who is sitting in the place where the Law is expounded, and when another person appears, the first person urges him to sit down and listen, or offers to share his seat and so persuades him to sit down. The benefits gained by this person will be such that when he is reborn he will be in a place where the lord Shakra is seated, where the heavenly king Brahma is seated, or where a wheel-turning sage king is seated.
(LSOC, 286–88)

Ikeda: Transmission is kosen-rufu, the spread of the Law. The transmission section that we have begun studying is full of guidelines pertaining to the propagation of the Mystic Law. It is remarkable that in the three thousand years of Buddhist history, we of the SGI, virtually alone, can understand this chapter based on actual experience. It seems, therefore, that the "Benefits of Responding with Joy" chapter was expounded for us.

In 1952, one year after his inauguration, the second Soka Gakkai president, Josei Toda, proclaimed: "At this auspicious time of the seven-hundredth anniversary of the establishment of

Nichiren Buddhism, I declare that kosen-rufu will increasingly flourish from this point forward."[3]

The SGI is an association dedicated to propagating the Mystic Law and accomplishing kosen-rufu. It is a body with a profound mission to realize the Daishonin's will and decree. To develop this profound awareness is of utmost importance.

Saito: I would like to read an excerpt from a speech titled "Toward the 704th Anniversary of the Founding," delivered by Nichijun (the sixty-fifth high priest) in 1956:

> I believe future historians will define the period leading up to the seven-hundredth anniversary of this school's founding as the age of protection [of the Law] by the priesthood, and the period thereafter as the age of widespread transmission. Looking over the history of the priesthood until now, while there have been times of some prosperity, in the final analysis it never went beyond safeguarding the teachings. . . .
>
> The fact that, with the seven-hundredth anniversary of the establishment of Nichiren Buddhism as the turning point, we have entered a period of widespread propagation indicates something preordained about the spread of the Law. I therefore believe that the emergence of the Soka Gakkai indicates its extraordinary relationship with the Buddha.[4]

Endo: His remarks bear great significance.

Suda: The "age of widespread transmission" that will unfold over the ten thousand years of the Latter Day of the Law has indeed begun.

In his speech at the eighteenth Soka Gakkai General Meeting on May 3, 1958, Nichijun also commented on the appearance of so many Soka Gakkai members in the dawning of this age:

In the assembly on Eagle Peak described in the Lotus Sutra, the four great bodhisattvas, with Bodhisattva Superior Practices in the vanguard, arrived one after another. They, in turn, were followed by great bodhisattvas as numerous as the sands of sixty thousand Ganges Rivers, who also gathered at Eagle Peak. There, they made a resolute vow to propagate Myoho-renge-kyo in the Latter Day of the Law. Those people are now here in accord with the promise they made at Eagle Peak. I believe that the Soka Gakkai, with President Toda in the vanguard, summoned them forth; in other words, I believe that the 750,000-strong membership built by President Toda represents the seven or five characters of Myoho-renge-kyo.[5]

He describes the Soka Gakkai as a great assemblage of Buddhas.

Saito: These are the words of a high priest. The current Nichiren Shoshu priesthood, in betraying these crystal-clear statements, is guilty of serious slander in turning against its own predecessors. It has attempted to obstruct kosen-rufu and consequently has become the archenemy of Nichiren Daishonin.

Ikeda: We chose to be born at this time in anticipation of the dawn of an "age of widespread transmission." From that standpoint, it is impossible to overstate the profundity and nobility of our mission in this life. We are in the forefront of a movement that will continue over the ten thousand years of the Latter Day of the Law. This thought fills me with profound emotion. My heart dances with joy. We must cultivate this awareness through strong prayer to the Gohonzon.

The "Benefits of Responding with Joy" chapter includes the

well-known explanation of the benefit enjoyed by the "fiftieth person." It is the SGI that is in actuality putting this teaching into practice. Propagation is not simply a matter of explaining theory; the key is to convey the confidence and sense of fulfillment we gain from putting Nichiren Daishonin's philosophy into practice. That is how we can touch people's lives.

THE BOUNDLESS BENEFIT OF THE FIFTIETH PERSON

Suda: The explanation of the benefit of the fiftieth person goes as follows: Bodhisattva Maitreya asks how much benefit will accrue to those who respond with joy upon hearing the Lotus Sutra. The Buddha replies that after his death—specifically, in the Latter Day of the Law—some will delight upon hearing the Lotus Sutra. He adds that no matter what their particular circumstances, whether old or young, they will go into the city and to the country, to quiet places and bustling places and, according to their ability, explain the teaching that they have heard to parents, relatives, friends and acquaintances. (The sutra says, "in accordance with what they have heard they put forth effort in preaching and expounding" [LSOC, 286].) Those who hear the teaching from such people will in turn share the teaching with others. In this way, the teaching spreads continuously until it reaches the fiftieth person.

Endo: One might wonder if the joy experienced would not be somewhat diminished by the time it reached the fiftieth person.

Suda: Even if that were so, the benefit would still be immense. That's the point of the principle of continuous propagation to the fiftieth person.

Ikeda: Addressing the question of just how vast that benefit is, the Daishonin says, "The benefit enjoyed by the fiftieth person who rejoices on hearing the Lotus Sutra is greater than that acquired by giving alms for eighty years" (WND-1, 60).

Endo: The idea of "giving alms for eighty years" supposes a wealthy person could possibly give all living beings in "four hundred ten thousand million asamkhya worlds" (LSOC, 287) anything and everything that they desire. According to the sutra, such alms include precious items—gold, silver, lapis lazuli, agate, coral, fine vehicles and palaces adorned with the seven kinds of treasure. This would go on for eighty years. Not only would the donors offer material objects, but when they saw that someone was growing old and approaching death, they would share with that person the teachings of the Buddha.

Saito: To give material things is to "make offerings of treasure." To expound the teachings is to "make offerings of the Law." No matter how wealthy one may be, material possessions themselves cannot enable one to grasp life's fundamental issues, like old age and death. That's why it is necessary to teach people about the Law.

Ikeda: Of course, the Law referred to in the sutra is a teaching prior to the Lotus Sutra.

Endo: Yes. And the beings who hear it are said to attain higher states of life, such as that of arhat. This is the sort of enlightenment sought by voice-hearers. Still, it represents a superior state of life to which people aspired.

Suda: The Buddha asks Maitreya whether he thinks that the benefit gained by a person who has thoroughly carried out such extensive offerings of treasure and of the Law would be sizable. Maitreya replies that the benefit of such a person would indeed be infinite and boundless. The Buddha then explains that the benefit of the fiftieth person who hears a verse of the Lotus Sutra and rejoices is even greater than that by hundreds, thousands, tens of millions of times.

Ikeda: And that is to say nothing of the benefit of those who hear the teaching before it reaches the fiftieth person. Such is the immense power of the Mystic Law.

Interpreted literally, the fiftieth person hears the teaching and rejoices but does not share it with anyone else. Even though he does not carry out the practice for others, however, his benefit is still immense. The sutra explains that the benefit gained by those who not only rejoice themselves but also endeavor to share the teaching with others is incomparably greater (see LSOC, 287).

From the standpoint of the Daishonin's teaching, the "one verse of the Lotus Sutra" (LSOC, 288) that these people hear is Nam-myoho-renge-kyo. In other words, they hear about the Gohonzon. This means that just hearing about the Gohonzon and thinking, "How wonderful!" "I am so fortunate to learn of this teaching!" produces enormous benefit. Those who respond this way and then embrace faith and share it with others according to their ability will have all their prayers answered, gain tremendous good fortune, and attain the state in which all desires are fulfilled without fail. The passage about the fiftieth person is documentary proof of this principle.

The Daishonin says that a person who chants Nam-myoho-renge-kyo only once a day or only once in the course of a lifetime or who hears someone else chant it only once in a lifetime and rejoices and so on to the fiftieth person will gain blessings "a hundred, thousand, ten thousand, million times greater" (WND-1, 68) than those gained by persons of excellent innate ability and superior wisdom such as Shariputra, Manjushri and Maitreya.

Saito: He also includes in this those who "rejoice in hearing the voice of someone else rejoice in the hearing" (WND-1, 68).

A Movement To Bring Happiness to All

Saito: In fact, there have been many instances where people living adjacent to homes where discussion meetings are held joined the SGI, their interest sparked by the sound of members' joyful voices.

Endo: I heard such an account from Toku Shirai, a women's leader of Niigata Prefecture. For many years, the Shirais' home was used for discussion meetings. A neighbor had for a long time thought it odd to see many people in high spirits coming and going. She could hear the vigorous recitation of the sutra at the beginning of the meetings, followed by singing and the sounds of laughter. She wondered why they always ended at 8:30 sharp and why everyone leaving looked elated and refreshed.

Whereas in the past, the Shirais' neighbors overheard nothing but continual fights between husband and wife, they now heard only cheerful voices. They were impressed by how polite the children had grown. This became the talk of the neighborhood.

After observing the Shirais for many years, the woman living next door came to the conclusion that the change must be due to the Soka Gakkai and decided to try practicing Nichiren Buddhism. So she asked Mrs. Shirai if she could join.

Suda: You hear about many cases in which people decide to join our movement simply because they see the joy exuded by SGI members and want to acquire this themselves.

Endo: I also heard from Mrs. Shirai about a member who had a speech impediment. When he reported on some activity at a discussion meeting, often he could only get out the words, "It was great!" He would try with all his might to speak, but he simply could say no more. So, in the end, he would just repeat, "It was great!" Although those listening didn't have any clear idea of what exactly was great, they could clearly sense his enthusiasm. Often guests attending the meeting would be so moved from what few words he said that they would decide to join.

Mrs. Shirai's conclusion, after having introduced more than a hundred families to the practice, is that dialogue means speaking with conviction and joy. This is just as you said a little earlier, President Ikeda.

Ikeda: She is truly noble. In this egoistic world, to offer prayers and work hard for the happiness of others, as well as for oneself, is magnificent. It is sublime. The fact that SGI members exert themselves for kosen-rufu day in and day out, even in the face of criticism and abuse, is proof that they are Bodhisattvas of the Earth. Of this, I have not the slightest doubt.

On the subject of joy, the Daishonin says, "'Joy' means that oneself and others together experience joy"; and "then both oneself and others together will take joy in their possession of wisdom and compassion" (OTT, 146). The key point is that joy is something we share with others. To be concerned only with one's own happiness is egoism. To claim you care only about the happiness of others is hypocrisy. Genuine happiness is becoming happy together with others.

President Toda said: "Just becoming happy oneself—there's nothing difficult to that. It's easy. Helping others become happy is the foundation of our faith."[6] The earlier passage by the Daishonin plainly states that such happiness is gained by sharing wisdom and compassion, sharing the life of the Buddha. To have wisdom but lack compassion is to lead a closed and constricted life. That is not true wisdom. To possess compassion but lack wisdom and be foolish is to be of no help to anyone, including oneself. One who cannot help another does not know compassion at all.

Saito: Both wisdom and compassion are vital.

Ikeda: And faith encompasses both. The Daishonin says: "Now, when Nichiren and his followers chant Nam-myoho-renge-kyo, they are expressing joy in the fact that they will inevitably become Buddhas eternally endowed with the three bodies" (OTT, 146). Attaining this state is itself "the greatest of all joys" (OTT, 212).

Saito: Sharing happiness with others—this is the benefit of talking to others about Buddhism. I think that the discussion of continuous propagation to the fiftieth person indicates a dynamic movement to propagate happiness. And the SGI has spread the Mystic Law literally to the ends of the earth.

The Daishonin says that the "fifty persons" represents all living beings:

> In its description of the continual propagation to the fiftieth person, the numeral 5 in the number 50 [which in Chinese is written with two characters standing for "5" and "10," thus 5 multiplied by 10] represents the five characters of the Wonderful Law, while the numerical 10 represents the living beings of the Ten Worlds. The words "continual propagation" stand for the principle of three thousand realms in a single moment of life.
>
> When one speaks in terms of the doctrinal studies of the sutra, this chapter estimates the amount of benefit received by the fiftieth person who responds with joy to the teachings. The fifty persons involved stand for all living beings. (OTT, 234–35)

This seems to suggest that when the living beings of the Ten Worlds embrace the five characters of the Mystic Law, that is, when kosen-rufu is in progress, then the actual principle of three thousand realms in a single moment of life is being realized.

ACHIEVING TRUE DEMOCRACY

Ikeda: Kosen-rufu also includes the struggle to transform the realm of the environment. This is the meaning of actual (as opposed to theoretical) three thousand realms in a single moment of life.

At any rate, propagation from one person to the next and so on to the fiftieth person is the democratic path of dialogue. Democracy is definitely not simply a matter of setting in place certain forms and institutions. Without content, democracy is an empty vessel that is easily crushed.

What is this content? It is individual self-reliance and self-improvement. It is individual happiness. Democracy must enable each person in society to live to the fullest. Without valuing the sanctity of the individual, democracy is a mere shell.

Endo: That would certainly describe the state of affairs in Japan today.

Ikeda: When people's hearts are vacant, democracy is imperiled, and the devilish potential of power can set in. That is when the dark shadow of nationalism begins to spread.

President Toda said that individual happiness and social prosperity must go hand in hand. It is a grave mistake for society to neglect the well-being of the individual while striving only for economic growth. Individual happiness is not self-centered; rather, it is the process of solidifying one's humanity, of developing wisdom and compassion in both oneself and others.

This is an issue of global importance, affecting socialist and democratic countries alike. The Lotus Sutra, however, has the power to enable all people to realize both individual happiness and social prosperity. This is the meaning of actual three thousand realms in a single moment of life.

In short, it is our efforts to pray for and help other people become happy that are the hallmark of the foremost popular movement and that directly contribute to the creation of a truly democratic society. We are engaged in transmitting joy from one person to another. No matter how long or broad the chain of transmission, the amount of fulfillment each person feels does not wane nor is anyone made to suffer. The propagation of Nichiren Daishonin's philosophy continues as each person becomes indestructibly happy. This is the path we have followed, raising our voices in a chorus of Gakkai songs along the way.

Over the years, in times of hardship and struggle and through bitter tears, we repeatedly revived our spirits by singing Gakkai songs. The remarkable task of spreading the Mystic Law that our pioneering members accomplished through their tenacious efforts could well be called the miracle of the twentieth century.

The Path of Indomitable Dignity

Saito: For most Soka Gakkai members, "Song of Indomitable Dignity" is laden with many memories. That shows just how widely it has been sung throughout the country.

Suda: President Ikeda, you once introduced the background of the person who wrote the lyrics, Yukie Ohashi, saying that the song was born from the Kyoto members' unwavering spirit to continue amid severe circumstances. You also described it as a wonderful part of the history of our kosen-rufu movement.

After Mr. Ohashi died, I asked a number of people in Kyoto

about him. He reportedly wrote the song in 1955 or 1956, shortly after taking faith. He operated a wholesale umbrella outlet, but the bankruptcy of a business associate resulted in his being saddled with enormous debt, making his daily life excruciatingly difficult. That was when he heard about this Buddhism.

The person who introduced him told him that this faith is truly remarkable and challenged him to give it a three-month trial. The friend guaranteed Mr. Ohashi that he would see results, promising that if he didn't, he would give him his head.

"I don't want your head," Mr. Ohashi replied. "I need money."

"How much do you need?"

"Thirty thousand yen," he said. That was the amount that the associate had failed to pay him.

The person responded: "I see. You can absolutely pay off your debts. The only condition is that you must do gongyo without missing a single day and attend discussion meetings for three months. And you have to tell others about the practice with me."

Endo: What confidence! Great confidence is the soul of propagation.

Suda: So for three months Mr. Ohashi joined his friend in sharing Nichiren Buddhism with others. Before three months had elapsed, the business associate who had absconded came back and returned the thirty thousand yen. Having gained confidence in faith through this experience, Mr. Ohashi told more and more people about Buddhism.

Around that time, there was a movement among districts in the organization to come up with their own songs. The Kyoto area had no song, and that made the members feel left out. When Mr. Ohashi pointed this out to one of his leaders, the leader handed him a pencil and paper and suggested that he go ahead and write one.

Mr. Ohashi had not an ounce of songwriting experience, but what he did possess was passion. Standing before a small desk in his shop, he thought it over. As soon as he had decided on indomitable dignity as the theme, it was as though his pencil began moving on its own and the words of the song flowed out. "Though I may currently be beaten down, when I enter the ranks of kosen-rufu, I stand up with indomitable courage." He also worked out the melody by trial and error. The song changed slightly every time he sang it, and it took him a month to complete it. One verse goes:

> *Into this defiled and evil world go*
> *We of the Gakkai*
> *Whoever may stand in our way.*
>
> *With indomitable dignity*
> *We summon our faith and advance.*
> *Herein lies our conviction.*

There were no tape recorders in those days. People who heard the song took to it, and soon it was being passed by word of mouth from one person to the next. When Kyoto Chapter was inaugurated, it was made the chapter song, and the members, singing it proudly and vigorously, went on to make their new chapter the first in propagation in the nation. This sparked the enthusiasm of members across Japan.

Ikeda: I, too, heard this song in Kyoto. The song itself is wonderful. Seeing the banner of the Law hoisted high in the city that was Japan's ancient capital for a thousand years by the Kyoto members with this song on their lips was more wonderful still. Immediately, I wanted to make this a song for members throughout Japan.

Suda: This episode is still a source of pride for the members of Kyoto. You proposed that the song be introduced to all members. Originally the third verse began, "Behold the peaceful land of Kyoto where we live." You suggested that it be changed to "Behold the paradise of Japan where we live." After that, the song spread around the country in no time at all.

Mr. Ohashi in the meantime saw his circumstances take a dramatic turn for the better. He started a silk-dyeing business, and it prospered. He never again had to endure privations. He eventually took up residence in an estate people called the Ohashi Palace, and he traveled overseas frequently.

When you related Mr. Ohashi's experience at a meeting in Kyoto (in 1989), he had been hospitalized with an advanced stage of cancer. Immediately afterwards, a senior leader visited him to tell him about the meeting. He reportedly listened with great satisfaction to what you had said at the meeting. Shortly after that, having completed his mission of sixty-nine years, he died in peace.

People widely recognized Mr. Ohashi as a master of dialogue and an expert at giving individual guidance. It is said that even those in whom no one else could stir any response would listen carefully to what Mr. Ohashi had to say.

Not long before he died, Mr. Ohashi remarked to someone who had come to visit him at the hospital, "There's more that I would like to do."

"Are there more places in the world you would like to see?" the person asked.

"No, I would like to do more home visits," he said. "I would like to do activities again together with everyone."

It seems to me that Mr. Ohashi was a genuine champion of the people, true to the words of "Song of Indomitable Dignity."

Saito: "I would like to do more activities"—SGI activities are truly the supreme "memory of your present life in this human world" (WND-1, 64).[7]

Rise Above Your Troubles

Endo: Though at the time they may not seem all that enjoyable, the feeling of satisfaction you get from putting forth your best effort in activities is unsurpassed. It's like how you feel after a nice hot bath!

Ikeda: We talk about experiencing joy, but that feeling itself does not last long. Emotions like excitement and joy tend to fade with time.

A Japanese author wrote: "The life of a flower is short. Of sufferings only are there many."[8] It's simply a fact of life that joy is short-lived while suffering endures. For precisely this reason, we are most fortunate to embrace the Mystic Law, which embodies the principle that earthly desires are enlightenment.

When faced with difficulties, we chant Nam-myoho-renge-kyo to solve our problems. When sad, we take our sadness to the Gohonzon. When happy, we chant with a profound sense of appreciation. As we do so, we continue moving forward, gazing down on our troubles from the vantage of a lofty state of life. When we pray to the Gohonzon, it is as though we are surveying the entire universe, allowing us to observe impassively our own sufferings.

"Responding with joy" doesn't mean that we are without worries or suffering. Precisely because we have worries, we can chant Nam-myoho-renge-kyo, bringing forth a strong life force. Because there is suffering, there is joy. It is impossible to experience only happiness in life.

Buddhism is a struggle. Life is also a struggle. That is why we must develop the inner fortitude to strive continuously to move forward. A life that has been tempered and made strong will savor eternal joy.

Through faith we can establish a state of life where, no matter what happens, we experience joy, hope and confidence in the depths of our being. That gives us the power to go among those who are suffering and together with them find true happiness.

While it is difficult for us to fathom Nichiren Daishonin's state of life, we can certainly discern such profound joy in his writings. President Toda once described the Daishonin's exile to Sado Island, saying, "In modern terms, exile to Sado is comparable to being banished to the Sahara Desert." And yet, in the midst of such great persecution, Nichiren said, "I feel immeasurable delight" (WND-1, 386).

Suda: It is hard to imagine how incredible his state of life must have been.

THE DAISHONIN'S IMMENSE STATE OF LIFE

Ikeda: Throughout his writings, we can hear the Daishonin declaring in a great voice: "How joyful!" "What happiness I feel!"

Why don't we look at some of these passages?

Saito: OK. Well, to begin with, the passage you cited earlier reads in full, "I feel immeasurable delight even though I am now an exile" (WND-1, 386). Elsewhere he says: "The greater the hardships befalling [the votary of the Lotus Sutra], the greater the delight he feels, because of his strong faith" (WND-1, 33); "Among all the persons since the beginning of our present kalpa who have incurred the wrath of their parents or their rulers and have been exiled to distant islands, there can be none who overflow with joy as we do" (WND-1, 313); "I have been condemned to exile, but it is a small suffering to undergo in this present life and not one worth lamenting. In future lives I will enjoy immense happiness, a thought that gives me great joy" (WND-1, 287); and "With this body of mine, I have fulfilled the prophecies of the sutra. The more the government authorities rage against me, the greater is my joy" (WND-1, 243).

Endo: There are countless examples. In other places the Daisho-nin says: "[Hearing that the government was discussing whether to behead me or banish me from Kamakura,] I rejoiced, saying that I had long expected it to come to this" (WND-1, 764); "What greater joy could there be? [that I am to be executed for the sake of the Lotus Sutra]" (WND-1, 767); "When my head is cut off, I will experience a special joy. Having encountered great bandits, I know I will exchange their great poison for a precious jewel" (WND-2, 432); "It is indeed a matter of joy that my situation perfectly fits the sutra passage that reads, 'Again and again we will be banished.' How delightful! How gratifying!" (WND-2, 463); and "What fortune is mine to expiate in one lifetime the offenses of slandering the Law I have accumulated from the infinite past! How destined I am to serve Shakyamu-ni Buddha, the lord of teachings, whom I have never seen!" (WND-1, 402).

Ikeda: These passages seem to reverberate with the rhythm of the Daishonin's heart, the rhythm of supreme joy that is Nam-myoho-renge-kyo.

To Be "Obedient" to the Gohonzon

Suda: Incidentally, the original meaning of the term *rejoice* or *delight* [as used in many of the above examples and in the title of the Lotus Sutra's eighteenth chapter] is "obediently believe and rejoice." I think it could be said that "obedience" means faith. If so, then what is the object of one's obedience referred to in the "Benefits of Responding with Joy" chapter?

That the benefit of the fiftieth person is so immense suggests that the teaching the fiftieth person "obeys" is incomparably broad—broader than the teaching offered by the wealthy per-son who makes offerings for eighty years, which we talked about earlier. But while the sutra makes reference to the idea that one should obey this Lotus Sutra, the substance of this teaching is never made clear in the text.

Saito: In other words, what does Shakyamuni indicate that we should believe and take as our object of fundamental devotion? This is not clear. It has been a point of serious debate in Buddhist communities from ancient times.

Ikeda: That's why it is necessary to elucidate the implicit teaching. At the start of this chapter, there is mention of those who will hear this sutra after the Buddha's passing. The question is: What are people to do after Shakyamuni has died? Does the Lotus Sutra say that they should make Shakyamuni their object of fundamental devotion? No, it does not say that anywhere. Rather, it indicates that they should take as the object of fundamental devotion the Law that enabled Shakyamuni himself to become a Buddha. This is the spirit of the Lotus Sutra.

"Obedience," therefore, means faith in the Gohonzon that embodies the oneness of the Person and the Law. And the benefit of this "obedience" is the "benefit of rejoicing."

Nichiren says: "The person is the ancient Buddha of numberless major world system dust particle kalpas ago. The Law is Nam-myoho-renge-kyo of the 'Life Span' chapter. To respond to them and take joy in them is what is meant by the words 'responding with joy'" (OTT, 146). The Great Teacher Dengyo of Japan says of those who fail to grasp this point, "Even though they praise the Lotus Sutra, they destroy its heart."[9]

Suda: High Priest Nichijun made an interesting comment on this passage: "What do the priests of the Tendai school say? If they understood this [the heart of the Lotus Sutra], they would say that the present age is that of Nichiren Daishonin. Those who don't [understand] continue to trample on the heart of the Lotus Sutra. That is why there are many priests from that school who have converted to the Daishonin's faith; because in the depths of their teaching lies the heart of the Lotus Sutra."[10]

Endo: In that sense, the latter half of the "Benefits of Responding with Joy" chapter should be read as describing the great benefit deriving from faith in the Gohonzon. Following the discussion of the fiftieth person, there is an explanation of three types of benefit received.

First, it says that a person who hears about the Mystic Law is sure to gain material happiness:

> As a result of the benefits so obtained, when he is reborn in his next existence he will enjoy the finest, most superior and wonderful elephants, horses, and carriages, and palanquins decked with rare treasures, and will mount up to the heavenly palaces. (LSOC, 288)

Second, it says that the person will acquire the merit to become a leader:

> The benefits gained by this person will be such that when he is reborn he will be in a place where the lord Shakra is seated, where the heavenly king Brahma is seated, or where a wheel-turning sage king is seated. (LSOC, 288)

It says the person will become Shakra, Brahma or a wheel-turning sage king. In modern terms, this means that if the person works in a company, he or she can become a manager or the company president or a leader in the community and a leader of propagation of the Mystic Law. This chapter is basically saying that those who take faith can become leaders in their realm of society.

Ikeda: That's right. The Lotus Sutra embodies the "science of leadership." The training that we receive in our efforts for kosen-rufu in the present is the cause that enables us to become great leaders in lifetime after lifetime and world after world. Absolutely no effort that we make in our Buddhist practice is wasted.

Endo: Third, it says that the person will acquire abundant wisdom and the benefit to enjoy excellent health in both body and mind.

The sutra goes on to describe fifty kinds of benefit the person will receive from encouraging others to learn about the Mystic Law. In addition to keen faculties and wisdom, it says that the person will be wholesome in appearance and healthy in mouth and tongue, teeth and nose, and in every respect. It concludes, "In each existence he is born into, he will see the Buddha, hear his Law, and have faith in his teachings" (LSOC, 289).

Saito: The person will possess an utterly free state of life, enjoying unsurpassed economic, spiritual and physical good fortune, wisdom and merit.

Ikeda: Last, it says that the person will enjoy a state in which all desires are fulfilled. In life, there are both mountains and valleys. But by maintaining faith throughout we attain a golden state where we can look back over our existence and say, "This was the best possible life I could have lived." Just as the fire produced by a single match can set a vast field of dry grass ablaze, our strenuous work for kosen-rufu produces benefit as expansive as the universe.

THE JOY OF LIVING BASED ON THE DAISHONIN'S TEACHINGS

Saito: I heard the experience of Fumiko Matsuda, who was a victim of the atomic bombing of Hiroshima. Mrs. Matsuda joined the Soka Gakkai in 1956. When she heard President Toda deliver his declaration calling for the abolition of nuclear weapons (in Yokohama in 1957), she was so moved that she decided to dedicate herself to spreading the Daishonin's teaching.

Although she suffered from seven ailments, including anemia, rheumatism and gastrointestinal obstructions—all aftereffects of radiation exposure—she overcame these one by one in the course of activities. She has in fact become so healthy that to this day she continues vigorously carrying out activities as a senior leader of Hiroshima Prefecture.

When she was sixty, she realized that she had not read all of Nichiren Daishonin's writings. Saying she felt ashamed that she had never even looked at some of the Daishonin's writings, she challenged herself to read all of them. The first time through, it took her five years. She gradually improved her speed and is now reportedly on her fifth reading.

As to the benefit she has received as a result of this effort, Mrs. Matsuda explains that she has stopped complaining. She never complains of being weary or tired. "Nowhere in his writings does the Daishonin express such sentiments," she notes, adding that her former complaints have now been replaced by a hardy optimism. I understand she is increasingly ardent in her passion to change the social environment, aware of the tendency of people to succumb to pessimism.

Ikeda: I have heard a great deal about Mrs. Matsuda. The fact that our membership includes countless such grass-roots champions is the pride of the SGI. This is wonderful.

"I will live exactly as the Daishonin teaches!" This is the faith of "rejoicing." The SGI has labored with the fundamental spirit to live according to Nichiren Daishonin's writings. By striving to do this, we can experience true joy and benefit.

In short, no benefit can compare to the joy of dedicating one's life to kosen-rufu. No joy is greater than the joy of propagating the Mystic Law. Nothing is greater than the joy of seeing other people become happy as a result of our efforts in dialogue. And when we rejoice at others' happiness, our own lives become increasingly pure.

Propagation has nothing to do with arrogance. On the contrary, it is motivated by a sincere desire to share Nichiren Buddhism with others, delighted at our good fortune to have been born as human beings and to be able to expound the Law. Whether the other person decides to take our advice is a separate matter.

SHARING BUDDHISM IS ITSELF GREAT BENEFIT

Ikeda: The "Benefits of Responding with Joy" chapter explains that just by inviting someone to listen to a discussion of the Lotus Sutra, we accumulate immense benefit. It says that the act itself of making room for a visitor in such a meeting place produces benefit. Accordingly, the benefit we receive by telling someone about Buddhism is truly enormous.

Whether or not the person begins practicing after hearing an explanation of the Mystic Law, our benefit is the same. President Toda once commented humorously about people who had difficulty taking faith no matter how many people talked to them, saying, "These people have given that many more members the opportunity to receive tremendous benefit."

Endo: So, if someone decides to take faith after seven people have spoken to him or her about Nam-myoho-renge-kyo, all seven receive benefit.

Ikeda: That's right. We receive benefit as a result of our efforts to enable others to hear about the Mystic Law, regardless of whether they practice or how many others talk to them. When we realize this, we know even greater joy.

Those carrying out the practice of propagation deserve

hearty praise from all. They are supremely noble emissaries of the Buddha. When we have this spirit to applaud those carrying out propagation, then everyone experiences profound happiness, and kosen-rufu expands still further.

When we possess the kind of strong faith where we love the Gohonzon, love chanting Nam-myoho-renge-kyo, and love SGI activities, our life overflows with the "benefits of responding with joy."

NOTES

1. Transmission section: One of the three divisions of a sutra, along with preparation and revelation.

2. Ajita: Another name for Bodhisattva Maitreya.

3. *Toda Josei zenshu* (Collected Writings of Josei Toda) (Tokyo: Seikyo Shimbunsha, 1983), vol. 3, p. 201.

4. From the January 1, 1956, *Seikyo Shimbun*.

5. From the May 9, 1958, *Seikyo Shimbun*.

6. *Toda Josei zenshu* (Collected Writings of Josei Toda) (Tokyo: Seikyo Shimbunsha, 1984), vol. 4, p. 378.

7. This passage reads in full: "Single-mindedly chant Nam-myoho-renge-kyo and urge others to do the same; that will remain as the only memory of your present life in this human world."

8. Fumiko Hayashi, *Horoki* (Journal of a Vagabond).

9. *Hokke Shuku* (The Outstanding Principles of the Lotus Sutra).

10. From the November 8, 1957, *Seikyo Shimbun*.

PART III

"Benefits of the Teacher of the Law" Chapter

3 Those Who Spread the Mystic Law Can Purify Their Senses

The words "teacher of the Law" mean the teacher of the Law who carries out the five practices. The word "ben efits" (kudoku) means the reward that is represented by the purification of the six sense organs. In general we may say that now Nichiren and his followers, who chant Nam-myoho-renge-kyo, are carrying out the purification of the six sense organs. Hence they are acting as teachers of the Law of Myoho-renge-kyo and possess great virtue (toku).

The element ku *in the word* kudoku *means good fortune or happiness.* (OTT, 147–48)

Ikeda: In this world of the Latter Day of the Law, none are more noble than those who pray and take action out of the desire to help others become happy.

Often when we tell another about Buddhism, even if it's with all sincerity, we find ourselves ridiculed and sometimes treated with outright contempt. SGI members nevertheless continue to engage people in dialogue with patience and compassion. They are carrying out the sacred work of the Bodhisattvas of the Earth.

It's important to remember that every time we are slighted or vilified on account of our efforts to tell others about Buddhism, our lives become purer. That's why President Toda used to say: "You should be filled with appreciation when you are treated badly as a result of your efforts to share Buddhism with others. That's because being subjected to such behavior enables us to rid our lives of negative karma and its effects and consequently move in the direction of absolute happiness."[1]

Endo: This is the concept of the "purification of the six sense organs,"[2] the central theme of the "Benefits of the Teacher of the Law" chapter we are now discussing.

Suda: This chapter explains the benefits received by teachers of the Law—those who propagate the teaching in addition to practicing it themselves.

Ikeda: Contrary to popular perception, the term *teacher of the Law* is not synonymous with the term *priest*. As we noted in discussing "Teacher of the Law," the tenth chapter, a teacher of the Law is a person who takes the Law as his or her teacher and who teaches others about it. Anyone, whether priest or layperson, who seeks out and propagates the Law is a teacher of the Law.

Saito: The "Teacher of the Law" chapter describes these teachers as "lay persons or monks or nuns who read and recite the Lotus Sutra" (LSOC, 201). Anyone who earnestly devotes him- or herself to Buddhist practice is a noble teacher of the Law. Someone who becomes idle or lazy, however, even if he or she wears the garments of a priest, is, as the Daishonin says, "no better than an animal dressed in priestly robes" (WND-1, 760). Dedication to Buddhism, not outward status, is the important distinction.

Ikeda: We can therefore state unequivocally that SGI members who single-mindedly apply and spread Nichiren Buddhism are the true teachers of the Law in this day and age. Where, outside of the SGI, can people declare confidently: "I have found the correct path in life!" "I have discovered the way to genuine happiness!"?

Teachers of the Law are spiritual leaders who, in a society overshadowed by darkness and confusion, strive to guide others toward happiness. They are beacons illuminating the community and society. There are countless such people in the great grass-roots organization that is the SGI. I'm sure each of you knows many of them.

Suda: Indeed. In Tokyo's Sumida Ward, where I live, there is a member named Chii Sekino who has personally converted 106 households to Nichiren Buddhism. She joined the Soka Gakkai in 1956. Last year [1997], she converted three households, and this year [1998] she has already converted two more. As a result, a tremendous surge of propagation has swept through her chapter. Moreover, the people she has introduced to the practice have realized steady growth, and many of them are currently active as chapter- and district-level leaders.

Ikeda: To help a hundred people completely transform their lives for the better is a great achievement that few scholars or business leaders could claim to match. Coming to see things this way, without being blinded by such considerations as social status, corresponds to the "purification of the eye" as explained by the principle of the purification of the six sense organs.

Suda: Mrs. Sekino operates a wholesale business in Sumida Ward specializing in shoe-manufacturing materials. Even now, past sixty, she continues to drive around town to conduct business.

Though she is very healthy today, when she joined the Soka Gakkai she suffered from a severe case of tuberculosis of the spine, or Pott's disease. Her mother died when she was five and for many years she lived in poverty. When she heard the guidance that there is no way to transform your destiny other than by sharing Buddhism with others, she determined to dedicate herself to doing just that.

Her first attempts at Buddhist dialogue consisted of talking to the people who visited her at the hospital. Although she had been told she would likely have to spend years in the hospital convalescing, she was discharged after just six months. Her recovery was so remarkable that she began working again only four days after her release. Through this experience, she gained supreme confidence and conviction in Nichiren Buddhism.

Saito: No one is stronger than a person of conviction.

Suda: Mrs. Sekino says, "I make efforts to spread Buddhism 365 days a year." Each morning and evening she prays to meet people with whom she shares some connection. As a result, she runs into people who are interested in learning about Buddhism. The people she introduced to the practice this year were old friends she had not seen for many years until she happened to run into them on the street.

She also writes down the names of those to whom she would like to introduce Nichiren Buddhism and offers prayers each day, thinking about how happy they would become if only they would take faith.

Endo: Nothing is more powerful than compassionate prayer. People cannot fail to listen to someone who has genuine concern for them. Doubtless Mrs. Sekino's friends can sense her strong concern and her prayers for their happiness.

Suda: Mrs. Sekino's method of propagation does not involve a lot of complex doctrine. She believes that even a few words will suffice. Most of the time, her friends readily decide to join. It's not a matter of theory; it comes down to using words that move a person's life.

THE LIFE FORCE TO WIN OVER
THE ENVIRONMENT

Ikeda: Sharing Buddhism with others means praying whole-heartedly that they will truly feel your sincerity. Then, regardless of how they respond at the time, they will be left with a deep sense of trust, knowing how much you care for their happiness. They will be profoundly moved. That's what's important.

Incidentally, why do more than a billion Chinese people to this day continue to cherish the memory of Zhou Enlai, born one hundred years ago this year [1998]? Many Chinese will tell you that just thinking of Premier Zhou brings tears to their eyes. The reason for this tremendous affection is that Zhou, more than anyone else, devoted himself heart and soul to working for the happiness of the Chinese people. This is the same kind of sincere dedication to the country as was exhibited by Chuke K'ung-ming, whose life a poet memorializes with these words: "Though some may argue his success or failure / He was loyal to the very end."[3] The happiness of the people was Zhou Enlai's only concern. That's why to this day, more than twenty-five years after his death [in January 1976], his memory still elicits feelings of warmth.

Endo: When you invited the Chinese Central Nationalities Song and Dance Ensemble to come to Japan to commemorate the hundredth anniversary of Zhou Enlai's birth, Masao Shimizu, director and president of the Matsuyama Ballet, wrote:

> Premier Zhou Enlai had a special feeling for the arts. That's because he had a rich sensitivity and a great love for the people. Though a person will eventually disappear from the world, love endures forever in the human heart. This is the source of the fondness of China's 1.4 billion people for Zhou Enlai.

Saito: In propagating Buddhism, too, it is important to pray until one's sincere desire for the happiness of the other person is conveyed.

Ikeda: When you have a strong spirit of compassion, you can understand the worries or difficulties others are experiencing, just as an excellent physician can immediately diagnose the cause of someone's illness. This is the benefit of purifying the sense organs.

Suda: In the forty-some years since she took faith, Mrs. Sekino has completely overcome both illness and poverty. She is fond of saying, "The strongest will win." With that conviction, to fortify her life force, she makes a point of always chanting Nam-myoho-renge-kyo sincerely before telling someone about Buddhism.

In her business activities, too, she has reportedly experienced setbacks, such as people defaulting on payment, but she explains that she has developed the strength to continue advancing no matter what happens.

Saito: Isn't such strength itself the benefit gained by a teacher of the Law?

Ikeda: You could say that. A strong person is happy. At the same time, strength is relative; it depends on the relationship between one's life force and the environment. If your life force is weak and frail, then even minor problems will cause you to worry and become overwhelmed, bringing you to a deadlock. This will only make you miserable.

When we strengthen our life force even a bit, we gain the vitality to resolve problems, such as those at home. Then we are not set back by such troubles. Once we step out into the community, however, we may find ourselves stymied by problems there. Going further, though we may have developed the life force to address the issues of the peace and prosperity of the country, we may still find ourselves bewildered when it comes to dealing with the sufferings of birth, old age, sickness and death.

The Lotus Sutra enables us to tap into the life force of the universe so that, no matter what happens, we are never bound by our difficulties. Nichiren Buddhism is the teaching that gives all people the power to experience incredible energy welling forth in their lives. A person who has solid faith in the Mystic Law, therefore, is the strongest and happiest of all.

Happiness does not rely solely on the environment. There are people living in luxurious mansions who spend their days in tears. Neither, however, is our happiness entirely independent of our environment. No one could honestly claim to be happy if unable to feed his or her children.

Happiness is determined by the connection between the environment, or outer world, and our life force. A person who is controlled by a negative environment will suffer. On the other hand, a person faced with a difficult situation who can control and influence it will be happy.

Endo: So we can say that a happy person is one who has developed a strong life force.

Ikeda: Such a person has purified his or her sense organs or, in modern terms, accomplished one's human revolution. The lives of teachers of the Law—that is to say, those who exert themselves for kosen-rufu—are purified, strengthened and greatly expanded. This is the benefit accrued by teachers of the Law. At the outset of the "Benefits of the Teacher of the Law" chapter, Shakyamuni addresses a bodhisattva called Constant Exertion.

Saito: Yes. In fact, Shakyamuni addresses his teaching in this chapter to this bodhisattva.

Ikeda: Regarding this figure, Nichiren Daishonin says:

> One should understand, however, that in the Latter Day of the Law, it is the votaries of the Lotus Sutra who act as the bodhisattva Constant Exertion. Of such persons who uphold the Lotus Sutra the sutra itself says, "This is what is meant by diligence." (OTT, 150)

Specifically, Bodhisattva Constant Exertion indicates Nichiren Daishonin. But in general, we, the Daishonin's true followers, are also the recipients of this teaching. That's because we are constantly working to propagate the Law.

Endo: The chapter begins:

> At that time the Buddha said to the bodhisattva mahasattva Constant Exertion: "If good men or good women accept and uphold this Lotus Sutra, if they read it, recite it, explain and preach it, or transcribe it, such people will obtain eight hundred eye benefits, twelve hundred ear benefits, eight hundred nose benefits, twelve hundred tongue benefits, eight hundred body benefits, and twelve hundred mind benefits. With these benefits they will be able to adorn their six sense organs, making all of them pure." (LSOC, 292)

Suda: It seems that "sense organs" here indicates powers or abilities as well as the organs invested with these powers.

Saito: For instance, the eye sense refers to the ability to see, as well as the physical eye and optic nerve.

Endo: Incidentally, each of the six sense organs (the eye, ear, nose, tongue, body and mind) has its respective object (color and form, sound, odor, taste, texture and mental or spiritual phenomena).

Also, these six sense organs are said to be operated by "six consciousnesses" (sight, hearing, smell, taste, touch and thought). Collectively, these organs, objects and consciousnesses are called the "eighteen worlds."

Saito: The above passage mentions accepting and upholding the Lotus Sutra, reading, reciting, explaining and preaching, and transcribing it. These are called the "five practices." Those who carry out these practices are called "teachers of the Law who carry out the five kinds of practice." But as we've already seen in our earlier discussions, in Nichiren Buddhism the one practice of accepting and upholding the Gohonzon includes the five practices in their entirety.

In "The Real Aspect of the Gohonzon," Nichiren says, "Embracing the Lotus Sutra and chanting Nam-myoho-renge-kyo in itself encompasses the five practices" (WND-I, 833).

Ikeda: "Accepting and upholding" means practicing faith with selfless dedication. It means wholeheartedly embracing the Gohonzon and thoroughly striving for kosen-rufu. This is "constant exertion." It is to work for kosen-rufu each day over the course of one's life. Through such faith, the six sense organs are purified. Let's start by considering the benefits of the eye.

PURIFYING THE EYE ENABLES US TO DISCERN THE ESSENCE OF ALL THINGS

Endo: OK. In the sutra, the Buddha says:

> These good men and good women, with the pure physical eyes they received from their parents at birth, will view all that exists in the inner and outer

parts of the major world system, its mountains, forests, rivers, and seas, down as far as the Avichi hell and up to the Summit of Being. And in their midst they will see all the living beings, and will also see and understand all the causes and conditions created by their deeds and the births that await them as a result and recompense for those deeds. (LSOC, 292)

Ikeda: This is basically referring to the "power of insight." It is not talking about clairvoyance or some mystical superhuman power.

Suda: The advancement of science has made it possible for human beings to see with their own eyes all of the mountains and seas of the world. Since science is also concerned with investigating the laws of life and the universe, we may also view science as part of Buddhism. It is certainly true that, as a result of scientific advances, our eyes and ears have acquired tremendous power.

Saito: The more important issue, however, is whether such power equals happiness. While the tendency of science has been to direct its investigative gaze ever outward, in the absence of a corresponding growth and maturation in the inner realm of life, it will only produce misfortune.

Ikeda: The capacity to discern this path to happiness is the benefit of the eye. This does not apply only to oneself. Like a skilled physician, we see what others are seeking and what we can do to help them break through their difficulties.

President Toda had extremely keen powers of insight. Just by observing a small detail—for example, how someone walked or opened a door—he could immediately fathom what was worrying the person or the nature of his or her situation.

Saito: I understand, President Ikeda, that from the time you were a young man people would say that you had X-ray vision.

Ikeda: The heart is invisible. Buddhism enables us to perceive the heart of another and thoroughly understand how it operates. It could be said that Buddhism is the science of the spirit and medicine for the heart.

It is not easy to do, but a Buddhist leader has to be able to deftly perceive the unseen principles or functions of the heart as though using radar.

Suda: Allow me to relate the experience of a young man who was once helping to manage a Gakkai meeting you attended. At the back of the stage area hung a large banner. The young man's task was to remain behind the banner with other staff throughout the entire meeting. He could not see you, and, of course, no one knew that they were behind the banner. But at the end of the meeting, you suddenly remarked, "I would also like to thank those members behind the banner for their efforts." He later told me that the surprise and emotion he felt at that moment have remained a cherished memory.

Ikeda: I'm not psychic or anything of the sort. It's just that I have the strong determination never to overlook those who are working behind the scenes and to show them my appreciation.

The Okinawa Training Center has an aquarium with rare tropical fish. Thinking that catching the fish must have been a difficult task, I lost no time sending a message of appreciation.

People might look at a display or something and say, "Isn't that beautiful," but rarely do they consider the effort of the person or people who prepared it. Probably there are those who, their hearts inert and cold as stone, won't be moved enough to say anything.

I always try to see the underlying essence, the invisible roots that lie buried and out of sight.

Endo: I often hear about how, when visiting a culture center, before even entering the building, you walk around the back to encourage those working behind the scenes—giving people quite a stir, I might add.

Ikeda: In doing so, I'm not trying to check up on people. When you observe things from an oblique angle, rather than from the front, you can usually grasp the entirety of the situation.

In the case of a magazine, for instance, publishers naturally put effort into the cover and the initial sections. This is probably true for the staff of *The Daibyakurenge*, too, I would imagine. By reading the articles in the back, however, you can accurately gauge just how much real effort is being put into the publication. It is the "power of vision" that enables us to discern this.

We should each strive to be attentive to the efforts of those around us.

Since I myself have worked behind the scenes, I understand people's inconspicuous efforts. It is in the wings rather than on center stage that you often find people of real strength and ability. I am always thinking about such people, and each day from morning to evening I do everything I can to encourage them.

Saito: I once heard someone describe you as "having many different sides," noting your multifarious activities—as a religious leader, a social activist, an author, a photographer, an educator. The person asked me how I would sum up your work. I answered simply that it is the work of encouraging people. I think we could also say that it is the work of fostering capable people.

Endo: Perhaps it is only through such constant exertion day in and day out that we can polish our lives and purify the eye.

Firm Resolve Brings Out the "Eye of Wisdom"

Ikeda: With regard to purifying the eye, in a verse section Shakyamuni says:

> *If in the midst of the great assembly*
> *someone with a fearless mind*
> *preaches this Lotus Sutra,*
> *listen to the benefits he will receive!* (LSOC, 292)

When we go out among others and dauntlessly spread the teaching, we receive the benefit of purifying the eye; we can develop the eye of wisdom without fail. This is another meaning of the opening of the eyes. Nichiren writes, "When the skies are clear, the ground is illuminated" (WND-1, 376).

In our daily lives, too, we need to plainly see the best direction in which to proceed. We mustn't live foolishly. When we exercise our ingenuity and tenaciously exert ourselves based on faith, never becoming impatient, we can discern the supreme path for our lives. We also develop insight into the future of our family, our community and society.

Nichiren Daishonin, as the Buddha of the Latter Day of the Law, could see clearly throughout past, present and future. Although we are ordinary people, the eye of wisdom comes to shine acutely as a result of our practice.

Suda: Today, it is clear that you have had great foresight, President Ikeda, but I understand that initially you faced much resistance because no one could fathom what you were doing.

Saito: I also heard there was a great deal of opposition to your plans to found Soka University, which today contributes greatly to education and culture, as well as the Min-On Concert Association and the Fuji Art Museum.

Ikeda: The holding of culture festivals, the formation of the fife and drum corps, the building of training centers—each of these initiatives was met with widespread opposition.

To help more people understand the wonder of Buddhism, we need to create a universal forum of culture, education and peace. If we use colors to describe the Soka Gakkai organization, I think we could say that in the past it had a gray tint. I have tried to change the organization to give it a colorful hue.

Fierce determination is key. When you are firmly resolved, you can open the eye of wisdom. The Daishonin says:

> If in a single moment of life we exhaust the pains and trials of millions of kalpas, then instant after instant there will arise in us the three Buddha bodies with which we are eternally endowed. Nammyoho-renge-kyo is just such a "diligent" practice. (OTT, 214)

Rather than feeling distressed over a lack of capable people in an area, for example, the first thing one should do is offer prayer. To secure peace based on the teachings of Buddhism is the Buddha's will. It is the Buddha's enterprise and the Buddha's work. As Nichiren Daishonin promised, Bodhisattvas of the Earth could therefore not fail to be in any given area, no matter how remote.

The problem isn't that there are no capable people; it's simply that we cannot "see" them. The solution is to offer earnest prayer. We also need to be determined to take full responsibility without anyone's help. Such resolve will without a doubt bring forth people able and willing to work for the same cause.

The Soka Gakkai is an organization of utmost sincerity. That is the meaning of faith; it is the way of purifying the six sense organs.

In this society rife with corruption and confusion, faith is the one absolute that will never betray a person of genuine sincerity. Such a person will triumph in the realm of faith. We are infinitely fortunate to have encountered such a wonderful realm.

This is what the Lotus Sutra means by "lotus flower in the water" (LSOC, 263)—though its roots are sunk in muddy water, the lotus itself remains pure. The Bodhisattvas of the Earth are the lotus. They exhibit the purification of the six sense organs.

The six sense organs are the interface between the small universe of our life and the cosmos. They are the portal connecting the microcosm and the macrocosm. Purifying the six sense organs means completely harmonizing one's life with the universe, tuning in to its rhythm.

Through our practice, we harmonize our lives with the rhythm, the wavelength, of the Mystic Law. We are then endowed with the power to advance confidently and without any hindrance, freed to live our lives in sync with the universe. This is what it means to attain Buddhahood in one's present form, to do one's human revolution, and to purify the six sense organs.

Saito: The sutra in one place speaks of "the pure physical eyes they received from their parents at birth" (LSOC, 292). The important point here is that we can actually change even such physical features.

Ikeda: Buddhism is concerned with reality. There's no such thing as Buddhism divorced from reality.

Practicing faith does not mean that your life will be free of the mud of suffering. It means acquiring the life force not to be defeated by suffering. In fact, it's necessary to have lots of struggles. Faith means developing the state of life in which you can enjoy even the challenge of facing and overcoming hardships.

Also, though we might speak of "purifying the eye," there are people who cannot physically see. Through faith in the Mystic Law, they can absolutely open the "eye of the heart."

Likewise, having perfect vision does not mean that a person can perceive the essence of things.

Endo: Helen Keller is renowned for her miraculous victory over the threefold disability of being unable to speak, hear or see. Mark Twain[1] told her: "Helen, the world is full of unseeing eyes, vacant, staring, soulless eyes."[4]

Ikeda: Twain and Keller were good friends. In her praise, Twain once remarked that the two most interesting characters of the nineteenth century were Napoleon and Helen Keller.[5] He also noted that while Napoleon had planned to conquer the world by means of force and failed, Helen Keller, while bearing the weight of a threefold disability, succeeded in winning the world over through her abundant spiritual strength.

Helen Keller inspired untold numbers of people with hope and courage. With enormous tenacity, by the sweat of her brow, she grappled her way up the mountain of learning, fell down, and climbed up again. Describing how she felt at the outset of her university studies, she proclaims: "In the wonderland of Mind I should be as free as another."[6]

The realm of the heart and mind is free. She calls it a "wonderland"—a mystical domain. She opened up a world filled with wonder in her heart. This is freedom, a state of true liberty.

Suda: President Ikeda, I recall that you gave the group in the Soka Gakkai for the vision impaired the name Freedom Group.

Ikeda: Helen Keller did not know about the Mystic Law. The members of the Freedom Group, who embrace the Mystic Law, cannot fail to open the supreme eye of wisdom and achieve boundless happiness. Indeed, this is my ardent hope; that's why I gave the group this name. The same of course also goes for other physically challenged people.

Purification of the Ears

Saito: Next, we come to the sense of hearing. The sutra explains in no uncertain terms that people who have purified the ears can hear all voices in the world. It says:

> They will gain twelve hundred ear benefits with which to purify their ears so they can hear all the different varieties of words and sounds in the major world system, down as far as the Avichi hell, up to the Summit of Being, and in its inner and outer parts. Elephant sounds, horse sounds, ox sounds, carriage sounds, weeping sounds, lamenting sounds, conch sounds, drum sounds, bell sounds, chime sounds, sounds of laughter, sounds of speaking, men's voices, women's voices, boys' voices, girls' voices, the voice of justice, the voice of injustice, bitter voices, merry voices, voices of ordinary people, voices of sages, happy voices, unhappy voices, voices of heavenly beings, dragon voices, yaksha voices, gandharva voices, asura voices, garuda voices, kimnara voices, mahoraga voices, the sound of fire, the sound of water, the sound of wind, voices of hell dwellers, voices of beasts, voices of hungry spirits, monks' voices, nuns' voices, voices of voice-hearers, voices of pratyekabuddhas, voices of bodhisattvas and voices of buddhas. In a word, although the person has not yet gained heavenly ears, with the pure and ordinary ears that he received at birth from his parents he will be able to hear and understand all the voices that exist in the inner and outer parts of the major world system. (LSOC, 293–94)

Ikeda: This covers all of the Ten Worlds. The world is filled with all kinds of voices, from the groans of beings in the realm of Hell to the compassionate voices of Buddhas leading people to happiness. Those who have gained the benefit of the ear can hear all these voices and clearly distinguish the essence of life that they express. Moreover, to hear the lion's roar of the Buddha, the powerful voice that defeats devilish forces, is the supreme happiness.

Endo: In his *Great Concentration and Insight*, the Great Teacher T'ien-t'ai of China says regarding the various grades of physicians, "The superior physician listens to the voice [of the patient], the common physician observes the color, the inferior physician examines the pulse."

Ikeda: This is from a section of *Great Concentration and Insight* titled "Observe the Patient." The Daishonin cites it in his well-known writing on the six causes of illness (WND-1, 631). Throughout its history, Buddhism has helped people address the four universal sufferings of birth, old age, sickness and death.

Certainly the voice clearly expresses the state or condition of a person's life. There are warm voices, cold voices, weak voices, spirited voices, voices resonating with profundity, voices ringing with shallowness, voices full of good fortune and benefit, voices reverberating with sincerity and voices revealing duplicity.

If we listen carefully, we will not be deceived. In a sense, the voice expresses even more about a person than what the person says.

Saito: People who excel at giving individual guidance emphasize the importance of careful listening. I think this means, in addition to hearing what the person has to say, compassionately opening one's ears and one's heart to the other person's voice.

Ikeda: The "Benefits of the Teacher of the Law" chapter says, "Because the faculties of his ears are so keen he can distinguish and understand all these sounds" (LSOC, 296).

A teacher of the Law can discern people's states of life from the sounds of their voices.

Keen here connotes sagacious. The first character of the Japanese word *somei* incorporates the element for ear. To have an ear that is acute is to have wisdom. The second character in the term *somei*, a character meaning "bright," expresses the idea of eyes that can clearly perceive the reality of things.

As Nichiren Daishonin indicates when he says, "Listen with the ears of Shih K'uang and observe with the eyes of Li Lou" (WND-I, 33),[7] we need to possess sharp ears and clear eyes. We live in an age teeming with information. This letter, which he composed and addressed to a follower named Shiiji Shiro just before the Izu Exile, can be interpreted as instruction to gather the most accurate information.

It is important to listen. The Chinese character for *holy, sage* or *sacred* consists of three elements, one of which signifies "ear." According to one explanation, the character denotes listening intently to the voice of heaven and praying. The virtue of listening to the voice of heaven—which can be interpreted as the fundamental voice of the universe—is called sagacity, and one possessing this virtue is called a sage.

Shih K'uang was in fact unable to see. He was a blind musician and a cultural figure. During the Spring and Autumn period (770–403 B.C.E.), when the kingdoms of Chin and Ch'u were at war, Shih K'uang, who served Chin, discerned the voice of death in the sound of the wind and divined the outcome of the battle, predicting the defeat of Ch'u.

Saito: The ability to recognize the tendency of the times by listening to the voices around us is part of the power gained from purifying the ears.

Ikeda: Nichiren condemned the melancholy drone of the Nembutsu as a death knell for the country and as beckoning people to take their own lives. [Nichiren writes, "It appears, therefore, that if one keeps on repeating the Nembutsu this will foster a desire to commit suicide" (WND-2, 500).]

It is said that songs follow the times, and the times follow the songs. President Toda used to point out that there was a surge in melancholy music around the time of the Great Kanto Earthquake [in 1923], such as the song that begins, "I am the withered eulalia grass of the dried riverbed. . . ."[8]

Suda: In contrast to this peal of death, Nam-myoho-renge-kyo is the peal of life. It is the rhythm of hope.

Ikeda: When this rhythm of hope enters our ears, the strife-ridden *saha* world becomes the place for us to attain Buddhahood. It becomes a land for attaining the Way through the sense of hearing.

Endo: This suggests that there are other worlds besides "lands for attaining the Way through the sense of hearing."

Ikeda: It seems to me that T'ien-t'ai addresses this in his *Profound Meaning of the Lotus Sutra*, when he says that there are, for example, "lands for attaining the Way through the sense of smell"—where you can attain the Way through fragrance.

Saito: Yes, there are lands of fragrance where the Buddha's work is carried out by means of scent, and teachings consist of fragrances.

Endo: Here, I suppose, smell is doing the Buddha's work rather than the voice.

Saito: Sutras explain that there are also "lands for attaining the Way through the sense of sight," where the teaching consists of lights and colors; "lands for attaining the Way through the sense of touch," where people attain Buddhahood through contact with heavenly garments; and "lands for attaining the Way through the sense of taste," where people attain enlightenment through food.

Suda: I imagine that people carrying out Buddhist practice in a "land for attaining the Way through the sense of taste" would all have difficulty maintaining their weight!

LETTING OTHERS HEAR "SINGING VOICES OF HOPE"

Ikeda: Buddhism is all-encompassing. While recognizing the vast potential inherent in all life, it is also cognizant of the prevalent needs of the world in which we live.

For beings on earth, the sense of hearing is very important. Of the sense organs, the ears are the first to become active at the beginning of our lives and the last to remain active at the end. It is said that a fetus in the mother's womb at about six months has completed the development of its ears and attendant nerves, so that even before birth it already knows the sound of its mother's voice.

President Makiguchi once said: "A child experiences the greatest tranquillity while in the mother's womb. If you practice faith at that time [when pregnant], it will bring great fortune to your child." Children in the womb clearly hear the sound of their mothers' voices chanting Nam-myoho-renge-kyo. Of course, the unborn child will also hear the sounds of its parents quarreling!

And, as I just mentioned, it is said that when we are approaching death, our sense of hearing is the last to go.

Endo: It is certainly true that while we can close our eyes or mouth voluntarily, our ears are always open.

Ikeda: The ears are the window of life opening from the small universe of the self onto the greater universe. They are also the gateway to the spirit through which direct access to the depths of a person's life may be gained. That is why music has the power to stir deep emotion in people.

Saito: A Soka Gakkai nurses group member told me about the experience of a terminal cancer patient, whom I will call Mr. K., who was receiving treatment at the hospital where she worked. Though only in his forties, his condition was deteriorating daily. The nurse told me she prayed that Mr. K., who was not a member, would lead the best possible existence to the very end of his life and that he would form a connection with Buddhism in this lifetime.

Having learned that the sense of hearing remains active to the end, she got a tape of Soka Gakkai songs for him as a present. Several days later, Mr. K. died. But she said that his mother told her that just before her son died he listened to the music with tears in his eyes.

Suda: His condition must have taken a turn for the worse by then.

Saito: Even so, it seems that he could hear the tape. The following day, the nurse received a phone call from Mr. K.'s wife, who wanted to use the tape that had so moved her husband. When the nurse heard this, she recalled your guidance, "It is the heart that moves the heart." She felt confident that Mr. K. and his family had understood her genuine concern.

Ikeda: Purifying the heart is the foundation for purifying the sense organs. It is purification of one's consciousness.

At any rate, since we attain the Way through the sense of hearing, it is vital that we speak, that we use our voices. We need to let people hear the voices of kosen-rufu: voices of warm encouragement, voices of justice deftly refuting falsehood, voices of conviction and joyful voices raised in song.

As Nichiren indicates in urging that we speak out vigorously and wholeheartedly (see WND-1, 394), kosen-rufu is a process whereby the single wave of one person's voice expands to produce ten thousand waves.

At the same time, since purifying the sense of hearing is vital, we need to listen attentively to the voices of the people, straining to hear if necessary. If communication is one-sided, then the sense of hearing is not at work. In this case, the ears are not purified but remain blocked.

Endo: Some politicians cannot hear a thing, even when the people are shouting right into their ears!

A Person Who Makes Steadfast Effort Has the "Fragrance of Tenacity"

Saito: With regard to the sense of smell, the sutra says, for example, "the upholder of the Lotus / by detecting their scents can know all this" (LSOC, 298). It explains that practitioners of the Lotus Sutra have the ability to distinguish keenly among all scents.

Suda: It is said that, ordinarily, a human being can distinguish several thousand smells. I understand that a perfume expert can identify as many as ten thousand!

Ikeda: The art of fragrance has long played an important role in Japanese culture. People would burn fragrant materials or wood and savor their scents. They would even hold contests in which people would compete to make the best perfume or try to determine from the scent what combination of ingredients had gone into a perfume. In Japanese, the phrase meaning *to smell incense* is also written with characters that literally mean "listening to fragrance."

Saito: The Lotus Sutra, too, uses the Chinese character for "listen" to indicate the verb *to smell.*

Ikeda: Since the Lotus Sutra is an important cornerstone of Japanese culture, a cultured person in ancient times would naturally have read the sutra repeatedly.

In any event, I think the point here is that each person has a unique fragrance. I'm not talking about perfume or body odor but a unique fragrance of the heart or fragrance of life. A person who studies, makes effort and strives to grow with single-minded diligence possesses the fragrance of tenacity. Such a person exudes a robust fragrance, like that of a fresh sapling.

On the other hand, people who spend their lives in decadent idleness seem to emit from their entire beings an unpleasant aroma, like that of something rotting. The difference is really striking.

Suda: It is the purification of the sense of smell that enables us to detect this.

VOICES THAT INVIGORATE PEOPLE

Saito: Next we come to the purification of the tongue. The benefits of the tongue are of two kinds. The first is that whatever a person eats tastes good. The second is the ability to explain Buddhism in such a way as to bring joy to the listener.

Ikeda: The first pertains to the mystery of state of life. A person who is healthy and full of vitality will find even simple fare delicious. To a person afflicted with grief, however, even the most sumptuous feast will taste like dirt. That's not to say, mind you, that we should forget about trying to cook nice meals! This merely shows that state of life is a mysterious phenomenon.

Likewise, a person who has purified the sense of sight will find a miracle in even the most mundane scene. And a person who has purified the sense of hearing will hear Mozart in the cacophony of a baby's cries.

Suda: Wouldn't it be wonderful to hear symphonic beauty in even the angry accusations of one's spouse!

Saito: President Toda used to emphasize that having a state of life of absolute happiness means experiencing joy under any circumstances. He would say: "When you achieve absolute happiness, you don't have money troubles, and you enjoy good health. Your home is peaceful, your business goes well, your heart is filled with a sense of abundance, and everything you see or hear makes you think, 'How delightful!' When the world appears to you in this way, then this world, this strife-ridden *saha* world, becomes a Buddha land. That is attaining Buddhahood."[9] He would say that even a quarrel with your spouse, for example, is joyful. And that when you get angry, it is with a feeling of contentment.

Ikeda: That description gives me a sense of leisurely looking down on the world from tufts of cottonlike clouds in a brilliant blue sky! To attain such a lofty state of life, we need to wholeheartedly and resolutely exert ourselves in faith with a singleness of purpose like that of a jetliner flying through the sky. That is the teaching of the "Benefits of the Teacher of the Law" chapter.

The "teacher of the Law" is a leader of kosen-rufu, a person who dedicates his or her life to working for peace and human happiness. When we become such a teacher of the Law, we receive the great benefit of absolute happiness.

Endo: Kyoko Terasawa, a group leader in Tokyo's Taito Ward, is renowned as a champion at promoting subscriptions to the *Seikyo Shimbun* newspaper. She doesn't have an environment that is particularly conducive to doing so; she is a regular wage-earner who works in a shop in the busy Akihabara area of Tokyo.

Ikeda: It is such individuals who sustain the Soka Gakkai. I am profoundly moved by their selfless dedication. They are heroes. They are kings and queens. They deserve everyone's heartfelt applause and praise. People with strong backgrounds in Buddhist study may be quick to toss around high-sounding words, but they are no match for such members when it comes to practice.

Endo: The eight-story building where Mrs. Terasawa works houses some forty shops and offices. She brightly greets the people she sees entering or leaving the building, developing friendly relationships with them.

In the process, of course, if there is anything she can do to assist people, for example, by helping tidy up, she readily lends a hand. She has tenaciously continued such efforts to build trust over the years. Many of the people she asks to subscribe to the newspaper do so solely on the basis of her recommendation.

Suda: She must have rock-solid determination to make such steadfast efforts.

Endo: Mrs. Terasawa was raised by her grandfather and has no recollection of her parents. When she was four, she learned that her parents had already died. When she was in the fourth grade, her grandfather died and she was taken in by a nearby family. Unable to receive even the most basic education, her early life was difficult.

She went on to work in a variety of jobs—as a maid, in retail, as a waitress. Ten years ago, at fifty-three, she got married. It was then that, at her husband's introduction, she joined the Soka Gakkai. Meeting her husband and encountering the Mystic Law changed Mrs. Terasawa's life completely. Up to that time, she had lived a solitary, uneasy existence. But after she started practicing, her worries disappeared, and she began to experience genuine fulfillment—both spiritually and in her day-to-day life.

Her sense of appreciation in developing a "state of life that I could never have imagined" has become the driving force in her practice. She stood up, determining that she could best contribute to kosen-rufu by promoting subscriptions and expanding the circle of those who understand the Soka Gakkai.

Saito: I know it's not a matter of method alone, but I wonder if she does something unique to get such outstanding results.

Endo: She says that since she made this determination, whether sleeping or waking, her thoughts have been constantly filled with the *Seikyo Shimbun*. Her sincerity is deeply moving. Mrs. Terasawa carefully cuts out members' experiences or other sections from the *Seikyo Shimbun*, like the "Daily Words," and presents them to people. In the course of reading the paper, she finds herself thinking: "This experience is perfect for that person. I'd really like him to read it."

She says that she can tell the state of people's lives just from hearing their voices. For instance, she might think, "This person sounds quite happy, but there is something missing behind that veil of energy." She can then say things that make a difference in the person's life.

Ikeda: This is truly an example of the purification of the sense of hearing. It is the state described by the line of the sutra: "Because the faculties of his ears are so keen / he can distinguish and understand all these sounds" (LSOC, 296). This is describing an expert on humanity, a master at dialogue. Also, these are the characteristics of someone who has purified the tongue. The sutra says:

If with these faculties of the tongue he undertakes to expound and preach in the midst of the great assembly, he will produce a deep and wonderful voice capable of penetrating the mind and causing all who hear it to rejoice and delight. (LSOC, 301)

Mrs. Terasawa is doubtless reaping the wonderful effects of all her efforts.

A LEADER SHOULD BE LIKE THE SUN

Saito: The sutra describes the benefit of the body as follows: "They will acquire pure bodies, like pure lapis lazuli, such as living beings delight to see" (LSOC, 302). In other words, a teacher of the Law acquires a dignified appearance to which people are naturally attracted.

Suda: Pure lapis lazuli is translucent when it has been thoroughly polished. Lapis lazuli, one of the seven kinds of gems,[10] is now thought to be either beryl or a type of glass.

Ikeda: This passage is saying that the person's life comes to shine like a crystal-clear mirror. Everyone around them feels joyful and refreshed. Such a person, in other words, becomes a sunlike presence.

A leader has to have a bright face and vitality like the rising sun.

Saito: A final benefit of the body, which is purified, is to discern the true nature of all life in the Ten Worlds as if reflected in a clear mirror.

Ikeda: This means the ability to tell people's life-tendency the moment you meet them. When we live out our lives based on the Mystic Law, we can clearly see the state of others' lives.

We can do so through having compassion. We must never be highhanded or arrogant, claiming to have the power to see through people. We are all ordinary people. We are all members of the family of the original Buddha and the family of the SGI. While we have to see through people with evil intentions, we must also make constant efforts to encourage and protect our fellow members.

A Relentless Fighting Spirit

Saito: Last, we come to purification of mind. The sutra says that one who hears just a single verse or phrase will understand "infinite and boundless teachings." Moreover, it says that the person can freely expound the meaning of that one verse or phrase over the course of a month, four months or a year. And the teaching he or she expounds "will never be contrary to the true aspect" (LSOC, 304).

Ikeda: The content of that person's speech accords entirely and perfectly with the truth of the universe.

Saito: Yes. The sutra further says: "If they should expound some text of the secular world or speak on matters of government or occupations that sustain life, they will in all cases conform to the correct Law" (LSOC, 304). This is the benefit of purifying the mind.

Ikeda: Through purifying the mind, practitioners become wiser. In lifetime after lifetime, they may become great scholars or people of unsurpassed insight.

In short, purifying the sense organs means transforming one's entire being into a vehicle of kosen-rufu. It's not a matter of shrewdness or calculation; when we work selflessly and wholeheartedly for kosen-rufu without begrudging our lives, then our entire being overflows with boundless life force. Wisdom, vitality and compassion all well forth.

Even after people grow old and their eyesight fades, they can still move their hands, so they can write letters. Since they can move their mouths, they can call people on the phone. This is not a matter of pushing oneself unreasonably. The important thing is that our hearts burn with a fighting spirit. Manifesting such faith purifies the sense organs.

No matter what worries or sufferings we might have, we can change them all into value and benefit. Such a great life force is the benefit gained by a teacher of the Law.

In conclusion, those who live out their lives together with the SGI, an organization dedicated to actualizing the Buddha's will and decree, and single-mindedly work for peace and the happiness of humankind are on the ultimate path in life.

A person who steadfastly moves forward is certain to win. A person who chants Nam-myoho-renge-kyo through everything will absolutely win.

NOTES

1. *Toda Josei zenshu* (Collected Writings of Josei Toda) (Tokyo: Seikyo Shimbunsha, 1981), vol. 1, p. 133.

2. Purification of the six sense organs: Also, purification of the six senses. Eradication of earthly desires caused by the working of the six sense organs—eyes, ears, nose, tongue, body and mind. According to the "Benefits of the Teacher of the Law" chapter, one can purify the functions of the six sense organs by carrying out the five practices of embracing, reading, reciting, teaching, and transcribing the Lotus Sutra.

3. A line from a poem by the Japanese poet Bansui Doi, "A Star Falls in the Autumn Wind on the Wuchang Plain," dedicated to the

legendary Chinese minister Chuke K'ung-ming (181–234), hero of the epic saga *Romance of the Three Kingdoms*.

4. Helen Keller, *Midstream: My Later Life* (New York: Doubleday, Doran & Company, Inc., 1929), p. 49.

5. Helen Keller, *The Story of My Life* (New York: Doubleday & Company, Inc., 1954), p. 225.

6. Ibid., p. 85.

7. Shih K'uang and Li Lou: Legendary figures in ancient China famed, respectively, for their extraordinary hearing and vision.

8. Lyrics from "Sendo Kouta" (The Ditty of a Boatman), which became popular around the early 1920s.

9. *Toda Josei zenshu* (Tokyo: Seikyo Shimbunsha, 1984), vol. 4, p. 259.

10. Seven kinds of gems: gold, silver, lapis lazuli, giant clam shell, coral, pearl and carnelia.

PART IV

"The Bodhisattva Never Disparaging" Chapter

4   A Struggle Against Arrogance

Ikeda: The seventeenth-century Japanese haiku poet Matsuo Basho wrote, "Myriads of things past / Are brought to my mind — / These cherry blossoms!"[1] Just as in Basho's verse, each time the cherry trees blossom I am reminded of how the blossoms looked on that day, that spring forty years ago, when Josei Toda died. On the day of the funeral, the air was filled with falling cherry petals. As they floated to the ground, each petal shone as if it were alive. It seemed as though the cherry trees, too, were saddened at the departure of this great champion of the Mystic Law.

Nichijun, the sixty-fifth high priest of Nichiren Shoshu, who had rushed to the scene when he learned of Mr. Toda's death, said: "President Toda was a truly remarkable person. . . . He was a Buddha." Throughout his life, Mr. Toda expended every ounce of energy for the sake of the people and struggled continually against the forces of nationalism.

During World War II, it seems even cherry blossoms were enlisted to serve Japanese nationalism. Propagandists glorified death for the nationalist cause with slogans like "To fall vigorously and suddenly like a cherry petal is what it means to be Japanese." This was appalling.

In fact, in Japan, cherry trees have traditionally symbolized living life to the fullest. In ancient times, people observed the cherry blossoms to ascertain the duration and extent to which they would be in bloom. It was held that if the cherry blossoms were numerous and stayed in bloom for a long time, there would be a rich harvest that year.

Saito: So if they bloomed in full force and then fell all at once, people would have had cause for concern.

Endo: The militants had turned the traditional view on its head.

Ikeda: From around the middle of the nineteenth century, a type of cherry tree called *Someiyoshino* (*Prunus yedoensis matsum*) was planted throughout the country. The rapidly scattering blossoms of this tree, in particular, were used to create the nationalistic image of suddenly falling in battle, which I mentioned earlier.

Suda: Cherry trees in places such as Tokyo characteristically blossom before the leaves appear, with the flowers blooming all at once and quickly scattering.

Endo: Power will twist anything it can to its advantage.

Saito: Moreover, after a while, people gradually forget the original meaning behind certain images and just accept the new meaning as a given.

Suda: Learning that cherry blossoms originally were not a symbol of death but of a resolute and fulfilling life comes as a shock. It never occurred to me that these blossoms had once been entrusted with people's hopes for an abundant harvest.

Ikeda: President Toda was committed throughout his life to realizing the hopes of the people. As a result of his two years in prison, he was physically in very bad shape. But summoning every ounce of strength, he dedicated himself fully as the disciple of Tsunesaburo Makiguchi, the first Soka Gakkai president, who had been killed by the state's injustice. Mr. Toda's life force was truly miraculous. His life epitomized the teaching of the "Life Span" chapter.

On January 1 of the year President Toda died (1958), he delivered what would be his last New Year's lecture. Although very weak from a long battle with illness, his voice was filled with energy. It is interesting that, on this occasion, he discussed the integration of the three mystic principles[2] in the "Life Span" chapter.

He emphasized the point that Nichiren Daishonin is the Buddha of true cause, and that the true Buddha does not exist anywhere apart from this real *saha* world, the world of suffering.

Endo: That pertains to the mystic principle of the true land, which is based on the passage, "Ever since then I have been constantly in this saha world, preaching the Law, teaching, and converting" (LSOC, 266).

Ikeda: Although mythical Buddhas were mentioned [by Shakyamuni] as expedient means, a Buddha is not an imaginary being. A genuine Buddha dwells in this real, impure world, going among those who are suffering the most, sharing their misery and sadness, and leading them to happiness. Only one who lives this way can be called a Buddha.

Moreover, because the Buddha is dedicated to helping people become happy, the Buddha meets persecution from arrogant forces of authority such as secular leaders and priests, and is hated even by the very people he is trying to help. He is subject to "curses and abuse" and is struck with "sticks of wood or tiles and stones" (LSOC, 309). The Buddha dwells in the midst of such great hardship.

A Buddha is not an otherworldly being basking in enlightenment. A Buddha is the first to dive in among the fierce waves of society. One who does so will absolutely encounter persecution and even be subjected to physical harm. Those who live in a calculating manner, on the other hand, disregarding the people and looking only to protect themselves, are something other than Buddhas. Such behavior is evil.

Soka Gakkai members, including President Toda himself, have ceaselessly striven to achieve peace and happiness for all humanity. The light of genuine Buddhism shines only upon such endeavors. That's what President Toda taught in what could be called his last lecture on the Lotus Sutra.

Saito: To struggle amid society and undergo persecution—this in itself is the teaching of the "Bodhisattva Never Disparaging" chapter.

Ikeda: Nichiren Daishonin says, "The heart of the Buddha's lifetime of teachings is the Lotus Sutra, and the heart of the practice of the Lotus Sutra is found in the 'Never Disparaging' chapter" (WND-1, 852). Basically, the ultimate teaching of Buddhism is the Lotus Sutra. And the concrete practice of the Lotus Sutra is explained in the "Bodhisattva Never Disparaging" chapter.

Suda: The passage you just cited is followed by the famous line: "What does Bodhisattva Never Disparaging's profound respect for people signify? The purpose of the appearance in this world of Shakyamuni Buddha, the lord of teachings, lies in his behavior as a human being" (WND-1, 852).

Endo: In other words, Shakyamuni appeared in the world and expounded the Law to instruct people how to conduct themselves as human beings, how they should live. The conclusion that he arrives at is the way of life of Bodhisattva Never Disparaging.

Ikeda: With these extraordinary words, Nichiren is explaining the essence of Buddhism. On that premise, let us commence our study of the "Bodhisattva Never Disparaging" chapter.

Helping Those Who Are Suffering the Most

Suda: To begin with, the three chapters that follow "Life Span of the Thus Come One," the sixteenth chapter—"Distinctions in Benefits," "Benefits of Responding with Joy" and "Benefits of the Teacher of the Law"—explain the benefit of propagation. The twentieth chapter, "Bodhisattva Never Disparaging," explains not only the good fortune and benefit that those who spread the Lotus Sutra receive, but also the unfortunate circumstances met by those who slander the sutra's votaries.

Saito: It explains this by recounting the experience of one practitioner, a bodhisattva named Never Disparaging.

Ikeda: There are various interesting explanations of this bodhisattva's name. In Kumarajiva's Chinese-language translation, the name means someone who never disparages or looks down on others. In contrast, I understand that in the original Sanskrit text it can be interpreted as meaning someone who is always disparaged.

Endo: That's right. Another Chinese translation of the sutra by Dharmaraksha renders the chapter title as "The One Who Is Always Scorned and Treated with Contempt."

Ikeda: This could certainly be said of the Soka Gakkai. We have been constantly ridiculed by Japanese society, where there is a pronounced tendency to revere the powerful and scorn the masses. Many once sneered at our organization as a gathering of the poor and the sick. But President Toda declared that helping the poor and the sick is the main focus of a genuine religion.

So-called religious organizations that aim only to make money wouldn't concern themselves in the least with people of scant resources, much less with sick people.

A true religion exists for those who are suffering. Its purpose is to enable those faced with severe hardship to achieve real happiness.

We have been constantly disparaged by people who fail to understand this sublime spirit. Nevertheless, we have courageously reached out to suffering people and offered them genuine support. While showing them we care, we have helped them realize that they can definitely become happy by cultivating the world of Buddhahood within their own lives. We have steadfastly encouraged them and made them aware of the Mystic Law. We have expended great energy in educating and caring for people one on one. This is the conduct of bodhisattvas who never disparage others.

Saito: It is certainly impossible to teach others Nichiren Buddhism and encourage their practice without genuinely respecting them. Once we disregard someone, thinking that they'll never listen, we close the door on any chance for meaningful exchange.

Ikeda: If we observe only the outer circumstances of Bodhisattva Never Disparaging, we can see without a doubt that he was constantly disparaged. But if we go a step further and consider the essence and spirit behind his actions, it becomes all the more apparent that the translation "never disparaging" is correct.

Endo: I think this translation, which takes into account the fundamental spirit of the sutra itself, shows the genius of Kumarajiva's translation.

Saito: President Ikeda, I recall that you once answered a question from a journalist on the reason for the SGI's development by saying, "It's because I continually meet and talk with individual members."

Ikeda: My intention at that time was not to speak about myself.

It goes without saying that the foundation for the SGI's development has been the hard work of all the members.

My point was that you cannot build such solid unity among many people simply by the power of organization or by giving orders. The SGI is strong because we have sincerely treasured each person. I wanted to emphasize that spirit.

Leaders in society tend to rely on giving orders. While carefully avoiding the hard, painstaking tasks, they steal the fruits of others' labors. There are all too many such leaders. The SGI is striving to revolutionize leadership as we know it.

Endo: Treasuring each person—that's hard work.

Ikeda: A leader who does not work hard is a fraud. Misery in the world largely stems from the fact that we have so many leaders who merely look out for themselves. When it comes down to it, such people are concerned only with protecting their positions and leading a comfortable existence.

The SGI exists to empower and help become happy those who are fatigued from their hard work and ardently striving to live their lives to the fullest. Leaders of such an organization must be willing and ready to take on even the most difficult tasks the best they can.

Of course, this is not to say we should push ourselves unreasonably. As we get older, we naturally need to exercise wisdom and common sense to safeguard our health. But if we lose the spirit to exert ourselves with selfless dedication, we are finished. This goes for leaders in our organization as well as in society.

The Twenty-four–character Lotus Sutra

For what reason was he named Never Disparaging? This monk, whatever persons he happened to meet, whether monks, nuns, laymen or laywomen, would bow in obeisance to all of them and speak words of praise, saying, "I have profound reverence for you, I would never dare treat you with disparagement or arrogance. Why? Because you will all practice the bodhisattva way and will then be able to attain Buddhahood." (LSOC, 308)

Suda: In summary, the "Bodhisattva Never Disparaging" chapter introduces a Buddha named Awesome Sound King Thus Come One living at a remote time described as "an immeasurable, boundless, inconceivable number of asamkhya kalpas in the past" (LSOC, 307). It relates how after the Former Day of the Law and toward the end of the Middle Day of the Law when this Buddha lived, his true teaching is lost and "monks of overbearing arrogance" (LSOC, 308) become all powerful. That is the state of affairs when Never Disparaging appears.

Ikeda: It is a time when the Law has perished. The Chinese character used to denote Middle Day of the Law means "likeness" or "image," referring to similarity of appearance. It is a time when the spirit of the Former Day has been lost and only the outward framework of the teaching remains, an age when Buddhism is reduced to a mere skeleton of its former self.

Endo: The designation "end of the Middle Day" corresponds to the start of the Latter Day of the Law, which is when Nichiren Daishonin lived. I think there is also significance in the fact that the Soka Gakkai began to flourish at a time when Nichiren Buddhism was clearly in crisis, when the Law was in danger of becoming extinct on account of the priesthood's negligence.

Suda: There are certainly a lot of "monks of overbearing arrogance" around. It is in such a time that Bodhisattva Never Disparaging appears.

Saito: He salutes all people, be they men or women, clergy or laity, with these words: "I have profound reverence for you, I would never dare treat you with disparagement or arrogance. Why? Because you will all practice the bodhisattva way and will then be able to attain Buddhahood" (LSOC, 308).

Endo: Since this passage is written with twenty-four characters in Chinese, we can say that the Lotus Sutra Bodhisattva Never Disparaging propagated is called the "twenty-four–character Lotus Sutra." In terms of the concept of the comprehensive, abbreviated and essential expositions of the sutra, the twenty-four–character passage represents the abbreviated Lotus Sutra.

The Record of the Orally Transmitted Teachings says: "These twenty-four Chinese characters that make up this passage are different [in wording] from the five characters of Myoho-renge-kyo, but the meaning is the same. These twenty-four characters represent the Lotus Sutra in miniature" (OTT, 152).

Ikeda: Just what does the Lotus Sutra teach? The sutra is condensed into this twenty-four–character passage: "I deeply respect you. I would never slight you or behave arrogantly toward you. For if you carry out the bodhisattva practice you can become a Buddha without fail." All living beings have the Buddha nature, the world of Buddhahood. It is this world of Buddhahood that Never Disparaging reveres.

The twenty-eight–chapter Lotus Sutra does not explicitly state that all people have the Buddha nature, but this is without doubt what it affirms. This is the highest philosophy of the sanctity of life.

While any number of religions preach equality, often what they mean by this is that human beings are all equally sinful. But the Lotus Sutra teaches that all people are noble children of the Buddha, that they are equal as entities of the world of Buddhahood. This is a very important difference.

Suda: Even if someone adheres to a different teaching and doesn't perceive the world of Buddhahood in his or her life, this does not in any way alter the fact that his or her life is an aspect of the world of Buddhahood. This is just as Never Disparaging states in his declaration. Therefore, the Lotus Sutra absolutely never condones violence.

Saito: Religious strife accompanied by violence would be totally antithetical to the sutra's spirit.

Ikeda: Bodhisattva Never Disparaging and the Lotus Sutra directly oppose all forms of violence. The Lotus Sutra is a teaching of spiritual struggle, not of violence.

Saito: Yes. And though totally nonviolent himself, Never Disparaging is showered with both physical and verbal abuse.

Endo: He is struck with sticks, tiles and stones and is slandered and mistreated. Seeing the four kinds of people[3] from afar, Never Disparaging approaches them, intoning the twenty-four–character passage and bowing in reverence.

Suda: To this day, it is a common practice in India for people to greet one another by joining their palms together and saying *namaste* in a sign of respect. I imagine Bodhisattva Never Disparaging as making a similar gesture.

Endo: But arrogant people, far from feeling any appreciation, only became angry and rebuked him: "This ignorant monk— where does he come from, presuming to declare that he does not disparage us and bestowing on us a prediction that we will attain buddhahood? We have no use for such vain and irresponsible predictions!" (LSOC, 308).

They would constantly berate him, saying in effect: "You're no Buddha. How presumptuous of you to talk about us becoming Buddhas. You are an ignoramus who doesn't know his place."

Ikeda: As the sutra indicates when it says "monks of overbearing arrogance exercised great authority and power" (LSOC, 308), these people commanded considerable power and influence. That probably made them all the more highhanded.

As long as people rely on some kind of force—be it authority, power, wealth, physical strength, position, organization, fame, talent or knowledge—they will have a hard time being humble. All too often, it is only after a person has lost everything that he or she can really listen for the first time. This is a tragic human failing.

Most people are destroyed by their own arrogance. Before that happens, we must ask ourselves what kind of human beings we would be if we were stripped of all such externals and ornamentation.

Saito: Even when arrogant people derided him, Never Disparaging was not the least taken aback. No matter how he might be mocked, without becoming angry he would simply repeat, "You will surely become a Buddha."

Ikeda: This is the practice of forbearance. The Buddha is called "One Who Can Forbear." Everything depends on whether we can endure the hardships that are an inevitable part of life and Buddhist practice.

Endo: Bodhisattva Never Disparaging underwent this treatment for many years. It did not stop with being vilified and mocked; he was also struck with sticks, tiles and rocks. When this happened, he would retreat to a safe distance and repeat in a loud voice the twenty-four–character passage.

Saito: That shows agility and strength of character.

Suda: There's no need to subject oneself to violence, to stand there and do nothing. While tactfully dodging the onslaught, he continues to spread the teaching without being the least intimidated. He is a dauntless practitioner.

Saito: And he steadfastly carries out a nonviolent struggle.

Ikeda: President Toda once said: "We ourselves are Nam-myoho-renge-kyo. Therefore, even if we should be struck or vilified, since we have determined to chant Nam-myoho-renge-kyo, as long as we are alive we should continue chanting Nam-myoho-renge-kyo through everything and exert ourselves for kosen-rufu, even if it means having to survive on water and grass. This is faith."

With regard to propagation, he said:

> There is no art or technique for carrying out prop-agation. There is no way to spread the teachings of Nichiren Daishonin without the solid conviction that you yourself are Nam-myoho-renge-kyo. Knowing this is the essence of propagation in the Latter Day of the Law. This is the only way.
>
> There are no rules for spreading Nam-myoho-renge-kyo or for sharing Nam-myoho-renge-kyo with others. We ourselves are Nam-myoho-renge-kyo! Nam-myoho-renge-kyo is all there is! We must be staunchly determined that Nam-myoho-renge-kyo is all we have and that, if that is not enough, then even if we should be killed or die, there is nothing else to do. Firmly convinced of this, we must continue to tell others about the Gohonzon.[4]

This is also the attitude of Bodhisattva Never Disparaging. Even when vilified or injured, he never ceases to plant the seed of the twenty-four–character Lotus Sutra. He continues struggling through all, having determined that this is how he will live regardless of other people's reaction. What becomes of him as a result?

Saito: The sutra says:

> When this monk was on the point of death, he heard up in the sky fully twenty thousand, ten thousand, a million verses of the Lotus Sutra that had previously been preached by the buddha Awesome Sound King, and he was able to accept and uphold them all. Immediately he gained the kind of purity of vision and purity of the faculties of the ear, nose, tongue, body, and mind that have been described above. Having gained this purity of the six faculties, his life span was increased by two hundred ten thousand million nayutas of years, and he went about widely preaching the Lotus Sutra for people. (LSOC, 309)

Ikeda: That's right. His life span is extended. He lives long, he survives. While "life span" here carries the literal meaning of longevity, it can also be interpreted as life force. Even if a person's life is short, if he or she lives with abundant life force and dies having created much value, then the person has had a long life. Also, there is no greater longevity than to have contributed to kosen-rufu and enabled many people to accrue strong life force.

In any event, Never Disparaging receives the benefit of the purification of the six sense organs. This indicates actual proof of human revolution. As a result, those around him come to view him in a new light.

Suda: The text continues:

> At that time, when the four kinds of believers who were overbearingly arrogant, the monks, nuns,

laymen, and laywomen who had looked with contempt on this monk and given him the name Never Disparaging—when they saw that he had gained great transcendental powers, the power to preach pleasingly and eloquently, the power of great goodness and tranquillity, and when they heard his preaching, they all took faith in him and willingly became his followers. (LSOC, 309–10)

Ikeda: Those people are very calculating!

Up to that time, Bodhisattva Never Disparaging was not an eloquent speaker. All he did was repeat the twenty-four–character passage and bow to people. That is probably the reason people ridiculed him so.

But the tables turn completely. The wretched person whom everyone had laughed at becomes splendid and dignified. At that point those who had ridiculed him may have all thought, "Oh, no! What have I done?"

President Toda once remarked, "When those who are now so arrogant toward us ask themselves, 'Oh, no! What have I done?'—that will be kosen-rufu."

Endo: These people who have a change of heart and come to believe in and follow Never Disparaging are in better shape than those who do not. Even so, they fall into the state of Hell because of their offense.

The Daishonin says:

> The people who cursed and struck Bodhisattva Never Disparaging at first behaved with such animosity, but later they took faith in him and became his followers, looking up to him and treating him with great respect, honoring him as the heavenly deities would the lord Shakra and standing in awe of him as we do the sun and moon. Despite this,

the great offense of their initial slander was difficult to extinguish, so they were condemned to the great Avichi hell for a thousand kalpas and abandoned by the three treasures for two hundred million kalpas. (WND-I, 435)

As for those who slandered Bodhisattva Never Disparaging but do not have a change of heart, their offense is so great as to defy comprehension.

THE BUDDHA LIVES IN THE PRESENT

Saito: In the meantime, lifetime after lifetime, Never Disparaging continues to serve various Buddhas and dauntlessly strives to widely propagate the Lotus Sutra. And finally he becomes a Buddha.

Ikeda: When Shakyamuni reaches this point in his discourse, he suddenly declares, "In fact he [Never Disparaging] was none other than I myself!" (LSOC, 310). This is a truly dramatic moment.

Suda: What had seemed like a discussion of events long past turns in a flash into a discussion of the reality before their eyes. Everyone is stunned.

Ikeda: Exactly. Nichiren Daishonin reads even deeper into the passage "In fact he was none other than I myself!," looking at it in terms of his own life. Having summoned forth the greatest persecution and facing imminent execution at Tatsunokuchi, he discards his transient status and reveals his true identity and so extends his life.

While at Teradomari en route to exile in Sado Island, he writes:

The Lotus Sutra accords with the fashion of the preaching employed by all Buddhas of the three existences. The past events described in the "Never Disparaging" chapter I am now experiencing as predicted in the "Encouraging Devotion" chapter; thus the present foretold in the "Encouraging Devotion" chapter corresponds to the past of the "Never Disparaging" chapter. The "Encouraging Devotion" chapter of the present will be the "Never Disparaging" chapter of the future. . . . (WND-1, 209)

Endo: He is saying in effect: "I have called forth the three powerful enemies[5] described in the 'Encouraging Devotion' chapter." He explains that he himself is now waging the battle that Never Disparaging carried out in the past. And, from the vantage of the future, people will recognize that his struggles are the same as those of Never Disparaging.

Saito: This is what he means by "The Lotus Sutra invariably concludes the Dharma preaching of all Buddhas of the three existences."

Ikeda: The Daishonin says, "The age of the Buddha is none other than today, and our present age is none other than that of the Buddha" (WND-1, 770). One must not vaguely think of the Lotus Sutra as simply a twenty-eight–chapter text. Buddhism exists only in the here and now, in the reality of people's lives. The Lotus Sutra teaches that in the depths of the present, we find the remote past. Fully grasping this profound truth is called attaining Buddhahood.

It's the present that counts. Myoho-renge-kyo lives only in the spirit and determination to work for kosen-rufu in the present, keeping in mind the words: "In fact he was none other than I myself!"

Nichiren teaches that just as Bodhisattva Never Disparaging is Shakyamuni, Nichiren himself, who was encountering incredible persecution at the time, is in fact also Shakyamuni—the Buddha. Unless we grasp this, he says, we have not deeply understood the Lotus Sutra.

Suda: By "Lotus Sutra," he does not mean a written text.

Ikeda: Someone once asked this question of President Toda: "It is said that Buddhism no longer exists in China and India, but isn't it true that many sutras remain in these countries?" President Toda replied: "The sutras are all that exist. Where there is no correct faith, there is no Buddhism. The sutras, just by themselves, are simply texts; they are not Buddhism."

Saito: The same can be said of Nichiren's writings. Unless we read them and take action with the spirit that the Daishonin lives today and this is the age of the Daishonin, we will not profit from their study. We will only be reading old texts.

For that matter, if we should become haughty because of the knowledge we gain from Buddhist study, then, far from doing us any good, it will result in our manifesting the nature of the four groups of arrogant people.

Ikeda: Bodhisattva Never Disparaging was not an eloquent speaker. He did not put on an air of greatness. He merely traveled around planting the seed of the Lotus Sutra in people's hearts with such direct simplicity that it bordered on naiveté. Across past, present and future, the spirit of the Lotus Sutra lives in such conduct.

In a word, this is the behavior of SGI members. Those struggling in the forefront of our movement are themselves Bodhisattva Never Disparaging. On the other hand, those who are widely revered in society and who are filled with self-importance belong to the four groups of arrogant people.

Whatever our standing in the organization, whether or not

we have a leadership position, we can vigorously take action and realize success in all endeavors because of the strength of the SGI, a wondrous body that is carrying out the Buddha's decree. Those who fall under the illusion that they can do everything on their own grow decadent and begin a downward spiral.

At any rate, we need to carry out the practice of never disparaging others, aware that we ourselves are Bodhisattva Never Disparaging and entities of Nam-myoho-renge-kyo.

Endo: Speaking of the practice of never disparaging, you once composed a poem, President Ikeda, in anticipation of the Soka Gakkai's seventieth anniversary:

> *The benefit of friends of kosen-rufu*
> *who embrace the brilliant spirit of never disparaging*
> *endures for millions of kalpas.*

> *Since the Mystic Law is the teaching*
> *without beginning or end,*
> *by dedicating our lives to it*
> *our offenses have all been expiated.*[6]

Suda: This is saying that the benefit received by SGI members, who in the spirit of never disparaging have blazed a path of kosen-rufu, is eternal. Also, the line "our offenses have all been expiated" points to a very important doctrine expounded in the "Bodhisattva Never Disparaging" chapter.

Endo: Yes. The sutra explains that the four kinds of believers persecuted Bodhisattva Never Disparaging because he had gone against the Lotus Sutra in the past, and that by spreading the Lotus Sutra while enduring such persecution, he expiates his past serious offenses.

Ikeda: This means that no matter how people might oppose or vilify us in our efforts to spread the Law, we should gladly accept this in the knowledge that we are thereby expiating our negative karma. We should not deplore such treatment.

I recall how President Toda described being struck four times while he was in prison. The jailer, brandishing his authority, punched President Toda once and then again for no reason. Though he burned with deep anger, since he was a prisoner he had no choice but to grit his teeth and endure it. Eventually, through studying the Lotus Sutra and intensively chanting Nam-myoho-renge-kyo in his cell, he realized that these blows enabled him to erase his negative karma.

The third time was on a day in early spring when he was bathing. The jailers herded the prisoners, forty to fifty in all, in to the tiny bathroom. Though he was chilled to the bone from having waited for thirty minutes, President Toda bathed carefully so as to waste as little hot water as possible out of consideration for the prisoners who would bathe later.

When a guard saw this, he started shouting at him: "Hey you! What are you doing taking such a leisurely bath! You must be a troublemaker!" And as he said this, he viciously struck President Toda in the face several times.

This time, while shedding bitter tears, he thought to himself with utmost conviction: "Yes! I have been hit again! When I am struck a fourth time, I will be free to leave!"

On another occasion, a furious guard gave President Toda twenty-some lashes on his back with a hemp rope. This was of course a horribly painful ordeal. But in his heart President Toda shouted with delight: "At last! The fourth time! Now my offenses are completely expiated!" Shortly thereafter, President Toda attained enlightenment in prison.

Saito: Just listening to this account gives me the shivers—both at the profundity of Buddhism and at the cruelty of power.

The Religion of Nationalism

Ikeda: What is nationalism? It is a way of thinking about the world that finds the worship of power at its root. This is the exact opposite of the spirit of Bodhisattva Never Disparaging.

Suda: Worship of power as the basis of nationalism—I never thought of it that way.

Ikeda: Nationalism could be described as a cult of power. It is based on the perverse notion that the state comes before the people. Nationalism is a "religion" that has existed since ancient times.

Suda: A "religion"?

Ikeda: I discussed this at length with the British historian Arnold Toynbee. As I think I have noted before, Dr. Toynbee remarked that the vacuum created in the West by the recession of Christianity was filled by three distinct religions: "belief in the inevitability of progress through the systematic application of science to technology, nationalism, and communism."[7]

What kind of religion, then, is nationalism? It takes collective human power as its object of worship. And worship of collective power is worship of the state.

Incidentally, Toynbee declared that nationalism, fascism and communism all share a common reverence for collective power.

In the religion of nationalism, people are nothing more than components of the state. They are turned into tools, means to an end. It is a religion in which the ego of the state tramples on the dignity of human beings.

Endo: I think we can find many signs of such nationalism today.

Ikeda: Toynbee also writes that the collective ego is dangerous "because it is . . . less patently unworthy of devotion." He says:

> Bad behaviour that would be condemned unhesitat-
> ingly by the conscience in an individual culprit is apt
> to be condoned . . . under the illusion that the first
> person is absolved from self-centredness by being
> transposed from the singular number into the plural.[8]

Suda: He is saying that when operating in numbers as a "we," people are more likely to carry out immoral acts that they could not possibly commit while acting as individuals.

Endo: This is the same mentality as thinking that it's safe to cross the street on a red light if you are in a group. It's frightening when you think about it.

Saito: The guards who tormented President Toda exemplify what becomes of people once they have been poisoned by nationalism. They identify with the great power of the state and carry on as though they themselves possess such power.

Endo: They borrow and hide behind the authority of a presumed higher power.

Ikeda: We see the same thing in war. Ordinarily, people regard killing another person as the most heinous of acts. But when it is "for the country," someone who kills many people becomes a hero.

Suda: The perverse religion of nationalism causes people to lose their senses.

Ikeda: President Toda wrote:

There are a number of things that have puzzled me since I was a boy. Among these, the thing that baffled me the most is how some relations between countries can be so far removed from culture.

What I mean is that people living in "civilized" countries receive a great deal of "cultural training," such as education in manners, language and attitudes. Despite the fact that such people live cultured lives based on a shared sense of value and awareness, when diplomacy between countries is the issue, although things may seem cultured on the surface, in actuality they are an exercise in brute force. Once diplomacy breaks down, isn't it often the case that countries discard courtesy and custom and become arenas of anger?[9]

President Toda declared that genuine religion is the driving force that can enable people to end this vicious cycle, including the wars that result from it, and construct an eternal paradise for humankind. The human being is most important. Society and the state exist for the sake of people, not the other way around.

The idea that the state takes precedence over people is worship of power. In short, such thinking produces a society of survival of the fittest. This is the exact opposite of the love of humankind exhibited by Bodhisattva Never Disparaging. Under such conditions, it is ultimately the people who suffer. People need to recognize this. They need to open their eyes.

REJECTION OF STATE WORSHIP

Ikeda: President Makiguchi keenly perceived that the iniquity of the state was something to be feared. When he refused to accept the Shinto talisman forced upon him by the authorities, some Nichiren Shoshu priests implored him to take it, saying that it was just a formality. But Mr. Makiguchi would not relent in the slightest.

Before Mr. Makiguchi was imprisoned, officers of the special police maintained a presence at Gakkai discussion meetings. If the talk turned to the talisman, they would immediately shout, "Stop!" When President Makiguchi, after discussing other subjects, came to the issue of household Shinto shrines, they would again shout for him to stop speaking.

The leaders around him wondered why Mr. Makiguchi returned time and again to these issues even though he was aware that he was in serious jeopardy. They failed to understand his spirit.

In rejecting the talisman, President Makiguchi was essentially rejecting worship of the state. "Aren't people more important than the state? We can't just sit back and watch everyone become miserable! Never!" This was his irrepressible cry.

Saito: Early Christianity also rejected worship of the state, firmly rebuffing the Roman Empire, which was the supreme collective power of the day.

Ikeda: Toynbee also discusses this history. In his work *Civilization on Trial*, he says: "The early Christians challenged the apparently irresistible might of the Roman Imperial Government rather than compromise with a Leviathan-worship that was persuasively commended to them as being nothing more sinister than an amiable formality."[10]

Hobbes uses Leviathan, an enormous mythical creature appearing in the Bible, to symbolize the power of the state.

Suda: Japan's religious denominations compromised with and gave in to the nationalists' efforts to control religion. In the name of protecting their organizations, they abandoned the essential spirit of faith and became utterly spineless.

Endo: This is true of the Nichiren Shoshu priesthood as well. It lost its soul.

Ikeda: Makiguchi and Toda safeguarded Nichiren's spirit by waging a magnificent struggle against the power of the state.

Saito: I think we could say that theirs was a fight against the erroneous religion of Japanese nationalism.

Endo: The state wielded enormous power.

Ikeda: Makiguchi and Toda fought to save people from becoming slaves to the state. Everyone has the right to become happy and the right to live freely. People are definitely not mere cogs in the machinery of the state. Because Makiguchi and Toda cherished such conviction, they were persecuted by the authorities. Theirs were truly actions of "never disparaging."

In any event, the four groups of arrogant people described in the account of Bodhisattva Never Disparaging, broadly speaking, can be identified with the evil of the state. None are more arrogant than people of power.

A passage in *The Record of the Orally Transmitted Teachings* says that the actions of the four groups are the conduct of the devil king of the sixth heaven:

> The four kinds of believers in their overbearing arrogance curse the bodhisattva Never Disparaging, calling him an "ignorant monk." To call "ignorant" the bodhisattva who bows in obeisance to whatever persons he happened to meet is the work of the devil king of the sixth heaven. (OTT, 154)

The four kinds of believers, priding themselves on their great authority and power, ridiculed and persecuted Never Disparaging, who had no such power. And Never Disparaging waged a spiritual struggle against their power and arrogance. He fought violence with nonviolence. He stood up alone to the tyranny being perpetuated against the people. In the modern age, this is reminiscent of the struggles of Mahatma Gandhi in India and Martin Luther King Jr. in the United States. It is a struggle for human rights motivated by love of humankind and championed by ordinary people.

THE ONENESS OF GOOD AND EVIL

"Self" and "others" are in fact not two different things.

For this reason, when the bodhisattva Never Disparaging makes his bow of obeisance to the four kinds of believers, the Buddha nature inherent in the four kinds of believers of overbearing arrogance is bowing in obeisance to the bodhisattva Never Disparaging. It is like the situation when one faces a mirror and makes a bow of obeisance: the image in the mirror likewise makes a bow of obeisance to oneself. (OTT, 165)

Ikeda: Let's examine the spirit of never disparaging in more depth and from other angles. For instance, Nichiren says regarding the relationship between the four groups of arrogant people and Bodhisattva Never Disparaging:

> To set up distinctions between good and bad by regarding the bodhisattva Never Disparaging as a "good" person and the arrogant ones as "bad" persons is a sign of ignorance.
>
> But when one recognizes this and performs a bow of obeisance, then one is bowing in obeisance to Nam-myoho-renge-kyo, the principle in which good and bad are not two different things, in which correct and incorrect are one and the same. (OTT, 162–63)

In terms of life tendency, Bodhisattva Never Disparaging is the opposite of the evil people who accost him. But both are human and both are entities of the Mystic Law. Evil people also possess the good of the world of Buddhahood, and good people likewise possess evil. Therefore, no matter how he might be persecuted, Bodhisattva Never Disparaging continues striving to achieve the widespread propagation of the Lotus Sutra. Confident that the world of Buddhahood lies dormant inside these evil people, he enables them to form a connection with Buddhism through a poison-drum relationship.[11]

Suda: In the Buddhism of sowing, enabling people to form a relation with Buddhism is very important. Nichiren says:

> Therefore, one should by all means persist in preaching the Lotus Sutra and causing them to hear it. Those who put their faith in it will surely attain Buddhahood, while those who slander it will establish a "poison-drum relationship" with it and will likewise attain Buddhahood. (WND-1, 882)

He says that we should "by all means persist" in this effort.

Saito: When people hear the Mystic Law being expounded, the Buddha nature in the depths of their lives is sure to be aroused. Whether one rejects this or is inspired to take faith depends on the individual. But without a doubt, such discourse stimulates their dormant Buddha nature.

Ikeda: That's right. The Daishonin says, "It is like the situation when one faces a mirror and makes a bow of obeisance: the image in the mirror likewise makes a bow of obeisance to oneself" (OTT, 165).

Put another way, respect invites respect, and contempt

breeds contempt. When we ourselves change, the other person changes, too.

The task of raising capable people also hinges on treating people with respect and believing wholeheartedly in their inherent ability. Treating people as though they are subordinate will not bring out their potential.

Those who genuinely respect their fellow members are great. Bodhisattva Never Disparaging reveres even people who do not embrace faith because he knows that the world of Buddhahood resides within them. Those who treat people poorly, especially their comrades in faith, will certainly suffer the consequences.

Saito: Leaders must be very careful about how they conduct themselves. To be inconsiderate of others or behave arrogantly goes against the teaching of the Lotus Sutra.

Ikeda: No matter what the other person's attitude, Bodhisattva Never Disparaging steadfastly maintained his convictions. And he won. It might seem on the surface that the powerful people who constantly abused him had won, but in terms of state of life, the difference between him and them could not have been greater.

Come to think of it, Nichiren Daishonin, while living in exile on Sado Island, said, "I pray that before anything else I can guide and lead the ruler and those others who persecuted me" (WND-1, 402). What sublime words! Like a peal of thunder and a grand symphony, this statement resounds high into the heavens and across tens of thousands of years of human history.

Saito: Those who irrationally attacked Nichiren, unaware of his profound and sincere spirit, were truly pitiful. And such people exist in the world today. Nichiren says of them, "But after they have been plunged into the hell of incessant suffering for a thousand kalpas and the time has come for their release, then they will meet Nichiren once again" (OTT, 157); and "But no matter how others may chant Nam-myoho-renge-kyo, if they are persons who show enmity toward Nichiren, then without fail they will fall into the hell of incessant suffering. And then, after countless kalpas have passed, they will become Nichiren's disciples and will succeed in attaining Buddhahood" (WND-2, 457).

Ikeda: The concept of the oneness of good and evil doesn't mean to simply recognize evil as evil. It means resolutely struggling against and defeating the negative functions in life and turning them into allies.

To practice Buddhism is to wage a decisive battle. If you allow good to be overpowered by evil, or if you are defeated by negative forces, you are not actualizing the oneness of good and evil in your life. By resolutely winning in our endeavors to vanquish evil, we can turn even the ill-intentioned into positive influences.

Endo: Nichiren says: "It is the lord of Sagami above all who has been a good friend to me. Hei no Saemon is to me what Devadatta was to Shakyamuni" (WND-1, 770). He says that Hojo Tokimune, the ruler of Japan who sent him into exile, is an ally, and that Hei no Saemon, his chief persecutor, is his Devadatta—an evil person whom Shakyamuni turned into a good friend of Buddhism.

Ikeda: A passage in the Lotus Sutra says, "Although the devil and the devil's people will be there, they will all protect the Buddhist Law" (LSOC, 145). Kosen-rufu becomes a reality when we turn even enemies into allies. And the only way to do this is for those who have this awareness to stand up with fierce resolve and forge an iron unity of the people.

At the outset of this discussion, we talked about how millions and tens of millions of noble irreplaceable lives have been destroyed by the perverse ideology of nationalism. It was President Makiguchi and President Toda who cried out for an end to the massacre. Theirs were actions of the ultimate patriotism.

They willingly devoted their lives to the Lotus Sutra, which can be called the religion of humankind. They gave their lives not for the state but for the sake of people. Thoroughly aware of this history, it is crucial that we stand up and oppose the new nationalism and cult of power that are now emerging. This is what it means to truly read the "Bodhisattva Never Disparaging" chapter.

NOTES

1. Makoto Ueda, *Matsuo Basho* (New York: Twayne Publishers, 1970), p. 28.

2. Integration of the three mystic principles: This refers to the fact that the three mystic principles of true cause, true effect and true land are all taught in the "Life Span" chapter.

3. Four kinds of believers: Monks, nuns, lay men and lay women. Broadly speaking, this refers to all people.

4. *Toda Josei zenshu* (Collected Writings of Josei Toda) (Tokyo: Seikyo Shimbunsha, 1982), vol. 2, pp. 466–67.

5. Three powerful enemies: Three groups of people who persecute the votaries of the Lotus Sutra after Shakyamuni's passing: arrogant lay people, arrogant priests and arrogant false sages.

6. *Our offenses have all been expiated:* This corresponds to the line from the sutra, "his offenses had been wiped out" (LSOC, 312).

7. *The Toynbee-Ikeda Dialogue: Man Himself Must Choose* (Tokyo: Kodansha International Ltd., 1976), p. 292.

8. Arnold Toynbee, *An Historian's Approach to Religion* (London: Oxford University Press, 1956), p. 34.

9. *Toda Josei zenshu* (Tokyo: Seikyo Shimbunsha, 1981),vol. 1, p. 20.

10. Arnold Toynbee, *Civilization on Trial / The World and the West* (New York: The World Publishing Company, 1964) p. 224.

11. Poison-drum relationship: Another term for reverse relationship, i.e., a bond formed with the Lotus Sutra by opposing or slandering it. The expression "poison drum" comes from the Nirvana Sutra, vol. 9, which states, "Once a poison drum is beaten, all the people who hear it will die, regardless of whether or not they have a mind to listen to it." Similarly, when one preaches the Lotus Sutra, both those who embrace it and those who oppose it will equally receive the seed of Buddhahood.

PART V

"Supernatural Powers of the
Thus Come One" Chapter

5   The Transmission to the Bodhisattvas of the Earth

As the light of the sun and moon
can banish all obscurity and gloom,
so this person as he advances through the world
can wipe out the darkness of living beings,
causing immeasurable numbers of bodhisattvas
in the end to dwell in the single vehicle.
Therefore a person of wisdom,
hearing how keen are the benefits to be gained,
after I have passed into extinction
should accept and uphold this sutra.
Such a person assuredly and without doubt
will attain the buddha way. (LSOC, 318)

Myoho-renge-kyo is not the Wonderful Law of Shakya-
muni Buddha, because when the action of this chapter takes
place, the essence of the sutra has already been transmitted
or entrusted to the bodhisattva Superior Practices. Generally
speaking, regarding this entrustment of Myoho-renge-kyo to
the bodhisattva, the ceremony for entrustment begins in the
"Treasure Tower" chapter (chapter eleven), the entity to
be entrusted becomes apparent in the "Life Span" chapter
(chapter sixteen), and the ceremony comes to an end in the
"Supernatural Powers" and "Entrustment" chapters (chap-
ters twenty-one and twenty-two).

The Thus Come One is the Thus Come One of the "Life Span" chapter, and the supernatural powers are the ten supernatural powers possessed by a Buddha. (OTT, 167)

Saito: At last, we begin discussing "Supernatural Powers of the Thus Come One" chapter of the Lotus Sutra. This is the climax of the entire sutra.

Ikeda: Nichiren Daishonin deemed "Supernatural Powers" one of the sutra's most important chapters, along with the "Emerging from the Earth" and the "Life Span of the Thus Come One" chapters. That's because it describes the ceremony in which Shakyamuni entrusts the Bodhisattvas of the Earth with achieving kosen-rufu in the Latter Day of the Law.

To begin, let's clarify just what the Lotus Sutra is. It is Shakyamuni's will and testament. It embodies the teaching he most wanted to leave to posterity.

So what was Shakyamuni's most ardent prayer? It was for all people to become happy. He says, "Just as a mother would protect her only child at the risk of her own life, even so, let him cultivate a boundless heart towards all beings."[1]

He is basically imploring us: "Strive to help all people, all living beings, become happy, just as a mother will put her life on the line to protect her only child!" This is what it means to stand up for kosen-rufu.

Shakyamuni continues: "May all beings be happy! Whether he stands, walks, sits or lies down, as long as he is awake, he should develop this mindfulness. This they say is the noblest living here."[2]

In our practice of reciting the sutra and Nam-myoho-renge-kyo each morning and evening, we continually pray for the happiness of all people. We pray for the happiness of all living beings. This is a truly lofty state of life.

Not only do we offer prayer, we also take action to see these prayers come to fruition. That is, we exert ourselves for kosen-rufu. What a noble way to live!

Endo: I believe that through my practice to the Gohonzon and participation in SGI activities, I have gradually come to such a state of life, even if only in some small measure. The fact that there are literally millions of people engaged in this process is wondrous; it is truly awe-inspiring.

Ikeda: Only Bodhisattvas of the Earth can carry out this practice of widely spreading the Law. In the "Supernatural Powers" chapter, Shakyamuni entrusts the Bodhisattvas of the Earth with achieving kosen-rufu in the Latter Day.

Saito: This is the ceremony of transmission or entrustment.

Suda: Transmission refers to the Buddha entrusting his disciples with the teaching and instructing them to spread it widely.

Ikeda: Without transmission, Buddhism would die out with the mentor's generation. No matter how great the teaching, it would have no lasting impact. It could not lead people to happiness.

Even if a teaching encourages compassion toward all living beings, if it cannot actually help those who are suffering, then it is nothing more than theory. Buddhism expounds the Law, and it leads the people to happiness.

After his release from prison, Josei Toda composed the following poem while gazing up at the starry sky, reminiscing about his mentor:

> *I clutch in my hand the wish-granting jewel.*
> *My heart cries out, "With this, I will save everyone!"*
> *My mentor smiles in peace.*

Carrying on the spirit of his mentor—President Tsunesaburo Makiguchi, who had died in prison—Mr. Toda stood up alone for kosen-rufu. The passing of the baton from Makiguchi to Toda occurred while they were in prison. The last time they saw each other was in September 1943 at the Metropolitan Police Department, when Makiguchi was being taken off to the Tokyo Prison in Sugamo. Given the circumstances, most likely they could not speak freely to each other.

President Toda recalled: "All I could say was 'Sensei, please take care of yourself.' You nodded without uttering a word. But from the way you carried yourself and from the look in your eyes, I sensed your boundless mercy and courage."[3]

Saito: This is a solemn and noble exchange between mentor and disciple. The ceremony on March 16, 1958, where Mr. Toda entrusted you with his vision, President Ikeda, also occurred in the midst of a heroic struggle against the devilish nature of power. That was during the turmoil surrounding the Yubari Coal Miners Union Incident[4] and the Osaka Incident.[5]

Suda: This certainly shows the solemn unity of mentor and disciple as they faced a life-or-death struggle.

Ikeda: That is, of course, on a different level from the ceremony of transmission in the "Supernatural Powers" chapter. Still, it can be said that without the mentor–disciple relationship, as exemplified in Soka Gakkai history, Buddhism simply would not exist.

Saito: Yes. Shakyamuni awakened to the Mystic Law and, perceiving the life force of the universe in the depths of his being, he experienced the greatest of all joys. The problem he faced was how to communicate the Law to humankind. He understood it himself and could share his insight with others while he was alive, but what would happen after his passing? This seems to be the great theme of Buddhism.

Buddhism is through and through a religion for human beings. It does not postulate the existence of a transcendent deity existing apart from people or of a creative deity that single-handedly generated the universe. Without departing from the human being, Buddhism continuously urges people: "Awaken to your own true nature!"

Things like "God's will" never become an issue; everything depends on the will of the individual. Consequently, without the transmission from mentor to disciple, Buddhism would lose its vitality. That's why transmission is so important.

Endo: Without mentor and disciple, the teaching would perish.

Ikeda: What we mean by the Law or teaching "perishing" is when there is no one who correctly inherits the teaching.

Saito: That certainly describes the state of affairs in the Nichiren Shoshu priesthood today.

Suda: The mentor–disciple relationship has ceased to exist in the priesthood. As a result, it has lost touch with Buddhism. Even so, it continues to arrogantly pose as a religious authority and is therefore acting as a devilish function, a force that aims to destroy the Law.

Ikeda: I imagine that when Shakyamuni thought about future generations, he worried about what he could do to help them. That is why in the end he taught his disciples to uphold and take as their mentor the eternal Mystic Law that had enabled him to become a Buddha. We discussed this in connection with the principle of "casting off the transient and revealing the true" (in volume 4, chapter 2).

Shakyamuni probably made this statement from time to time during his later years, and it was most likely incorporated into the Lotus Sutra.

Endo: Shakyamuni's mentor is the eternal Mystic Law that is itself the eternal true Buddha. In modern terms, we sometimes refer to this as the "universal life."

By practicing with this eternal Law as one's mentor, anyone can become a Buddha just as Shakyamuni did. It is the "great beneficial medicine" that enables all living beings to become happy. "Since I am teaching you this, you should take this great beneficial medicine and share it with others"—this is the teaching of the Lotus Sutra and the spirit of the "Life Span" chapter.

Ikeda: The focus is solely on the period after Shakyamuni's death. It is on the future; the future of kosen-rufu. To lose sight of this one point is to fail to grasp the heart of the Lotus Sutra.

Saito: Transmission is the central theme of not only the "Supernatural Powers" chapter but of the Lotus Sutra in its entirety. This is particularly evident in the description of the Ceremony in the Air. The appearance of an enormous tower in the "Emergence of the Treasure Tower" chapter, the portrayal of countless Bodhisattvas of the Earth dancing from the earth in the "Emerging from the Earth" chapter, and the discussion of the eternal Buddha in the "Life Span" chapter are all for the sake of transmission.

Suda: In *The Record of the Orally Transmitted Teachings*, Nichiren says, "Regarding this entrustment of Myoho-renge-kyo to the bodhisattva, the ceremony for entrustment begins in the 'Treasure Tower' chapter (chapter eleven), the entity to be entrusted becomes apparent in the 'Life Span' chapter (chapter sixteen), and the ceremony comes to an end in the 'Supernatural Powers' and 'Entrustment' chapters (chapters twenty-one and twenty-two)" (OTT, 167). Unless we understand the meaning of transmission, the Ceremony in the Air, with all of its extraordinary circumstances, becomes little more than a fairy tale.

Buddhas Who Carry Out the Practice of Bodhisattvas

Endo: Let's consider the outline of the "Supernatural Powers" chapter. As the title "Supernatural Powers of the Thus Come One" suggests, this chapter reveals the Buddha's ten great supernatural or mystic powers, which are so awesome as to move the universe.

It begins with the Bodhisattvas of the Earth making a vow. They pledge to preach the Lotus Sutra far and wide in this *saha* world after Shakyamuni has passed into extinction, as well as in lands where other Buddhas have ceased to exist.

Ikeda: They promise to widely propagate the teachings of all Buddhas after the Buddhas have died. In this we find the great and mystic significance of the Bodhisattvas of the Earth.

To start from the conclusion: In any land, the Bodhisattvas of the Earth shoulder the task of widely propagating the Law from the Buddha to all people. Why is that? It's because while the Bodhisattvas of the Earth have the same state of life as the Buddha, their conduct is thoroughly that of bodhisattvas. They could therefore be described as "bodhisattva-Buddhas."

If the life state of the bodhisattva is not one with that of the Buddha, he or she cannot correctly propagate the Law. At the same time, in a defiled age, unless bodhisattvas go out into the world and assimilate themselves to society, kosen-rufu cannot be achieved. The Bodhisattvas of the Earth are endowed with these qualities. That's probably why at the close of the "Supernatural Powers" chapter they are described as passing "through the world." It is in the world and among the people that they carry out their practice.

Suda: The passage reads:

> *As the light of the sun and moon*
> *can banish all obscurity and gloom,*
> *so this person as he advances through the world*
> *can wipe out the darkness of living beings,*
> *causing immeasurable numbers of bodhisattvas*
> *in the end to dwell in the single vehicle.*
> *Therefore a person of wisdom,*
> *hearing how keen are the benefits to be gained,*
> *after I have passed into extinction*
> *should accept and uphold this sutra.*
> *Such a person assuredly and without doubt*
> *will attain the buddha way.* (LSOC, 318)

It describes the Bodhisattvas of the Earth as taking action in the world, illuminating all beings and removing the gloom of suffering from their lives, just as the light of the sun and moon banishes darkness. It also says that they inspire countless bodhisattvas and ultimately enable them to become Buddhas. In other words, they make kosen-rufu a reality.

Ikeda: The Bodhisattvas of the Earth are like so many suns. And, as indicated by the description "like the lotus flower in the water" (LSOC, 263), they dwell in society but are not sullied by its evils.

Saito: They are suns and lotus flowers—from this we see the profound meaning that attaches to the Daishonin's name *Nichiren,* which literally means "Sun Lotus."

Ikeda: The sun and the white lotus are consistently used as symbols of the Buddha in the Lotus Sutra. This has been the subject of some research.

Endo: In a study of the Sanskrit text of the sutra, the Indologist scholar Shuntaro Matsuyama contends that from the "Treasure Tower" chapter on, Shakyamuni is identified with the white lotus as the embodiment of the true Law and also with the light of the sun.

Saito: Nichiren says:

> The Lotus Sutra is the sun and moon and the lotus flower. Therefore it is called the Lotus Sutra of the Wonderful Law. Nichiren, too, is like the sun and moon and the lotus flower. (WND-I, 186)

Ikeda: This is very profound.

Suda: Continuing with the summary of the chapter, in response to the vows of the Bodhisattvas of the Earth, Shakyamuni uses his supernatural powers to reveal various mystic phenomena to Bodhisattva Manjushri and countless other bodhisattvas. These are termed the "ten supernatural powers."

The Ten Supernatural Powers: Symbols of Kosen-rufu

Ikeda: There might seem to be something fantastic about this display of supernatural powers. But we should bear in mind that they represent functions of life.

Suda: Yes. For the first of these, it says that the Buddha "extended his long broad tongue upward till it reached the Brahma heaven" (LSOC, 314). In ancient India, people would stick out their tongues in a gesture to testify to the truth of their words. By extending his tongue, Shakyamuni is indicating that the Lotus Sutra is entirely free of falsehood.

Ikeda: The Daishonin says that the tongue being broad indicates that the Mystic Law can save all beings in the Ten Worlds, and the tongue being long indicates that the Law has existed from time without beginning (see OTT, 167).

Saito: In regard to the second supernatural power, the sutra says:

> From all his pores he [Shakyamuni] emitted immea-
> surable, countless colored beams of light that illumi-
> nated all the worlds in the ten directions.
>   The other Buddhas . . . did likewise, extending
> their long broad tongues and emitting immeasurable
> beams of light. (LSOC, 314–15)

Ikeda: The universe is completely illuminated. It is a magnificent image.

This is the world of kosen-rufu. We shine, too. When we truly burn with a spirit of faith, our entire lives radiate with character, wisdom and hope, and we can illuminate the lives of others.

Endo: Next, it says that Shakyamuni and the other Buddhas drew their tongues together and, exhibiting the third and fourth supernatural powers, "coughed in unison, and all together snapped their fingers" (LSOC, 315). According to Indian custom, people would also snap their fingers to give evidence of the truth of their words.

Suda: These sounds reverberate throughout the universe. As for the fifth power, it says, "The sounds made by these two actions filled all the buddha worlds in the ten directions, and the earth in all of them quaked and trembled in six different ways" (LSOC, 315).

Ikeda: The universe trembles with joy. In other words, even the land attains Buddhahood. This is the principle of three thousand realms in a single moment of life; it symbolizes the great drama of kosen-rufu.

Saito: After the land trembled with joy, the sixth supernatural power manifests itself:

> The living beings in their midst . . . all saw in this saha world the immeasurable, boundless hundreds, thousands, ten thousands, millions of buddhas seated on lion seats . . . and also saw Shakyamuni Buddha and Many Treasures Thus Come One seated together on a lion seat in the treasure tower. Moreover, they saw immeasurable, boundless hundreds, thousands, ten thousands, millions of bodhisattvas mahasattva and the four kinds of believers who reverently surrounded Shakyamuni Buddha.
>
> When they had seen these things, they were all filled with great joy, having gained what they had never had before. (LSOC, 315)

Ikeda: The multitude of Buddhas, sitting upon lion thrones, stretch out as far as the eye can see. The term *lion* is written with two Chinese characters; the first stands for *mentor* and the second for *disciple*. This indicates that when mentor and disciple are one, any realm can be transformed into a Land of Eternally Tranquil Light.

Suda: The original meaning of the term used for the place the high priest sits is *lion's chair*, suggesting that it is the seat of a practitioner who upholds the path of the oneness of mentor and disciple. One who betrays one's predecessors has no right to occupy this chair.

Saito: The worlds in the ten directions could be said to refer to the realms where all beings of the Ten Worlds dwell. The seventh supernatural power is displayed when, upon seeing this, these "heavenly beings in the midst of the sky cried out with loud voices" (LSOC, 315).

The heavenly beings declare:

> There is a land named saha, and in it a buddha named Shakyamuni. Now for the sake of the bodhisattvas mahasattva he is preaching the great vehicle sutra called the Lotus of the Wonderful Law, a teaching to instruct the bodhisattvas, one that is guarded and kept in mind by the buddhas. You must respond with joy from the depths of your hearts, and also offer obeisance and alms to Shakyamuni Buddha! (LSOC, 315)

Endo: The eighth supernatural power then takes place in response to these voices. The sutra says: "The various living beings . . . pressed their palms together, faced the saha world, and spoke these words: 'Hail, Shakyamuni Buddha! Hail, Shakyamuni Buddha!'" (LSOC, 315).

Ikeda: The Daishonin notes that "Shakyamuni Buddha" here represents the spirit of endurance. This expresses a wonderful doctrine of life.

To live in the *saha* world requires tremendous forbearance; it is a place where one must steadfastly persevere. It is a land inhabited with people of poor capacity, people who cannot accept something true at face value. Instead, they are inclined to persecute those who stand up for justice.

Suda: Japan is a case in point.

Ikeda: Those who cast aside self-interest and devote themselves to helping others become happy are slandered and abused. We live in a truly befuddled world.

To withstand such persecution and contempt and still persist in spreading the Mystic Law calls for endurance. Even if we should be persecuted time and again, we need to continue struggling with dauntless resolve, repeatedly pushing back devilish forces. Nichiren Daishonin teaches that doing so is itself the world of Buddhahood and the life state of Shakyamuni Buddha.

The living beings in the worlds in the ten directions revere this world of Buddhahood. That is, they hold in high esteem a thorough dedication to kosen-rufu. Without a doubt, the Buddhas and bodhisattvas throughout the universe applaud us who are now fighting for kosen-rufu.

Suda: Up until the preaching of the Lotus Sutra, the *saha* world was viewed as an undesirable place filled with people of extreme evil who can be led to Buddhism only with great difficulty. But the Lotus Sutra changed things entirely.

As for the ninth supernatural power, it says:

> Then they [the living beings in the worlds in the ten directions] took different kinds of flowers, incense, necklaces, banners, and canopies, and the ornaments, rare jewels and other wonderful articles that adorned their persons, and all together scattered them far off in the direction of the saha world. The objects thus scattered poured in from the ten directions like clouds gathering together. Then they changed into a jeweled curtain that completely covered the area where the buddhas were. (LSOC, 315–16)

And in regard to the tenth power, it says: "At that time the worlds in the ten directions were opened up so that there was unobstructed passage from one to the other and they were like a single buddha land" (LSOC, 316).

Endo: It was already explained in the "Life Span" chapter that the *saha* world itself has been the True Land of Shakyamuni since the remote past. In this scene, the *saha* world actually becomes the Land of Eternally Tranquil Light.

THOSE WHO PRACTICE WITH ENDURANCE ARE BUDDHAS

Ikeda: The Buddha goes to the place where people are suffering the most—to the *saha* world. A real Buddha shares everyone's sufferings. Anything short of this is not the genuine article.

Is a priest automatically respectable? No, definitely not. Does being a politician or a celebrity make someone great? Certainly not. Nor does having a high position in our organization. Commendable are those who exert themselves alongside the people facing the most hardship.

Women's division members on the forefront who pray for the happiness of all and work tirelessly to spread the Daishonin's teaching, sometimes even over the chiding and opposition of their husbands and the bad-mouthing of others, are truly great. That spirit to endure is what we mean when we say "Buddha."

Referring to the principle that the *saha* world itself is the Land of Eternally Tranquil Light, President Toda once said, "Buddhism at this point has refuted everything it had expounded." This is because, contrary to what had previously been taught, this concept reveals that the ideal is not to eventually reach some distant pure land. Rather, it is to eternally strive for peace and human happiness while living in this world, which is filled with suffering. The Buddha exists nowhere apart from such endurance.

That the *saha* world is the Land of Eternally Tranquil Light is stating this revelation from the standpoint of the environment. From the standpoint of the person, it implies that the Buddha is in reality a "bodhisattva-Buddha." Shakyamuni was a bodhisattva and at the same time a Buddha.

The idea of the bodhisattva is said to refer originally to the way of life Shakyamuni followed while he was striving for enlightenment. But it is not the case that Shakyamuni was a bodhisattva only during his years of practice. Even after he had attained the Way, Shakyamuni continued to carry out the actions of a bodhisattva to spread the great Law to which he had awakened. While boundlessly rejoicing in the awareness of the eternity of life that filled his being, he spread that Law to others. This is what is meant by a "bodhisattva-Buddha."

That's why Mr. Toda said that this revelation turned Buddhism on its head. The essential point is that even after attaining enlightenment, Shakyamuni continued to exist as a human being. The Lotus Sutra thus appeals: "Restore your humanity!"

THE TRUE BUDDHA IS A COMMON MORTAL

Saito: It occurs to me that the notion that Shakyamuni attained enlightenment for the first time during his lifetime in India, which is refuted in the "Life Span" chapter, must contain extremely misleading implications. It suggests that Shakyamuni was an ordinary person "before" and a Buddha "afterwards," making it difficult to recognize him as a human being.

In fact, it is because he earnestly sought the correct path *as a human being* that he awakened to the world of Buddhahood within his own life. And because he became enlightened in this fashion, he followed the supreme way of life *as a human being*. From start to finish, Shakyamuni was human. This consistency is severed by the misguided notion that Shakyamuni attained enlightenment for the first time during his preaching in India.

Endo: Such a view could easily cause people to think that attaining enlightenment made Shakyamuni some kind of special or superhuman being. While this might not have been a problem for those alive during Shakyamuni's lifetime who could see his humanity for themselves, I imagine that, for people after his passing, the temptation to see him as otherworldly would have been very strong.

Suda: Giving in to that temptation leads to Shakyamuni's deification and the tendency for people to think of themselves as unworthy. Though it may sound like humility, self-deprecation is actually an expression of arrogance, for it suggests that one pretends to know the full potential of human life, while in fact being ignorant of it. It equates to a lack of faith in one's humanity.

Ikeda: To think of oneself as just an ordinary person is indeed a great mistake. The fresh breeze of the Lotus Sutra dispels such dark clouds of illusion. It does not discriminate against the ordinary person but says that all people are themselves Buddhas, that the human being is supremely worthy of respect. Nichiren Daishonin gives ultimate expression to this spirit when he says:

> A common mortal is an entity of the three bodies, and a true Buddha. A Buddha is a function of the three bodies, and a provisional Buddha. In that case, though it is thought that Shakyamuni Buddha possesses the three virtues of sovereign, teacher, and parent for the sake of all of us living beings, that is not so. On the contrary, it is common mortals who endow him with the three virtues. . . . The "true Buddha" here means common mortals, whereas "provisional Buddhas" means Buddhas. (WND-I, 384)

These words certainly overturn all the assumptions of Buddhism up to that point. The common mortal is the true Buddha, the Daishonin says, and the Buddha is a provisional Buddha, a projected image of the common mortal. He is asserting that the existence of the common mortal is not subordinate to that of the Buddha, but the existence of the Buddha is predicated on that of the common mortal.

This is a declaration of extreme significance not only in the history of Buddhism but in the history of all religion. Religions, in general, place absolute beings such as gods and Buddhas "above" and human beings "below." Nichiren states unequivocally, however, that gods and Buddhas exist because of people, and that they are merely means to enable people to become happy. This is the mammoth declaration of a religion that exists for human beings.

History has witnessed countless instances of religions becoming slaves to authority, though their original intent was to bring happiness to the people. The philosophical roots of such transformation lie in the assumption that gods and Buddhas are superior to human beings.

Suda: I suspect the notion that clergy are above other people has the same origin. People are taken in by the illusion that since gods and Buddhas are superior to people, then clergy, who are supposed to be intermediaries between people and those higher beings, must also be better than ordinary believers.

Saito: In that sense, the idea that priests have an intrinsically higher standing than lay people is fundamentally alien to Nichiren Buddhism.

Ikeda: That is true, but it's important to remember that thought and philosophy depend on people. If the mentor-disciple spirit should be forgotten, then even Nichiren Buddhism could be used to suppress people, instead of existing for their benefit. This is an issue with which we have become very familiar.

In any event, I think we can say without a doubt that in

proclaiming that the once-exalted Buddha is merely provisional, Nichiren has made a landmark declaration in religious history. What enables him to say this? This is actually the key point of the "Supernatural Powers" chapter.

This may be jumping ahead, but the transmission from Shakyamuni to the Bodhisattvas of the Earth is a ceremony signifying that the common mortal is a true Buddha.

Nichiren Daishonin explains all teachings, even those like the ten supernatural powers that seem to have little to do with regular people, in terms of human life. From the standpoint of the Buddhist philosophy of life, "Thus Come One" in the chapter's title refers to the life of the universe and therefore indicates the lives of all beings. Nichiren says, "The Thus Come One refers to all living beings, as has already been explained in the section on the 'Life Span' chapter" (OTT, 167). And "supernatural powers" means the power of the spirit or of life. In particular, it refers to the great life force of Buddhahood. The life force of the universe that is inherent in the lives of all living beings is called the "supernatural powers of the Thus Come One." The Bodhisattvas of the Earth carry out the task of kosen-rufu manifesting this great life force.

Kosen-rufu means awakening all people to the supreme life force of the "supernatural powers of the Thus Come One." In other words, it means expanding the ranks of the Bodhisattvas of the Earth and perpetuating the chain reaction of human revolution, the momentous movement of human happiness. The teaching of the ten supernatural powers is a prophetic revelation of this aspect of kosen-rufu.

Saito: Certainly, the description at the end of the "Supernatural Powers" chapter of the worlds in the ten directions all becoming one and of all beings devoting themselves to the Buddha is a vision of kosen-rufu.

Suda: "Great events never have minor omens" (WND-1, 1119),

Nichiren says. Nowhere else do we find mention of such "omens" occurring in all worlds in the ten directions.

Endo: Nichiren clearly indicates this when he says, "The great omens of the 'Supernatural Powers' chapter foretold that the essence of the Lotus Sutra would spread widely after the Buddha's demise, when the two thousand years of the Former and Middle Days of the Law had passed and the Latter Day of the Law had begun" (WND-1, 646).

Ikeda: We are now making this a reality. It's remarkable—truly mystic. We are leading exciting lives.

In general, people associate supernatural powers with psychic or supernatural abilities. But that is not what it means in this context. Nichiren admonishes, "Whether they are correct or incorrect in their views is to be judged solely on the basis of the doctrines they expound. It is not to be decided on the basis of whether or not they have keen capacity or can display supernatural powers" (WND-2, 234). To make psychic powers or the like the standard is to set people with extraordinary abilities apart from regular human beings. This is dangerous.

We must also keep in mind that possessing supernatural powers is no guarantee of happiness. As a matter of fact, those who rely on special ability may neglect their own growth as human beings and actually become miserable as a result.

Endo: I seem to recall that some years ago there was a lot of interest in people who could bend spoons using psychokinetic powers. My friend, after seeing a number of demonstrations on television, remarked: "Just what on earth is it good for? I could see that it might have some value if they could return the spoon to its original shape!"

Suda: Our human tendency is to forget the purpose behind our actions.

Ikeda: In any undertaking, we should ask, "Why am I doing this?" The most important reason, of course, is happiness. Such things as supernatural abilities that do nothing to promote human happiness ultimately have no significance.

The Daishonin says, "Outside of the attainment of Buddhahood, there is no 'secret' and no 'transcendental powers'" (OTT, 125). Attaining Buddhahood, achieving a state of life of absolute and eternal happiness, is the Buddha's supernatural power. For this is itself the supreme power according with the law of life.

CARL JUNG: DO NOT BECOME A "SLAVE" OF THE STATE

Ikeda: Let's take up the profound meaning of this transmission next time. If we were to try to cover the entire chapter all at once, it might be too much for our readers to digest.

The main point of the various supernatural powers that we have discussed this time is to alert all people to the dignity of their lives. The "Supernatural Powers" chapter cries out to people in a dynamic voice that reverberates throughout the universe. It is an appeal for kosen-rufu. It calls for the realization of the compassionate prayer of Shakyamuni for all beings to become happy.

On a global scale, there is a gaping void in people's hearts, and it seems that spiritual desolation is only becoming more widespread.

A hundred years ago, the German philosopher Friedrich Nietzsche[6] declared that "God is dead." This century has seen other icons occupy the vacant seat of a god in which people have lost faith.

Endo: One of these would be worship of the state, which we discussed in connection with the "Bodhisattva Never Disparaging" chapter.

Suda: Faith in science would be another candidate. Worship of wealth is also a kind of faith. We can also plainly see the result of the Japanese belief that money brings happiness, or that the path to happiness lies in economic abundance.

Saito: An expert notes that during the chaotic postwar era, money in Japan was seen as a means to ensure a peaceful and secure existence. In other words, people believed that only money could bring peace and security. As a result, he argues, people have developed an inordinately strong attachment to money, which has thus taken on the role of a religion.

Ikeda: With the "death of God" has come the "death of the human being." This is perhaps the reality of the twentieth century. Not only have we seen the death of spirituality, but worship of the state has brought with it unprecedented cases of "megadeath." The twentieth century has been the most murderous century ever.

We must overturn this situation and make the next century an age in which the human being is highly revered. That is the purpose of the kosen-rufu movement. We need to call out to all people to open up the great life force of the "supernatural powers of the Thus Come One" within them. We mustn't allow the iniquity of nationalism to fill the spiritual void in people's hearts today.

Endo: It is said that the sudden rise of Nazi Germany was preceded by a widespread nihilistic sentiment.

Ikeda: The famous Swiss psychologist Carl Jung,[7] in an essay titled "The Undiscovered Self," writes: "If the individual . . . should feel that his life has lost its meaning . . . then he is already on the road to State slavery."[8]

That's because someone who feels this way lacks the strength to resist the enormous power of nationalism. Once we fail to oppose evil, we are on our way to becoming its slave.

Jung says that for authoritarians who want to fill people with a sense of reverence for the state, the greatest source of trouble is religion that does not compromise with the state.[9]

Therefore, he says, the state will "try to cut the ground from under [such] religion."[10]

Because religions that do not kowtow to authority teach "another authority opposed to that of the 'world,'"[11] they are a thorn in the sides of those who would turn people into slaves of the state. Jung declares without reservation: "The dictator State . . . along with the individual . . . swallows up his religious forces. The State takes the place of God."[12]

Suda: To say that a state "takes the place of God" certainly sounds like worship of the state.

Endo: The frightening thing is that many people fail to realize that they have been taken in by nationalism. While remaining apathetic, they are herded down this slippery path unawares. When they finally understand what has happened, it is already too late. This is the fundamental problem.

Ikeda: Jung's conclusion is that the sole power to resist the devilish nature of nationalism lies in individual awareness of the dignity of human life, in the sense that "man is a microcosm, a reflection of the great cosmos in miniature."[13]

Saito: That is in complete agreement with the philosophy of the Lotus Sutra.

Ikeda: By contrast, Jung lamented that in the modern age, "the insignificance of the individual is rubbed into him so thoroughly that he loses all hope of making himself heard."[14]

Suda: Certainly there is a spreading sense of helplessness; people feel that nothing they do will amount to anything. People are also growing isolated from one another, having become uninterested in sharing their thoughts and feelings. There is a lack of solidarity.

Endo: Consequently, people withdraw and grow silent. But this is just what those in power want. This confirms to me how important our movement is.

Tagore: A Life "Gushing" with Joy

Ikeda: While the "Supernatural Powers" chapter describes omens of kosen-rufu on a universal scale, human revolution is kosen-rufu in the microcosm of the individual. It means to bring forth great vitality, like the image of the Bodhisattvas of the Earth who emerge bursting through the ground.

While on a different level from the sutras, I would like to cite a few famous remarks by the Indian poet Rabindranath Tagore.[15]

When he was around twenty, Tagore one morning had a remarkable experience. Looking out from the veranda, he writes, "All of a sudden a covering seemed to fall away from my eyes, and I found the world bathed in a wonderful radiance, with waves of beauty and joy swelling on every side."[16]

He describes this experience in the famous poem "The Waterfall Awakens":

> *Oh, why—I myself do not know —*
> *has my life now awakened from its slumber*
> *after the course of many years?*
>
> *My life has now awakened from its slumber.*
> *There is much water; the waves rise and swell.*

The longing of life, the passion of life —
I could not remain closed and hold it back.
The mountain, rumbling, causes the earth to shake
and tremble.
Rocks, rumbling, crash down.
Foaming waves, roaring, swell
and roar with fury.[17]

Endo: He says that the world shakes and sways—this is reminiscent of the "Supernatural Powers" chapter.

Ikeda: He is describing the powerful quaking of life. While the "Supernatural Powers" chapter certainly speaks of the earth trembling with boundless joy, Tagore here is probably describing a fitful struggle to awaken to and bring out his greater self.

But toward the end of the poem, welling with joy, he sings:

Speaking the thoughts of my heart,
singing the melody of my heart,
the more generously I give of my life, the more it
surges forth.
It is inexhaustible.
I have many words to speak, many songs to sing.
My life overflows: I have an abundance of joy, an
abundance of dreams.
Life overflows and in ecstasy.
What can compare with such joy?
Such beauty?[18]

Saito: He literally depicts the joy of one who has awakened to the greater self. I sense in this the spirit of India that resonates through the Lotus Sutra.

Ikeda: Everyone has the ability to achieve an awakening even more profound than Tagore. The substance of such an awakening—of the supernatural powers of the Thus Come One—is Nam-myoho-renge-kyo.

When we chant Nam-myoho-renge-kyo to the Gohonzon each morning and evening, we cause a magnificent drama like that described in the "Supernatural Powers" chapter to arise in the microcosm of our lives. When we then cause that drama of change to unfold in society, we are grasping the chapter's true meaning.

To do that, we need courage. We have to take the initiative. When we do so, we change and society changes, too.

Tagore, having awakened to the greater self, bids us to break through our own narrow limitations!

NOTES

1. *The Sutta-Nipata,* trans. H. Saddhatissa (London: Curon Press, 1994), p. 16.

2. Ibid.

3. From his remarks at the third memorial for Mr. Makiguchi, marking the second anniversary of the latter's death. *Toda Josei zenshu* (Collected Writings of Josei Toda) (Tokyo: Seikyo Shimbunsha, 1983), vol. 3, p. 385.

4. Yubari Coal Miners Union Incident: In 1957, Soka Gakkai members working as coal miners in the town of Yubari, Hokkaido, were barred from joining the workers' union.

5. Osaka Incident: This refers to Mr. Ikeda's arrest in 1957 on trumped-up charges of violating election law. He was later cleared of any wrongdoing.

6. (1844–1900).

7. (1875–1961).

8. *The Collected Works of C.G. Jung,* vol. 10, trans. R.F.C. Hull (Rockville, Md.: Princeton University Press, 1964), p. 254.

9. Ibid., p. 257.

10. Ibid., p. 256.

11. Ibid.

12. Ibid., p. 259.

13. Ibid., p. 258.

14. Ibid.

15. (1861–1941).

16. Rabindranath Tagore, *Reminiscences* (London: Macmillan and Co., Limited, 1961), p. 217.

17. Translated from Japanese: *Togoru chosakushu* (Collected Works of Tagore), trans. Tatsuo Morimoto (Tokyo: Daisan Bunmeisha, 1990), vol. 1, pp. 501–02.

18. Ibid., p. 504.

6 The Dawn of "Humanistic Buddhism"

The people living at the same time as Shakyamuni Buddha had already formed profound karmic ties with him in the past; hence they were able to attain the way. Shakyamuni, however, was so concerned about how to save those who would live after his passing that he put his eighty thousand sacred teachings into written form. Then, among his lifetime of sacred teachings, he entrusted the Hinayana sutras to the Venerable Mahakashyapa, and both the Mahayana sutras and the Lotus and Nirvana sutras to Bodhisattva Manjushri. But the five characters of Myoho-renge-kyo, the heart of the eighty thousand sacred teachings and the core of the Lotus Sutra, he neither entrusted to Mahakashyapa or Ananda, nor transferred to great bodhisattvas such as Manjushri, Universal Worthy, Perceiver of the World's Sounds, Maitreya, Earth Repository, or Nagarjuna. Even though these great bodhisattvas hoped that he would do so and requested it of him, the Buddha would not consent. He summoned forth a venerable old man called Bodhisattva Superior Practices from the depths of the earth,[1] and then, in the presence of the Buddha Many Treasures and the Buddhas of the ten directions, from within the tower adorned with the seven kinds of treasures, the Thus Come One Shakyamuni entrusted the five characters of Myoho-renge-kyo to him. (WND-1, 605)

Ikeda: I recently heard a wonderful poem by the Uruguayan poet Eduardo Galeano:

> *Utopia lies at the horizon.*
> *When I draw nearer by two steps, it retreats two steps.*
> *If I proceed ten steps forward, it swiftly slips ten steps ahead.*
> *No matter how far I go, I can never reach it.*
> *What, then, is the purpose of utopia?*
> *It is to cause us to advance.*[2]

Saito: For SGI members, "utopia" could represent kosen-rufu, the establishment of a peaceful world based on Buddhist thought. Of course, kosen-rufu is not the kind of surreal dream world implied by the term *utopia*. It's an ideal we continually challenge ourselves to advance toward. The power to inspire others to join in the struggle and enable them to move forward in their lives is an intrinsic aspect of the movement for kosen-rufu.

Suda: Without the aim of kosen-rufu, we could neither practice with a selfless spirit nor attain Buddhahood in this lifetime.

Ikeda: Kosen-rufu and attaining Buddhahood in this lifetime could be compared to the two types of motion of the earth, revolution [on its axis] and rotation [around the sun]. They are intrinsically related.

I think this poem is wonderful because it explains the spirit of the Buddhism of true cause in a way that is very easy to understand. To paraphrase the meaning in Buddhist terms, it is saying: "With our sights on the distant true effect, we continually advance. We are constantly setting forth. We ceaselessly burn with hope. With our sights on the future, we are ever moving on from the beginningless past. Each day, each moment, we experience time without beginning."

"True effect," in this context, indicates kosen-rufu and

attaining Buddhahood. While it may be possible to think of these concepts as final destinations beyond which there is no need to proceed any further, in reality, this is not the case.

Saito: Indeed. Someone who has attained Buddhahood would not just sit back and relax, thinking, "I've achieved enough already," but would tirelessly press on.

Ikeda: Of course, there is no denying that someone who has accomplished his or her mission in this life will feel immense satisfaction and fulfillment—a sense of "I've done it!" A Buddha is someone who even then continues working for the welfare of others.

The true effect is an ideal, while the true cause is reality. This brings us to the "Supernatural Powers of the Thus Come One" chapter.

The ceremony of transmission that takes place in this chapter is basically the passing of the baton from the "teacher of the mystic principle of the true effect" to the "teacher of the mystic principle of the true cause." This signifies a great transition from a Buddhism centering on the ideal image of the wonderful effect of Buddhahood, represented by the thirty-two features,[3] to a Buddhism focused on the cause of Buddhahood, or the Buddha nature inherent in the lives of all people. It is a move toward a Buddhism that exists solely in the reality of human life.

Saito: The "teacher of the mystic principle of the true effect" is Shakyamuni, who attained enlightenment in the remote past described as numberless major world system dust particle *kalpas* ago.

Endo: The "teacher of the mystic principle of the true cause" is Bodhisattva Superior Practices, the leader of the Bodhisattvas of the Earth.

Suda: I think it could be said that Shakyamuni, who attained enlightenment in the remote past, represents the world of Buddhahood, while Superior Practices represents the nine worlds. Just what does this transmission from the representative of the world of Buddhahood to the representative of the nine worlds signify? This has been a source of much controversy since ancient times.

THE MYSTIC LAW IS THE "ORIGINAL MENTOR"

> *Because after the Buddha has passed into extinction*
> *there will be those who can uphold this sutra,*
> *the buddhas are all delighted*
> *and manifest immeasurable supernatural powers.*
> *Because they wish to entrust this sutra,*
> *they praise and extol the person who accepts and upholds it,*
> *and though they should do so for immeasurable kalpas*
> *they could never exhaust their praises.*
> *The benefits gained by such a person*
> *are boundless and inexhaustible,*
> *like the vast sky in the ten directions*
> *that no one can set a limit to.* (LSOC, 317)

Ikeda: Last time, we studied the ten supernatural powers described in this chapter. Let's pick up our discussion from that point.

Endo: All right. To review, the ten supernatural or mystic powers of the Buddha are:

(1) Shakyamuni Buddha extends his long broad tongue until it reaches the Brahma heaven.
(2) He emits countless beams of light from every pore of his body, illuminating all the worlds in the ten directions.

(3) He clears his throat, causing the sound to reach the worlds in the ten directions;

(4) He snaps his fingers, causing the sound to reach the worlds in the ten directions;

(5) All the lands in the ten directions tremble in six different ways.

(6) All beings in the worlds of the ten directions behold the Ceremony in the Air and rejoice.

(7) Heavenly gods proclaim with loud voices to the beings in the ten directions that the Buddha is now expounding a great vehicle sutra called the Lotus Sutra of the Wonderful Law, and they should therefore rejoice and make offerings to him.

(8) On hearing this proclamation, all the beings in the worlds of the ten directions convert to the Buddha's teaching and become his disciples.

(9) The beings scatter offerings of various treasures over the *saha* world, and these gather together like a cloud and form a jeweled curtain over the Buddhas assembled there.

(10) Passage between all worlds in the ten directions becomes unobstructed, as though they were one Buddha land.

In short, this is describing the *saha* world itself manifesting as the Land of Eternally Tranquil Light. It is also a picture of the world of kosen-rufu. This time we will look at what follows the description of the Buddha's ten supernatural powers.

First, I would like to note that Shakyamuni says something surprising here:

The supernatural powers of the buddhas, as you have seen, are immeasurable, boundless, inconceivable. If in the process of entrusting this sutra to others I were to employ these supernatural powers for immeasurable,

boundless hundreds, thousands, ten thousands, millions of asamkhya kalpas to describe the benefits of
the sutra, I could never finish doing so. (LSOC, 316)

Saito: It seems to me that, in a sense, the ten supernatural powers
are explained in order to express this idea.

Ikeda: Shakyamuni is not simply praising the benefit of the
Lotus Sutra. He is in fact praising the benefit accrued by the
person who will uphold this sutra after his passing, that is to say,
the benefit of Bodhisattva Superior Practices. That is the point.

Suda: This is indicated in the verse section of the "Supernatural
Powers" chapter where it says:

> *Because they wish to entrust this sutra,*
> *they praise and extol the person who accepts*
> *and upholds it,*
> *and though they should do so for immeasurable kalpas*
> *they could never exhaust their praises.*
> *The benefits gained by such a person*
> *are boundless and inexhaustible,*
> *like the vast sky in the ten directions*
> *that no one can set a limit to.* (LSOC, 317)

Endo: Right before this, it says:

> *Because after the Buddha has passed into extinction*
> *there will be those who can uphold this sutra,*
> *the buddhas are all delighted*
> *and manifest immeasurable supernatural powers.* (LSOC, 317)

This passage is lauding those who uphold the sutra after the
Buddha's passing, meaning the Bodhisattvas of the Earth and
Superior Practices in particular.

Suda: Their benefit is described as "boundless." It is infinite, like the universe.

Ikeda: Even though the Buddhas possess such incredible powers that they can move the universe itself, they cannot praise enough the benefits of Superior Practices. This is extraordinary.

The sutra says, moreover, that all Buddhas manifest their "immeasurable supernatural powers" because they are delighted that Superior Practices will uphold this teaching after the Buddha's passing. The ten supernatural powers therefore celebrate the future activities of Bodhisattva Superior Practices.

Saito: From this part alone, we can see that Bodhisattva Superior Practices is a being of extreme significance.

What's more, all of Shakyamuni's preaching since the appearance of the treasure tower in "The Emergence of the Treasure Tower" chapter has been building up toward this transmission of the Law to Superior Practices. You could say that Superior Practices holds the key to understanding the Lotus Sutra.

Endo: In the prose section preceding the verse section of the "Supernatural Powers" chapter, Shakyamuni says that he could never finish illustrating the benefits of the sutra, even employing these supernatural powers, whereas in the verse section he speaks of the benefit of the person who upholds the sutra as similarly defying description. In the former instance he is talking about the "Law"; in the latter, he is talking about the "Person."

Ikeda: I'm jumping ahead, but Shakyamuni is ultimately extolling the benefit of the "Nam-myoho-renge-kyo Thus Come One," which embodies the oneness of the Person and the Law.

Shakyamuni, who attained enlightenment in the remote past, and Bodhisattva Superior Practices are both transient manifestations of the Nam-myoho-renge-kyo Thus Come One, the fundamental Buddha of the universe.

The Nam-myoho-renge-kyo Thus Come One is the Buddha whose life is without beginning or end; the universal life itself; the origin of all Buddhas throughout time and space; the entity of the eternally inherent Ten Worlds and their mutual possession.

Of the Ten Worlds, the Lotus Sutra identifies the world of Buddhahood with Shakyamuni and with Many Treasures, who accompanies Shakyamuni in the treasure tower. And it identifies the nine worlds of the Nam-myoho-renge-kyo Thus Come One with Bodhisattva Superior Practices and other beings. This signifies that the worlds of Buddhahood and Bodhisattva exist in the life of the same fundamental Buddha.

It is for all of these reasons that Shakyamuni cannot fully elucidate the magnificence of the Nam-myoho-renge-kyo Thus Come One. And, since the Nam-myoho-renge-kyo Thus Come One is the "original mentor" who allows all Buddhas to attain enlightenment, this means that Shakyamuni is in fact also praising the mentor.

Suda: Then it makes sense that, in spite of his supernatural powers capable of moving the universe, Shakyamuni cannot pay tribute enough to the Nam-myoho-renge-kyo Thus Come One. That's because the Thus Come One of "the supernatural powers of the Thus Come One" is the "body," and the supernatural powers are that body's innate functions. The Nam-myoho-renge-kyo Thus Come One is the ultimate source from which the body, or enlightened entity, of the Buddha arises.

Ikeda: What is more, since the Nam-myoho-renge-kyo Thus Come One is one with the universe, we ourselves and all living beings are entities of the Nam-myoho-renge-kyo Thus Come One. The Nam-myoho-renge-kyo Thus Come One is the true aspect of the lives of all beings of the Ten Worlds.

It is Nichiren Daishonin who teaches this, and who is therefore called the "lord of the teachings." When we chant

Nam-myoho-renge-kyo just as Nichiren instructs, our voices resonate throughout the entire universe. Just as a soft voice can be transformed into a booming voice through the use of a good megaphone, when we chant Nam-myoho-renge-kyo with heartfelt prayer, we can move the entire universe. As Nichikan, the twenty-sixth high priest, says: "[If you have faith in this Gohonzon and chant Nam-myoho-renge-kyo even for a short while] no prayer will go unanswered, no offense unexpiated, no good fortune unbestowed, and all righteousness proven."[4]

Nichiren says that it is not difficult for those who chant the daimoku of the Lotus Sutra (in other words, Nam-myoho-renge-kyo) to become Buddhas equal to Shakyamuni (see WND-I, 1030). This statement is very significant. He says this because the Mystic Law is the origin of all Buddhas.

We must absolutely never give up on prayer. He declares: "Muster your faith, and pray to this Gohonzon. Then what is there that cannot be achieved?" (WND-I, 412). We need to pray "as though to produce fire from damp wood or to obtain water from parched ground" (WND-I, 444).

Endo: Yet there are those who say that even though they are praying, they see no results.

Ikeda: As Nichikan points out, there is an important distinction between "daimoku of faith" and "daimoku of practice." The act of chanting Nam-myoho-renge-kyo is "daimoku of practice," but the results of our efforts vary greatly depending on whether we truly have confidence in the benefit of the Gohonzon. Offering "daimoku of faith" is what makes the difference.

THE BOUNDLESS POWER OF THE MYSTIC LAW

Suda: I heard the following experience from a member of the Kanagawa Nurses Group that I think illustrates this perfectly. Ms. H., the chief nurse of a hospital attached to a university medical school, was asked for advice on a couple, Mr. and Mrs. T., who were facing a grave and difficult situation.

In autumn of 1996, Mr. T., who was in his forties and worked for a construction company, underwent surgery for a tumor in his brain stem. It seems, however, that it was not possible to remove the tumor in its entirety. Mrs. T., who had joined the Soka Gakkai as a result of her husband's illness, was praying for his recovery. But from around the summer of 1997, Mr. T.'s headaches and nausea worsened, and he began having consistent convulsions. The doctors informed Mrs. T. that, while the tumor had not metastasized or spread, he was experiencing these symptoms because water had built up in his brain and that surgery to remove this fluid would be necessary. Mr. T. could only walk with a great deal of assistance, and his speech was limited to grunts and moans.

Mrs. T. told her district women's leader that although she had been chanting Nam-myoho-renge-kyo for her husband's recovery for a year, she could not see any improvement in his condition. The leader then discussed her situation with Ms. H., the nurse. Ms. H. gave the following advice: "The fact that the tumor has not metastasized is the benefit of chanting Nam-myoho-renge-kyo. This is really remarkable. Mrs. T.'s questions about whether he will recover, or whether her prayers will be effective, are simply barriers she has created in her own life. But there is no barrier, there is no limit, to the great power of Nam-myoho-renge-kyo. Now is the time when she needs to offer strong prayers! It's a matter of overcoming any feelings of confusion or doubt and offering wholehearted prayer with the strongest possible determination and focus. She needs to pray in such a way as to shower the diseased area with Nam-myoho-renge-kyo!"

Endo: That's very clear guidance. The advice of the members of the nurses group, based as it is on their experience, is very compelling.

Suda: Indeed. When the district leader related all this to Mrs. T., her prayers became all the more earnest. That very evening, there was a change in Mr. T.'s condition. He suddenly started producing more urine, and a continuous stream of tears and mucus began flowing from his eyes and nose—so much so that his pillow became soaked.

This went on for three days. On the fourth day, he showed startling signs of recovery. He could carry on ordinary conversations with the members of his family and could walk about without any help. The doctors were surprised at this change in his condition and brought him in for more tests. They concluded that he had fully recovered and that surgery was no longer necessary.

Mr. T. made a complete recovery. On seeing this, his son, who was in the seventh grade, remarked: "Nam-myoho-renge-kyo is incredible! I want to join the Soka Gakkai, too. I want to start right away." He urged his sister, who was in elementary school, to practice Buddhism also, and the siblings joined together.

Saito: That's a wonderful experience. I am reminded of just how important it is to offer resolute prayer.

VICTORY OF MENTOR AND DISCIPLE! VICTORY OF FAITH!

Endo: It's true that people sometimes limit the beneficial power of Nam-myoho-renge-kyo without realizing it. We need to be confident that, just as Nichikan says, "no prayer will go unanswered."

Ikeda: That's right. In particular, the prayers of those who are exerting themselves to accomplish the propagation of the Mystic Law cannot fail to be answered. The Daishonin says, "If you are of the same mind as Nichiren, you must be a Bodhisattva of the Earth" (WND-1, 385). To be "of the same mind as Nichiren" means to cherish the same determination for kosen-rufu. When we work for kosen-rufu and we stand up with the resolve to demonstrate the victory of faith, our lives overflow with benefit beyond belief.

We receive benefit *because* we work for kosen-rufu, which is the wish of the Buddha. This is analogous to how someone who works for a company receives a salary.

Second Soka Gakkai president Josei Toda characterized those who chant with a laundry list of things that they want, as though it were the duty of the Gohonzon to supply benefit, as having "beggar's faith." And he urged that instead they should stand up with the determination: "I will stake my life on the struggle for kosen-rufu!"

When we muster the faith to uphold the Gohonzon and the Mystic Law with our very lives, we are protected by the Buddhas and bodhisattvas throughout time and space. In response to our earnest efforts in faith to score a resounding victory for the SGI, an organization dedicated to the widespread propagation of the Mystic Law, all the protective functions of the universe come to our aid.

What was Mr. Toda's prayer when he was imprisoned alongside his mentor, Mr. Makiguchi? Each day, morning and evening, he prayed: "I am young and my mentor is old. If only my mentor could be released even one day sooner, it would not matter how long I remained. May my mentor be quickly released!"[5]

How noble!

The wisdom of the Buddha is vast and boundless. Although President Makiguchi died in prison, Mr. Toda, his faithful disciple, survived the ordeal and went on to prove the greatness of his mentor. Now, because of his selfless struggle against nationalism, the SGI has gained immense trust in Asia and throughout the world.

Saito: President Makiguchi is lauded across the globe. In Brazil, for example, schools in increasing numbers are implementing his value-creating pedagogy. And a number of municipalities have named parks and streets after him.

Ikeda: President Makiguchi triumphed. President Toda's prayers were victorious. Their struggle transcended life and death.

Japan, with its parochial, island-nation mentality, confined the truly great Mr. Makiguchi to a tiny, one-person cell. However, due to the unyielding determination of his disciple, Mr. Toda, Mr. Makiguchi's greatness has broken free of such shackles and reached the far corners of the earth. This is a genuine united struggle of mentor and disciple. Buddhism comes down to the relationship of mentor and disciple. In the "Supernatural Powers" chapter, too, we have a ceremony of mentor and disciple.

Endo: Yes. The Bodhisattvas of the Earth are disciples whom Shakyamuni has instructed since the remote past. In this chapter Shakyamuni entrusts them with the propagation of the Lotus Sutra in the Latter Day of the Law.

Saito: This is the key point. If we only look at the literal meaning of the chapter's text, we wind up with the simple interpretation that Nichiren Daishonin, as the reincarnation of Bodhisattva Superior Practices, spread the twenty-eight–chapter Lotus Sutra of Shakyamuni.

Suda: That is, in fact, the standard interpretation.

Saito: But Nichiren Daishonin says: "Myoho-renge-kyo is not the Wonderful Law of Shakyamuni Buddha, because when the action of this ['Supernatural Powers'] chapter takes place, the essence of the sutra has already been transmitted or entrusted to the bodhisattva Superior Practices" (OTT, 167). Nichiren is clearly stating here that the teaching he is spreading is not that of Shakyamuni.

Endo: Even so, some still interpret these words of Nichiren to mean that he is saying that Myoho-renge-kyo is not Shakyamuni's teaching because Bodhisattva Superior Practices inherited the teaching in the same way that a son inherits the estate of his father and insists: "Since the tenure of my father is over and I am now head of the household, everything belongs to me and no longer to my father."

Saito: How can we further clarify this?

Ikeda: The analogy of a family estate expresses one side of the truth. Namely, that the Latter Day of the Law is the age of Bodhisattva Superior Practices and not the age of Shakyamuni. In the "Supernatural Powers" chapter, Shakyamuni transfers his teaching in its entirety; it's as though he is saying, "From here on, I leave everything in your hands."

Let's look at the passage.

Suda: OK. Shakyamuni says:

> To put it briefly, all the doctrines possessed by the thus come one, all the freely exercised supernatural powers of the thus come one, the storehouse of all the secret essentials of the thus come one, all the most profound matters of the thus come one—all these are proclaimed, revealed, and clearly expounded in this sutra. (LSOC, 316)

This is a well-known description of the transmission of the essence of the Lotus Sutra.

Saito: In short, it means that the Lotus Sutra reveals the life of the Thus Come One in its totality. Shakyamuni then says that he transfers this to Bodhisattva Superior Practices.

The Great Teacher T'ien-t'ai of China describes this transmission as summing up the entirety of the Lotus Sutra. And he explains the significance of the Lotus Sutra based on this passage. This is the doctrine of the five major principles of name, essence, quality, function and teaching.

T'ien-t'ai associated "name" with "all the doctrines possessed by the thus come one," or the sutra's title, Myoho-renge-kyo; "essence" with "the storehouse of all the secret essentials of the thus come one," or the ultimate Law itself; "quality" with "all the most profound matters of the thus come one," or the causality of the enlightenment of the Thus Come One; "function" with "all the freely exercised supernatural powers of the thus come one," or the power to benefit all people; and "teaching" signifies that "all these are proclaimed, revealed, and clearly expounded in this sutra."

It seems to me that T'ien-t'ai is explaining the reason that the Lotus Sutra is endowed with infinite benefit; in other words, he is elucidating that it is the ultimate source of all benefit.

Suda: Put another way, it is the very life of the Thus Come One.

Endo: This is what is transferred to Bodhisattva Superior Practices.

SUPERIOR PRACTICES IS A BODHISATTVA-BUDDHA

Ikeda: The question then becomes: Just what is this bodhisattva who "receives and embodies the entirety of the Thus Come One?"

Ordinarily, when we speak of a bodhisattva we mean someone who is practicing the teachings with the aim of becoming a Buddha. But this is clearly not the case with Bodhisattva Superior Practices. Although he embodies the entirety of the Thus Come One, he is still called a bodhisattva. Superior Practices is a "bodhisattva–Buddha."

Let's go back to the analogy of a son inheriting the family estate from his father. We must assume that father and son are equal, that if the father is a Buddha, the son who inherits the family estate is also a Buddha. Otherwise, this analogy is illogical.

Endo: Certainly, a person who inherits sovereignty over a country from a king is also a king.

Ikeda: At the time of their appearance, Superior Practices and the other Bodhisattvas of the Earth are described as follows: "The bodies of these bodhisattvas were all golden in hue, with the thirty-two features and an immeasurable brightness" (LSOC, 252).

Suda: The thirty-two features are special characteristics of Buddhas. This therefore seems to indicate that the Bodhisattvas of the Earth are Buddhas.

Saito: What's more, they are described as even more splendid in appearance than Shakyamuni. The sutra likens Shakyamuni to a young man of twenty-five with a hint of immaturity, and the Bodhisattvas of the Earth as venerable seasoned elders of a hundred years (see LSOC, 262).

Ikeda: Therefore, the ceremony of essential transmission in the "Supernatural Powers" chapter is fundamentally a transmission from a Buddha to a Buddha. This is a state of life that "can only be understood and shared between buddhas" (LSOC, 57).

Why, then, does Superior Practices appear as a bodhisattva? Well, for one thing, it is so this sutra would not contradict the traditional idea that in any given world there can be only one Buddha. People would be confused if two Buddhas were to appear at the same time.

Saito: This is the view that Superior Practices assumes the position of a disciple who is helping Shakyamuni expound his teaching.

Endo: When the Bodhisattvas of the Earth make their appearance, everyone else, including Bodhisattva Maitreya, is startled. This is what prompts Shakyamuni to begin preaching the "Life Span" chapter. In that sense, the Bodhisattvas of the Earth certainly assisted in his preaching.

Ikeda: But this takes on still greater significance, given that Bodhisattva Superior Practices appears unequivocally as the representative of the nine worlds. This point virtually transforms the entire history of Buddhism. It is a recognition of the virtues (or effect) of Buddhahood existing within the practice (or cause) of a bodhisattva.

Up to this juncture, Buddhism had taught that the effect was superior and that practice, which is the cause of enlightenment, was inferior, which seems like common sense.

Endo: I think we intuitively think of the world of Buddhahood as above, or better than, the nine worlds.

Ikeda: But with the appearance of Bodhisattva Superior Practices, it becomes evident that the cause (the nine worlds) contains the effect (the world of Buddhahood).

Why is this important? Let's try to recall the teaching of the "Life Span" chapter. There, Shakyamuni explains that he attained Buddhahood in the extremely remote time described as numberless major world system dust particle *kalpas* ago. This implies that all Buddhas in the universe are disciples of Shakyamuni who attained enlightenment in the remote past. Then what about before that time?

Saito: Shakyamuni's statement, "originally I practiced the bodhisattva way" (LSOC, 268), indicates that, before numberless major world system dust particles *kalpas* ago, he carried out a bodhisattva practice.

Ikeda: From there we can infer that since he carried out the Buddhist practice, there was a Buddhist Law. There was a Law, but no Buddha, which means that there was no Buddha who is at one with the universe and whose life is without beginning or end.

Suda: It goes without saying that if the time when the Buddha appeared could be pinpointed, he could not be called the "Buddha eternally existing throughout past, present and future."

Endo: The view that Shakyamuni had first attained enlightenment during his lifetime in India is refuted as without origin and existing only in the present. Such a Buddha is like grass without roots. But the Shakyamuni of the "Life Span" chapter, who revealed that he attained enlightenment in the remote past, also became enlightened at some specific time. Strictly speaking, this view also fails on the grounds that it is "without origin and existing only in the present." It does not present Buddhahood as originally inherent.

Saito: If a Buddha's enlightenment is not originally inherent, then that Buddha cannot be called the true Buddha who exists eternally.

Ikeda: While this is an important point for our present discussion, it is somewhat challenging. Those who find this a bit confusing should feel free to just skip ahead! It's a concept that can be studied throughout one's life. Even if we don't fully comprehend the fine points of Buddhist theory, the main thing is that we understand the importance of chanting Nam-myoho-renge-kyo.

Suda: I, for one, am relieved to hear you say that!

Ikeda: To return to the topic at hand, there are two ways of explaining the fundamental Buddha at one with the universe whose life is without beginning or end. The first involves ignoring the workings of causality. By doing so, we can assume the existence of a Buddha whose life is without beginning or end and leave it at that. That's because once causality is brought into the picture, the question arises regarding what happened before the effect of Buddhahood was attained.

If the issue of causality is simply passed over, however, then what we are talking about is not Buddhism. It is precisely this explanation of the workings of cause and effect that distinguishes a teaching as Buddhist, while the absence of causality marks a teaching as non-Buddhist.

In particular, the cause of Buddhahood and effect of Buddhahood are Buddhism's main concern. It could be said that, after Shakyamuni's passing, Mahayana Buddhism itself originated out of the people's quest for the cause that had enabled Shakyamuni to attain Buddhahood.

Saito: Yes. Having lost Shakyamuni, they must have sought to become Buddhas themselves by grasping the cause that enabled him to attain enlightenment.

Ikeda: To put it another way, it was an investigation into the true nature of Shakyamuni's life, which yielded a variety of doctrines expounding an eternal Buddha.

Suda: These would include a discussion of Shakyamuni's eternal life as a "Buddha of the Dharma body," in contrast to the living Shakyamuni. A number of arguments were further advanced as to the properties of the Buddha's life, including the doctrine of the three bodies of a Buddha (the Dharma body, or body of the Law; .the reward body, related to wisdom; and the manifested body, or the physical form that a Buddha assumes in order to save people, related to action).

Endo: Perhaps an argument could be made that the various Buddhas of Mahayana Buddhism—Vairochana[6] of the Kegon Sutra, Amida[7] of the Pure Land sutras, and Dainichi[8] of the Dainichi Sutra—each reveal one side of the Buddha while pointing toward the fundamental Buddha whose life is without beginning or end.

Ikeda: But no matter how these teachings might deal with the eternal life of the Buddha, they were greatly limited. In the first place, because they described the world of the Buddha as a grand and beautiful realm, they departed from Shakyamuni the human being. This signifies their having moved away from the reality of human life.

Another limitation has to do with the issue of cause and effect we are now discussing. If the cause of Buddhahood comes first and the effect of Buddhahood comes later, then it follows that the Buddha appears at some particular time.

In short, to explain the Buddha without beginning or end, the effect of Buddhahood (benefit) has to be recognized as being inherent in the cause of Buddhahood (practice). This is the second approach and the only one that can suffice to explain the reality of the original Buddha being eternally present throughout past, present and future.

Saito: This seems to be the most logical conclusion.

Ikeda: Bodhisattva Superior Practices is actually a Buddha who is exerting himself at the level of Buddhist practice that enables one to attain enlightenment. In other words, he is the Buddha embodying the simultaneity of cause and effect.

The original Buddha whose life is without beginning or end could not be revealed without the appearance of Superior Practices. His emergence points to the existence of the "true Buddha of *kuon ganjo*," the Buddha enlightened from time without beginning, which far surpasses the idea of an unimaginably remote time called "numberless major world system dust particle *kalpas* ago."

Suda: I am much clearer now on a number of points that had been somewhat ambiguous.

This original Buddha whose life is without beginning or end is then the Nam-myoho-renge-kyo Thus Come One that we refer to as the Buddha of absolute freedom of *kuon ganjo,* or time without beginning.

Ikeda: That's correct.

Suda: So it becomes clear that time without beginning in this context does not mean the remote past. It transcends the framework, indeed the very concept of time.

Ikeda: Yes, time without beginning is another name for life that is without beginning or end. It pertains not to the doctrine of time but to the doctrine of life.

The truth in the depths of life, the very life of the universe that continues to function ceaselessly, is referred to by the term *time without beginning*. This can also be called the "Thus Come One originally endowed with the three bodies."

Regarding the term *time without beginning*, which in Japanese is *kuon ganjo*, Nichiren says, "*Kuon* means something that was not worked for, that was not improved upon, but that exists just as it always has" (OTT, 141). "Not worked for" means inherently endowed; it does not indicate a specific time. "Not improved upon" means not possessing the thirty-two features and eighty characteristics; it refers to ordinary people just as they are. "Exists just as it always has" means eternally existing.

Kuon signifies Nam-myoho-renge-kyo; it signifies the Gohonzon. When we pray to the Gohonzon, that very instant is beginningless time. For us, each day is beginningless time. Each day we can cause the supreme, pure, eternal life of time without beginning to well forth from our entire being. Each day we start anew from time without beginning, the starting point of life.

Saito: This is what it means to live based on the mystic principle of the true cause.

Ikeda: That's why the present time is the most important. We should not dwell on the past; there is no need to do so. Those who exert themselves fully in the present moment and burn with great hope for the future are the true sages in life.

In transmitting the essence of the Lotus Sutra to Bodhisattva Superior Practices, Shakyamuni entrusts him with achieving kosen-rufu in the Latter Day of the Law. Therefore, when we stand up in earnest and work for the propagation of the eternal Mystic Law, we experience the eternity of time without beginning in each moment.

President Toda always regarded propagation of the Mystic Law as his personal responsibility, vowing to realize it without relying on anyone else. And he prayed that youth would rise up with the same great spirit of faith.

On one occasion before a gathering of about twenty youth, he suddenly called out in a powerful voice: "I will accomplish kosen-rufu!" He then had each person there repeat these words:

One after another they fervently exclaimed, "I will achieve kosen-rufu by myself!" Some spoke with weak and unsure voices. Some were taken aback. And some later abandoned their faith. President Toda's sole wish was for young people to stand up with the same determination as he himself cherished. This was his strict compassion. My feelings toward the members of the youth division are exactly the same.

At any rate, although the doctrine concerning Bodhisattva Superior Practices is extremely difficult, since it is the very heart and essence of the Lotus Sutra, let's pursue our investigation a little further.

Saito: So to confirm what we've covered so far, while the Lotus Sutra expounds the essential transmission from Shakyamuni as the Buddha enlightened since the remote past to Bodhisattva Superior Practices, the Law that is thus handed down is not the twenty-eight–chapter Lotus Sutra but the Law of Nam-myoho-renge-kyo that is contained in the sutra's depths.

Ikeda: That's right. But I think the expression "handed down" may invite misunderstanding. Fundamentally, Bodhisattva Superior Practices is already an entity of Nam-myoho-renge-kyo. Since he has possessed this Law eternally, the purpose of the ceremony is merely to verify that he is qualified and charged with spreading Nam-myoho-renge-kyo in the Latter Day; it provides proof of his status.

Endo: Then if I may return once again to the analogy of inheritance of a family estate, it's something like a document from the parent certifying the transfer of assets.

Ikeda: I think you could say that. The "Supernatural Powers" chapter is the letter of certification. Compared to the Mystic Law itself, it is merely a shadow. To illustrate, let us say that a child receives ¥10 million from his parents. That would also be a kind of transmission. The ¥10 million is the essential teaching (body), and the certificate attesting that he has received it is the theoretical teaching (shadow). The difference between essential and theoretical is like day and night. This is also stated in the Daishonin's writing, "The One Hundred and Six Comparisons."

> The Mystic Law which Shakyamuni received in the remote past when he was practicing the Bodhisattva Way at the level of hearing the name and words of the truth is essential (the body), whereas Superior Practices and the others are theoretical (the shadow). The transmission of the essential teaching of the Lotus Sutra from beginningless time is the same as Nichiren's present inheritance of the "Life Span" chapter. (GZ, 865)

This is complex. In essence Nichiren Daishonin says that since time without beginning, he—as a common mortal at the stage of hearing the name and words of the truth—has been upholding the true Law of Nam-myoho-renge-kyo, that is, the body, or the essential teaching. From that standpoint, the ceremony involving Superior Practices and the other bodhisattvas is the shadow, or the theoretical teaching. The sutra is a prophecy; it is documentary proof authorizing the Daishonin to carry out widespread propagation of the Mystic Law.

The Nam-myoho-renge-kyo Thus Come One reflected on the canvas of the twenty-eight–chapter Lotus Sutra manifests both as Shakyamuni who attained enlightenment in the remote past (the world of Buddhahood) and as Bodhisattva Superior Practices (the nine worlds). We must never forget that the Mystic Law is the "body," and Bodhisattva Superior Practices, the "shadow."

There Are No Buddhas
Apart from Human Beings

Endo: So the ceremony of transmission boils down to a passing of the eternal Law from the world of Buddhahood to the nine worlds. But what is its significance?

Ikeda: It indicates that the common mortal is a Buddha.

The point I wish to stress is that while we might speak of the Buddha as a "perfected being" possessing the thirty-two features, this is an ideal image that recedes the closer you get, as in the poem about a utopia that I cited earlier.

Although we might make assumptions about what a "perfect Buddha" is, in actuality this is nothing more than a target. In other words, there is no such thing as a Buddha living apart from the nine worlds of the ordinary person; an idealized Buddha possessing the thirty-two features simply does not exist. In reality, the Buddha can be found only in the life and activities of a bodhisattva. There is no Buddha other than the bodhisattva-Buddha.

The effect resides within the cause. That is to say, the simultaneity of cause and effect is the true aspect of attaining Buddhahood. This is the reality of the original Buddha's enlightenment; therefore, apart from this there is no attainment of Buddhahood. Nichiren says: "Shakyamuni's practices and the virtues he consequently attained are all contained within the five characters of Myoho-renge-kyo. If we believe in these five characters, we will naturally be granted the same benefits as he was" (WND-I, 365).

Saito: What, then, is the reason for the description of perfect Buddhas possessing the thirty-two features? Is it simply to prompt people to practice, much as utopian ideals cause people to seek to advance humanity?

Ikeda: It is to motivate people to persevere in Buddhist practice. Descriptions of Buddhas endowed with wonderful and grand attributes generate within people a yearning to know such beings, which subsequently inspires them to strive to attain Buddhahood themselves. Such images are meant to awaken within people the desire to advance and seek self-improvement.

To say that the Buddha does not exist only means that ordinary people cannot see the Buddha with their own eyes. The world of Buddhahood is undeniably inherent in our lives; it just is not manifested anywhere other than in the nine worlds.

As the Great Teacher Dengyo of Japan says, "The bliss body of the Buddha, which is created by causes, represents the provisional result obtained in a dream, while the uncreated, eternally endowed three enlightened bodies represent the eternal true Buddha."[9]

Suda: "Created" means that it is not inherent; it is something achieved that had not existed previously. The "bliss body of the Buddha" is a property of the Buddha achieved as the result of Buddhist practice. With the exception of the Buddha inherently endowed with three bodies, all Buddhas adorned with idealized features and characteristics are provisional Buddhas who symbolize the effects of Buddhist practice; they are but illusions.

Endo: An actual Buddha is inherently endowed with the three bodies; it is an eternally existing condition of life, not something attained as a result of countless aeons of practice.

Saito: I have read this passage many times, but now I have an entirely fresh sense of its meaning.

Ikeda: Majestic Buddhas are but illusions that have nothing to do with reality. The only actual Buddhas are ordinary people who each moment bring forth the eternal life force of time without beginning. There is no Buddha existing apart from the people. A Buddha set above the people is a fake, an expedient means. Therefore, the correct way is to live with dignity as a human being and to continue along the supreme path in life; to do so is to be a Buddha.

This is what the Lotus Sutra teaches. The transmission to Bodhisattva Superior Practices in the "Supernatural Powers" chapter signifies such a transformation toward a Buddhism focused on the human being. As Nichiren indicates when he says, "If you are of the same mind as Nichiren. . .." we, who are endeavoring to spread the Mystic Law and thereby bring happiness to all humanity, are the Buddhas of the modern age. There are no others.

For this reason, those who use SGI members for personal gain will without fail experience retribution for acting against the Law of the Buddha. On the other hand, to work for the welfare of SGI members and strive to see them become ultimately happy is to cause wonderful benefit to bloom in one's life.

NOTES

1. In chapter 15 of the Lotus Sutra, the Bodhisattvas of the Earth are described as being like venerable hundred-year-olds.

2. Translated from Spanish: Eduardo Galeano, "Ventana sobre la utopia" (Window on Utopia), *Las palabras andantes* (Walking Words) (Mexico: Siglo Veintiuno Editores, 1993).

3. Thirty-two features: Remarkable physical characteristics said to be possessed by Buddhas symbolizing their superiority over ordinary people.

4. "Kanjin no Honzon Sho Mondan" (Commentary on "The Object of Devotion for Observing the Mind").

5. *Toda Josei zenshu* (Collected Writings of Josei Toda) (Tokyo: Seikyo Shimbunsha, 1983), vol. 3, p. 419.

6. Vairochana: A Buddha who appears in the Kegon, Bommo and Dainichi sutras. The Shingon sect equates this Buddha with its central deity, Mahavairochana.

7. Amida: Skt. Amitayus or Amitabh, Infinite Life. The Buddha of the Pure Land of Perfect Bliss in the western region of the universe.

8. Dainichi: Skt. Mahavairochana. A Buddha mentioned in the Dainichi and Kongocho sutras, worshipped by adherents of esoteric Buddhism.

9. *Shugo Kokkai Sho*, one of the most important works of the Japanese Tendai school. This passage is cited in the *Gosho zenshu* on pages 382, 560, and 783.

7   Ordinary People Are the True Buddha

Ikeda: The Lotus Sutra exists to enable ordinary people—who have been oppressed, made to suffer and derided throughout history—to stand up and advance with their heads held high. It aims to help people develop a strong life force, encouraging them: "You who have suffered the most will become the happiest!" It opens the eyes and raises the chins of those who deprecate themselves as worthless, telling them instead, "You are most noble and respectworthy."

The Lotus Sutra empowers us ordinary people to unite and advance proudly for the happiness of all. The "Supernatural Powers" chapter is the prelude, as it were, to this triumphal march. We in the SGI are now setting in motion our goal of achieving a victory of the people in the twenty-first century. We are paving the way and building a bridge.

While this is an extremely laborious and inconspicuous undertaking, we should be confident that our accomplishments will only increase in brilliance with the passage of time.

Endo: What you're talking about, I would call the "living Lotus Sutra."

Suda: The transmission of the Lotus Sutra's essence from Shakyamuni to Bodhisattva Superior Practices is a ceremony in which Buddhism in its entirety and the very life of the Thus Come One are transferred to Superior Practices. It amounts to a declaration that the Latter Day of the Law is not the age of Shakyamuni but the age of Bodhisattva Superior Practices.

Endo: The age of Bodhisattva Superior Practices means an age when the truth that ordinary people are Buddhas is revealed. This is a new era that completely revamps Buddhism as it had existed previously; it overturns the assumption that the Buddha (conceived as a being possessing all manner of remarkable characteristics) is superior to the common mortal.

Saito: The idea that there is no Buddha apart from ordinary people, apart from human beings, points to a profound and genuine humanism.

Ikeda: I heard someone make the following argument: "Fundamentally, doctors exist to serve patients. It is their effort to serve patients that makes them doctors. Yet, all too often, doctors arrogantly think themselves superior to their patients.

"Lawyers exist to help those facing legal troubles. Yet often lawyers become haughty, thinking themselves better than others.

"Politicians exist for the sake of citizens. They are public servants. Yet politicians tend to grow insolent, supposing themselves above their constituents, whom they exploit.

"The role of journalists should be to protect the rights of the people. Yet the mass media is sometimes at the forefront in violating those rights.

"Clergy exist for the sake of the faithful. Yet it happens that priests think of themselves as higher, asserting superiority over believers."

Endo: It's a topsy-turvy situation.

Ikeda: Indeed. What is needed to right this state of affairs is a humanistic revolution.

Saito: As in the original meaning of the term *revolution*, to reverse or overturn.

Ikeda: I think we could say that Nichiren Daishonin and Shakyamuni were revolutionaries of the most radical and fundamental kind. Shakyamuni toppled the prevalent notion that people exist for the sake of the gods, teaching instead that the gods exist for the sake of the people. At the same time, he rejected the Brahman caste, which arrogantly took advantage of people's faith, and the caste system itself. Proclaiming that all people are equal, he put that assertion into practice.

Endo: It seems only natural, therefore, that he should have been persecuted by conservative elements.

Ikeda: In later times, the adherents of Buddhism forgot Shakyamuni's spirit, and consequently Buddhism ceased to be a humanistic teaching.

It was then that Nichiren Daishonin appeared, declaring that people don't exist for the sake of the Buddha; rather, the Buddha exists for the sake of people.

Saito: This was an earthshaking declaration.

Suda: The designation of the present time as the age of Bodhisattva Superior Practices has truly profound meaning.

Ikeda: Since religion is the very foundation of society, a revolution in the realm of religion will rectify all of society's ills on a fundamental level.

In any event, whatever our station in life, we need to be aware that arrogance strips us of our humanity. The more we think ourselves better than others, the less humanistic we become, and the lower our life condition falls.

Endo: In other words, the higher we place ourselves above others, the lower we in fact become.

Saito: This is the case among those with an elitist attitude. In addition to the examples mentioned earlier of lawyers, politicians, doctors and priests, we also find elitism among graduates of leading universities, the wealthy, those who work for major corporations, or even those who have leadership positions in our organization. Such identifiers are but adornments, however, that have nothing to do with our basic identity as human beings. The Lotus Sutra urges us to win in life not based on such superficial laurels but through our humanity.

Suda: Since even the Buddha's august attributes are rejected by the Lotus Sutra, the same goes without saying for all other external adornments.

Ikeda: Those who think themselves above others do not toil selflessly. To avoid personal harm, they shrewdly get others to do the hard work, while taking all the credit themselves. This is cowardice, and it is despicable.

The fundamental teaching of the Lotus Sutra and of the Buddhism of Nichiren Daishonin is that ordinary people—just as they are—should live, assert themselves and strive wholeheartedly for happiness while fully expressing their humanity. To do so is to throw oneself completely into the struggle, to stand up against adversity. This is what it means to practice without begrudging one's life. Apart from this, there is no "living Lotus Sutra."

The social elite has not advanced the movement for kosen-rufu. The path has been opened up by the fully engaged efforts of ordinary people. Herein lies the true practice of the "Supernatural Powers" chapter.

A Struggle for Human Rights
Led by Ordinary People

Endo: One example of ordinary people effecting change was during the so-called Yubari Coal Miners Union Incident in 1957 in Yubari, Hokkaido. I have heard the experiences of two people involved, Masayo and Kazuo Daimon. Masayo, who now lives in Tomakomai, Hokkaido, is over seventy. Her husband, Kazuo, died in 1995.

Ikeda: I am familiar with her experience. I will never forget my friends in Yubari who fought at my side during that difficult period.

Endo: Volume eleven of *The Human Revolution* gives a detailed description of the series of events that took place. It is a moving account of the struggle for human rights waged by unidentified individuals against the devilish nature of power.

Mr. and Mrs. Daimon joined the Soka Gakkai at the urging of Masayo's parents, who were concerned about Kazuo's immoral ways. Though they joined the Soka Gakkai, they did so in name only, however, and did not actually begin practicing. Because of Kazuo's spending on alcohol and their excessive debts, the couple lost their home twice.

Endo: They relocated from Tokyo to Osaka, but Kazuo's business failed, and so he returned alone to his hometown of Yubari. Masayo thought hard about leaving him, but with her mother's encouragement to give their marriage another chance for the sake of the children, she followed Kazuo to Yubari. Immediately after that, however, her mother, on whom she had depended so greatly, died.

Saito: She must have felt terribly lonely.

Endo: Dazed by this turn of events, she stood by the bridge in Yubari one day gazing blankly out into space. As she did so, she heard an unfamiliar voice. "There is someone who is very concerned about you," a woman said. Following at the woman's behest, she found that it was President Toda who wanted to see her.

From the window of the inn where he was staying, President Toda, who had come to Yubari on a guidance tour of the area, had seen Masayo looking so dejected and downcast that he was concerned she might take her life by throwing herself into the water. And so he asked someone to call her over.

Ikeda: President Toda was truly perceptive.

Endo: That was in August 1955.

Hearing President Toda's warm guidance enabled Masayo to turn over a new leaf, and she and her husband began energetically participating daily in activities for kosen-rufu. When Masayo asked President Toda why her mother had died even though she was practicing, he strictly reprimanded her: "How foolish! I have never seen anyone as negligent of her responsibility toward her parents as you. Have you practiced earnestly enough to be able to say such a thing? Your mother was using her death as an expedient means to teach you, her daughter, about faith."

Saito: President Toda put all of his energy into encouraging and revitalizing each person faced with hardship. This kind of compassion has given so many people the strength to stand up—knowing that there is someone who truly cares about their happiness.

Suda: Wasn't the crux of the Yubari Coal Miners Union Incident the contempt, jealousy and fear directed at the solidarity of ordinary people by the union leadership?

Saito: These feelings became particularly acute when, in the Upper House election of July 1956, the candidate supported by the Soka Gakkai received many times more votes from Yubari than had been projected. It seems that this gave the union leaders quite a start.

Endo: They used their powerful influence to threaten Soka Gakkai members who belonged to the union, trying to get them to renounce their faith. This was an outrageous violation of their rights as citizens, rights guaranteed them by the country's constitution.

Suda: At both its national convention and at the local convention in Hokkaido, the Yubari Coal Miners Union announced with great fanfare its policy to staunchly oppose the Soka Gakkai.

Ikeda: Union leaders said things like: "Since disasters and illnesses such as silicosis are quite common in coal mines, and because the workers are uneducated, it is not surprising that a religion of this kind should find a ready reception among our membership." In other words, they were saying that sick and unintelligent people join the Soka Gakkai. What an arrogant and disparaging attitude toward the people!

Saito: They threatened Soka Gakkai members with expulsion unless they obeyed the rules of the union. And to be excluded from the union in those days meant losing one's job.

Suda: If our members tried to borrow money from their credit union, they would be told flat out, "We will make the loan if you quit the Soka Gakkai." The union also used cable broadcasting, leaflets and other means to attack the Soka Gakkai, issuing messages that said things like, "Beware of phony religions!"

Ikeda: There were many such examples of insidious harassment and coercion.

Endo: The Soka Gakkai members of Yubari fought on, enduring everything, united in spirit with you, President Ikeda.

At one union meeting, Kazuo Daimon boldly confronted the leadership, stating: "If there are any Soka Gakkai members who have damaged the union or any of its activities, I would like to hear the facts of such allegations!" There were, of course, no such examples.

The leaders of the union grew unsteady and their true colors were revealed.

AN ORGANIZATION NOT BASED ON THE PEOPLE WILL PERISH

Saito: President Ikeda, you assured the members of Yubari, saying, "This is a struggle for the people, so victory is certain." Also, "The Union will no doubt resort to all kinds of means to harass Soka Gakkai members. We must therefore forge on now to ensure that the members of Yubari are never again subjected to such abuse."

Suda: The Soka Gakkai's historic Sapporo Convention was held on July 1 and the Yubari Convention on July 2, 1956. An account of one of these meetings in a local newspaper described the event as follows: "Conspicuous at the gathering was the large number of women with young children, and junior and senior high school students. I have never before witnessed a scene like it, with each comment by speakers greeted with unanimous applause in a packed auditorium."

Ikeda: At the time, it was probably quite unusual for women with young children to have anything to do with issues of politics or labor unions. But it was just such ordinary people who stood up to actualize politics for the happiness of all people, in contrast to the egoistic politics of the privileged. I simply could not abide the thought of these heroic members just swallowing such treatment in silence.

Which side would win, the powerful, with their tactics of intimidation, or the people, who stood on the side of justice? The problem with the Yubari Coal Miners Union Incident might have seemed like a local occurrence, but it was an important struggle for Buddhism and for the victory of the people.

Endo: The Coal Miners Union had requested to be allowed to observe the Gakkai's Yubari Convention. But midway through the event, the union representatives quietly slipped away.

Kikutaro Mitobe, who was then a chapter leader, gave this testimony: "Of all the guidance I have received from President Ikeda, I am most deeply impressed by something he said to me at the time of the Yubari Coal Miners Union Incident when we were riding in a car together. He told me, 'The union, which does not draw its strength from the people, is really rather pathetic. Someday it will crumble. I hope each of you will carry out a strong practice and solidify your foundation in life.' Just as he predicted, in November 1978 the Yubari Coal Miners Union disbanded, and so its thirty-two-year history came to an end."

Ikeda: Of course, it was not only the union that was at fault. No one had ever taught the union members a correct view of democracy and of humanity. So in a sense, they were victims.

Endo: The Soka Gakkai members of Yubari who created this history all have significantly developed and cultivated their lives. Mrs. Daimon showed actual proof in her work as a calligrapher and is still quite active. She says unequivocally of her late husband, who had once caused her so much grief, "He was my greatest friend and comrade."

Suda: A scholar who read about the Yubari Coal Miners Union Incident in *The Human Revolution* remarked that, in the final analysis, the postwar labor movement was based on nothing more than reactionary conservatism, which could not become a force for genuine change. It was this particular incident, he added, that first made this apparent to the Japanese public.

Professor Koichi Murao of Ehime University also said, regarding the incident: "It vividly illustrates that it was the poor, anonymous, ordinary people who supported Toda at the time of this persecution. It clearly reveals that the Buddha nature dwells within 'ordinary people.' One could not find a better example of the behavior of Bodhisattvas of the Earth."

Ikeda: Anonymous and poor "ordinary people" are themselves most noble and respectworthy. Ordinary people who strive for kosen-rufu are themselves Buddhas. This is the secret of the Thus Come One. It was to teach this that the Thus Come One—the Buddha—appeared.

Saito: Indeed, Buddhism is itself humanism. President Ikeda, in your dialogue with the noted Hong Kong author Jin Yong, Mr. Jin explains how he came to have faith in Buddhism. His words are most impressive and profound.

From Great Pain to Great Joy: One Person's Encounter with the Mystic Law

Ikeda: That's right. His remarks provide a valuable reference for considering the question, "What is Buddhism?" He says that as a result of his lifelong investigations, he came to realize that the truth is to be found within Buddhism.

Saito: Yes. Mr. Jin describes it as an extremely painful process that led him to dedicate himself to the teachings of the Buddha.

His eldest son, an outstanding student who was studying at Columbia University in the United States, had committed suicide. Nothing could have been more devastating for Mr. Jin.

Suda: How old was Mr. Jin then?

Saito: Fifty-two.

Suda: By that time he had already realized considerable success as an author and journalist.

Ikeda: He said that he considered committing suicide himself and following his son in death.

Saito: Plagued with questions about what could have driven his son to take his own life—about why he suddenly chose to throw away all that he had—Mr. Jin spent a year investigating the issue of life and death, reading countless books on the subject. But for a long time he simply could not find any explanation of the significance of death that was truly convincing and persuasive. He says that though he repeatedly pondered the teaching of Christianity on the matter, he never really felt comfortable with it.

Ikeda: That is when he began studying Buddhism.

Saito: He started by taking up the Agama sutras, which are a part of the so-called Hinayana teachings. For months he poured his energy into studying and pondering their meaning, even to the point of neglecting to sleep and eat properly. Then he suddenly had a revelation: "The truth was in Buddhism all along. Its teachings are true beyond any doubt."

Mr. Jin, reading English- and Chinese-language translations of Buddhist texts side by side, says that "I accepted Buddhism from the bottom of my heart with all my body and soul."

Endo: He also says: "Buddhism resolved the huge doubts that had burrowed into my heart. Thinking, 'So that's it! Finally I understand!' my heart overflowed with joy. My happiness knew no bounds."

Ikeda: That is wonderful.

Early Buddhist canons (to which the Agama sutras belong) repeatedly talk about immortality. They are filled with statements like the following: "Immersed in the state of immortality you merge [with the universe] without dying . . . you experience the joy of peace";[1] "The one who reaches the foundation of immortality is the enlightened person";[2] "Better than a hundred years not seeing one's own immortality is one single day of life if one sees one's own immortality";[3] "Enter the realm of immortality";[4] and, "I will surely beat the drum of immortality."[5]

As we see from such passages, Shakyamuni was trying to teach people about a state of eternal happiness that transcends life and death. With keen and subtle insight, Mr. Jin must have sensed this essential meaning.

Saito: He next studied a number of Mahayana texts including the Vimalakirti, Lankavatara and Prajnaparamita sutras. But he says that he found these hard to accept because they contain so much that is mysterious and fantastical.

Suda: It is certainly true that Mahayana Buddhist texts display rich imagination, depicting many miracles and supernatural phenomena.

Endo: They read almost like science fiction! The content may even appear absurd. I think this is one reason the Mahayana sutras have been regarded by many as not being Shakyamuni's teachings at all but apocryphal works by people of later generations. The fact that, from a historical perspective, Mahayana

Buddhism appeared several hundred years after Shakyamuni's death (around the start of the Common Era) seems to lend support to such a view.

Ikeda: The question is, what is Mahayana Buddhism trying to express? In the case of the Lotus Sutra, such events as the Ceremony in the Air or the emergence of the Bodhisattvas of the Earth from within the ground sound preposterous if we only read them literally.

But there are three different levels to the sutra: the words (the text itself), the teaching (the meaning that follows from the words), and the intent (the true intention behind the sutra). We need to understand the intent or "heart" of the sutra.

Saito: Although Mr. Jin was at first puzzled by the Lotus Sutra, he says after lengthy reflection, he finally grasped its true meaning. He says, "I understood that this 'Mystic Law' fundamentally encompasses everything that the Mahayana sutras are trying to teach."

Endo: That's a remarkable insight. Certainly the sutras all have the Mystic Law as their common focus.

Ikeda: They are directed toward the great life that is the oneness of life and death, the Mystic Law. "Mystic" refers to death, and "Law," to life. "Mystic Law" expresses the oneness of life and death. The state of immortality, or "no death," that Shakyamuni talks about in early texts is the state of someone who is awakened to this eternal great life.

Saito: That's the world of Buddhahood.

Ikeda: Yes. When we dedicate ourselves to the Mystic Law, the tremendous life force of Buddhahood, which neither ages nor dies, wells forth.

Suda: "Beating the drum of immortality" could be taken to mean causing the great voice of the Mystic Law to resound.

Endo: Mr. Jin says: "In the Lotus Sutra, the Buddha uses a variety of familiar metaphors such as a burning house, an ox cart and heavy rains to explain Buddhism to people. There are also instances where he uses 'expedient means' to guide people. There are even scenes where the Buddha causes people to think that he has died. This, too, is to cause Buddhism to spread among people.

"I began thinking deeply about the meaning of 'Mystic Law.' In time, I ceased to feel repelled by the illusions that fill the Mahayana sutras. It took about two years for the immense pain I felt to turn into immense joy."

Suda: These are striking comments. It's as though he undertook an odyssey through the stages of the fivefold comparison.[6] From Christianity he turned to Buddhism; from the Hinayana teachings he turned to the Mahayana and then to the Lotus Sutra.

Ikeda: This clearly demonstrates the earnestness with which Mr. Jin pursued his investigation of life and death. Guided by his son, he approached the Mystic Law.

The true intent that the "Supernatural Powers" chapter is trying to express is the Mystic Law; it seeks to convey the eternal and supreme life that is without beginning or end from time without beginning.

Who Is the True Protagonist of the Lotus Sutra?

Endo: Last time, we learned that the appearance of Bodhisattva Superior Practices refers to the original Buddha of time without beginning whose life is without beginning or end.

Saito: To reiterate, Superior Practices is a "bodhisattva-Buddha," a bodhisattva in his outward conduct but a Buddha in his inner state of life. His true identity is that of a Buddha exerting himself at the initial stage of Buddhist practice when the cause to attain enlightenment is made; in other words, he is a Buddha embodying the simultaneity of cause and effect. Such a figure had never before been known in the history of Buddhism.

Suda: Through the appearance of this "Buddha of the simultaneity of cause and effect," the original Buddha of time without beginning finally could be identified. As long as the discussion was premised on the notion that the cause comes first and the effect later, it was assumed that a person became a Buddha at some particular time; such enlightenment, therefore, could not be "without beginning or end."

Ikeda: The lotus flower represents the principle of the simultaneity of cause and effect. The *renge* of Myoho-renge-kyo, the lotus flower, symbolizes the Buddha of the simultaneity of cause and effect.

Endo: This idea seems quite complicated.

Ikeda: Certainly. The important thing is, however, to have the spirit to learn. As long as we have such a seeking mind, we will continue to advance in our human revolution.

President Toda often said, "changing is more important than understanding." Even if we should intellectually comprehend the so-called eighty thousand teachings, unless we can use this knowledge to grow as human beings, it will not benefit us in the least. We study Buddhism to do our human revolution and strengthen our faith. It's enough that we have the faith to continue our Buddhist study, even if only a little at a time.

Saito: Superior Practices is a truly wondrous being. His appearance overturns the prevailing understanding of Buddhism.

Ikeda: That's right. In fact, the question of the identity and nature of Bodhisattva Superior Practices is the main theme of the essential teaching (or second half) of the Lotus Sutra. In that sense, he is the true protagonist of the Lotus Sutra. While Shakyamuni might appear to be the protagonist, in fact Superior Practices more deeply embodies the sutra's spirit.

This is first and foremost revealed by the development of the Lotus Sutra itself. Shakyamuni calls out, "After my death, who will spread the Mystic Law in the *saha* world?" Many bodhisattvas announce their "candidacy," beseeching him to entrust them with the teaching. But Shakyamuni refuses.

Suda: He flatly turns them down, saying, "Leave off, good men! There is no need for you to protect and embrace this sutra" (LSOC, 252). He then calls forth the Bodhisattvas of the Earth.

Ikeda: Saying "Leave off" is significant. With this, he refutes all the teachings he has expounded up to that point. Nichiren Daishonin says, "With this single expression 'leave off,' Shakyamuni Buddha settled once and for all that there is no need for any bodhisattvas other than Bodhisattva Superior Practices and his followers [to spread the Mystic Law]" (GZ, 840).

Endo: This is a declaration that the Latter Day of the Law—the period indicated by references to the time after Shakyamuni's passing—is the age of Bodhisattva Superior Practices. Tremendous weight attaches to the expression "Leave off."

Saito: Shakyamuni then calls forth the Bodhisattvas of the Earth, led by Superior Practices, from below the ground. The entire assembly is thunderstruck, for these bodhisattvas are even more splendid in appearance than Shakyamuni.

On behalf of all those gathered, Bodhisattva Maitreya entreats Shakyamuni to explain where these bodhisattvas have come from and what "causes and conditions" bring them together (LSOC, 256). By way of reply, Shakyamuni expounds the "Life Span of the Thus Come One" chapter. This is the general progression of events.

Suda: Shakyamuni uses the question of the identity of Superior Practices to reveal that he has been enlightened since the remote past. And in the "Supernatural Powers" chapter, he transfers the life of the Thus Come One in its entirety to Superior Practices. In this light, we can see just how central is the role played by Superior Practices.

It may be that he is on a par with Shakyamuni during the Ceremony in the Air. But after the Buddha's passing, Superior Practices becomes the undisputed "star."

Saito: You might say that Shakyamuni and Superior Practices, the eternal mentor and disciple, are the protagonists of the Lotus Sutra.

Ikeda: The issue is, what does this eternal oneness of mentor and disciple signify? It indicates the life of the original Buddha without beginning or end, which is one with the universe.

In the twenty-eight–chapter Lotus Sutra, Bodhisattva Superior Practices personifies the true cause of the original Buddha, and Shakyamuni who attained enlightenment in the remote past personifies the true effect.

Endo: So they are both functions of the same original Buddha.

Ikeda: That's right. Shakyamuni and Superior Practices are one Buddha, not two. They are two sides of the same Buddha.

Therefore, while we may speak of transmission, this is nothing more than a formality. To think that this transmission itself has any substance is to misunderstand the Lotus Sutra.

What Shakyamuni Ultimately Wanted to Communicate

Suda: What is the purpose of the ceremony?

Ikeda: Fundamentally, it is to announce that Superior Practices will appear in the Latter Day and propagate the Mystic Law of time without beginning. Because of this "announcement" or "prophecy," people could recognize the person who was to spread the true Mystic Law when he appeared.

Endo: That suggests that those who compiled the Lotus Sutra distinctly knew that someone would appear in the future who would spread the Mystic Law. But how did they know?

Saito: I think they knew because they grasped the limitations of the twenty-eight–chapter Lotus Sutra.

Endo: In other words, they knew there were things not made explicit in the sutra's text.

Suda: This brings us to the question of the sutra's "implicit meaning."

Ikeda: The conversation has again taken a difficult turn. But since this is an important point, let's try to set things straight.

First, what was the enlightenment of the historical Shakyamuni?

Endo: I believe it was that he perceived the state of life of immortality.

Saito: He opened his eyes to the eternal life, the eternal Law.

Suda: The Pali term for immortality (*amata*) originally also indicated the mystic elixir of heaven (*amrita*) that is said to bestow immortality.

Saito: The Mystic Law is the true mystic elixir of immortality.

Ikeda: The Daishonin says in his writings:

> *Amrita* is said to be the elixir of immortality. In the first place, *myo* is the elixir of immortality. . . . That the behavior and actions of beings in each of the Ten Worlds are in themselves eternally dwelling and unchanging is called *amrita*, the Mystic Law, mystic, the original Law, or concentration and insight [as taught by the Great Teacher T'ien-t'ai]. In the Latter Day of the Law, *amrita* is Nam-myoho-renge-kyo. (GZ, 831–32)

Endo: This is saying that the lives of all beings in the Ten Worlds, or all phenomena of the entire universe, while undergoing constant change, are eternal.

Ikeda: Viewed through the eye of the Lotus Sutra, all phenomena manifest the eternal original Buddha, the universal life that is without beginning or end. That is the true aspect of all phenomena. Therefore, all beings are themselves, just as they are, the Thus Come One. This is what is meant by "The Thus Come One refers to all living beings" (OTT, 167).

Suda: Shakyamuni awakened to the fact that this eternal Law is itself the eternal Buddha. He called it the Dharma or (in Pali) Danma, and the Tathagata or Thus Come One.

Saito: This Dharma manifested through and pervaded his life. He perceived it as a state of life at one with himself and called it a state of immortality. I think that in this we find the basic paradigm of the "Life Span" chapter.

Ikeda: That may be. Shakyamuni dedicated his entire life to communicating this realization to others. But he could not succinctly express all that he wanted to convey in words.

While expounding various teachings according to people's suffering or their capacity, he was ultimately trying to open their eyes to this state of life, to the great life force of eternal youth and immortality. Through a lifetime of teaching, he gradually developed the people's capacity, and in the end he taught them the Lotus Sutra.

Of course, the content of Shakyamuni's sermon may not be identical to what is written in the twenty-eight–chapter Lotus Sutra itself. But he certainly expounded the truth that constitutes the sutra's core, because a Buddha who does not expound the Lotus Sutra is not a Buddha.

Suda: This "core" is the real existence of the great life that is the eternal Mystic Law, which is itself the eternal Buddha.

Ikeda: It is the principle that this great life manifests in ordinary human beings. This is the purpose of the living Lotus Sutra. It could be said that the progression and advancement seen over the entire history of Buddhism come down to the question of how to express and open people's eyes to this one point. From that standpoint, I think the advent of Mahayana Buddhism was inevitable.

What was Shakyamuni's last wish for his followers when he died? It was: "In this world be an island to yourself, be a refuge to yourself and take refuge in no other. Make the Dharma your island, the Dharma your refuge and no other."[7] In other words, depend on no one other than yourself. With the Law as your sole foundation, rely on yourself alone. Amid the turbulent currents of the sufferings of life and death, he is saying, we should live with the Law and the self as our only support. The pursuit of this "self" and this "Law" became the task of adherents of Buddhism after Shakyamuni's passing.

Suda: In terms of the Person and the Law, the self corresponds to the Person. And the goal of our pursuit is the eternal Buddha and the eternal Law, the entity of the oneness of the Person and the Law.

Endo: In other words, after Shakyamuni's passing, Buddhism became a search for the cause of enlightenment that enabled him to become a Buddha. This of course was not just a theoretical pursuit but an all-out struggle on which people staked their very lives.

Saito: It has been a search for the eternal life that could be called "Shakyamuni's mentor."

Ikeda: The pursuit of the cause of enlightenment is also summed up in the *Jataka.*

Suda: This is a collection of tales describing Shakyamuni's activities during past lives and the benefits that he accumulated.

Endo: There are a number of remarkable tales, such as how, as a bodhisattva, he once gave up his life to save others, or how he became a king of animals so as to lead other animals to happiness.

Ikeda: Many of these stories are cited in the Daishonin's writings. They include accounts of his incarnations as King Shibi (who gave his own flesh to a hawk in order to save a dove), as the hermit Ninniku (who does not bear a grudge even when his hands and legs are cut off by King Kali), as the king of the deer (who allows himself to be eaten to save the lives of the other deer), as Prince Satta (who gives his body to feed a famished tigress), and as Sessen Doji (who throws himself into the mouth of a demon to learn half a Buddhist verse).

Saito: These accounts are also well known in Japan from early collections of folklore such as the *Tales of Times Now Past.*

Ikeda: These might seem like mere fairy tales of old. But we are in fact composing many such "bodhisattva tales" through our SGI activities, which constitute bodhisattva practice for the modern age.

Nichiren Daishonin praised the united struggles of the Ikegami brothers, saying, "Could there ever be a more wonderful story than your own?" (WND-1, 499). People of later generations will certainly talk about and relate our efforts for kosen-rufu. They will doubtless become "tales" that are broadly praised.

Saito: The fierce struggles of the first three presidents of the Soka Gakkai certainly constitute a glorious tale that will endure throughout the ten thousand years and more of the Latter Day of the Law.

Endo: To be directly connected to this legacy is the greatest honor.

THE BUDDHA APPEARS IN RESPONSE TO THE PEOPLE'S LONGING

Suda: Speaking of the *Jataka*, when I visited India, I saw many stupas with carvings and reliefs depicting scenes from such tales.

Ikeda: Stupas, as you know, have much to do with this pursuit of the cause of enlightenment.

Endo: Yes. After Shakyamuni's death, lay followers held a funeral in which they cremated his remains. It was conducted by lay people because Shakyamuni had admonished the monks and nuns that they should not have anything to do with the holding of funerals. "If you have that kind of free time, then you ought to spend it on your practice," he told them in his final words. His ashes were divided up and interred in stupas set up for that purpose.

Thereafter, a faith centering on stupas spread widely. While the details of how exactly this came about remain unclear, it has become generally accepted that the spread of stupas is closely linked to the rise of Mahayana Buddhism.

Saito: What belief was upheld by those who prayed to these stupas? While unsubstantiated, it is thought that their actions were motivated by a sense of longing for the deceased Shakyamuni.[8]

Ikeda: The "Life Span" chapter says, "Then when their minds are filled with yearning, / at last I appear and preach the Law for them" (LSOC, 271). In other words, the eternal Buddha appears and expounds the Law in response to the longing in people's hearts.

After Shakyamuni's passing, weren't people seeking an "essential" or "true" Shakyamuni that transcended even his death? I think this is also evident in the emergence of teachings articulating theories about the Buddha body.

Saito: Yes. As scholars such as Nagarjuna indicate, it seems that early Buddhist theorists postulated the existence of two bodies: the manifested body of the person Shakyamuni and the Dharma body of the Buddha. The historical Shakyamuni Buddha who died at the age of eighty is termed the manifested body. By contrast, the eternal state of enlightenment that made Shakyamuni the Buddha is called the Buddha's Dharma body.

Ikeda: The Dharma body is later said to possess the two properties of the Dharma body (objective reality) and the reward body (subjective wisdom). This further gives us the doctrine of the three bodies—the Law (Dharma body), wisdom (reward body) and action (manifested Body). While such theories concerning the nature of the Buddha body developed, the basic spirit to view the eternal Buddha as existing in the depths of the life of the actual person Shakyamuni remained unchanged.

Suda: In like manner, I imagine that people's faith in stupas was sustained by the belief of people "single-mindedly desiring to see" (LSOC, 271) an eternal Buddha transcending the corporeal Shakyamuni.

Endo: Several passages in the Lotus Sutra refer to such practices. The "Expedient Means" chapter says things like: "If . . . they pile up earth to make a mortuary temple for the buddhas, / or even if little boys at play / should collect sand to make a buddha tower, / then persons such as these/ have all attained the buddha way" (LSOC, 72–73).

Saito: The appearance of the treasure tower probably also reflects the practice of building stupas.

Endo: Many Treasures Buddha who appears with the treasure tower is a "Buddha of the past." Shakyamuni is the "Buddha of the present." And Bodhisattva Superior Practices is the "Buddha of the future." Together, obviously they represent the Buddhas of past, present and future.

Ikeda: In any event, stupas were built as expressions of people's yearning for the eternal Buddha who transcends past, present and future. The truth is that the life of the ordinary person is itself the treasure tower. Ordinary people who embrace the Mystic Law are themselves treasure towers; they are one with the eternal Buddha. Nichiren writes to his follower Abutsu-bo, "Abutsu-bo is therefore the treasure tower itself, and the treasure tower is Abutsu-bo himself" (WND-I, 299).

Suda: Tracing the matter in this way, it becomes that much clearer why Mahayana Buddhism postulated the existence of various eternal Buddhas. The Mahayana teachings are often blamed for wanting to turn the deceased founder Shakyamuni into a divine being. But even though there may be an element of truth to this charge, this is not the main point. The driving force of Mahayana Buddhism is the pursuit of the "cause of enlightenment" that enabled Shakyamuni to become a Buddha; and this turned into the pursuit of the eternal Buddha.

Ikeda: We should note that the eternal Buddha is another name for the "cause of enlightenment." All Buddhas are born of the "Nam-myoho-renge-kyo Thus Come One." Of course, while this is the cause of Buddhahood, it is simultaneously the effect of Buddhahood.

Saito: In connection with the two bodies doctrine of the living body and the Dharma body that we talked about a moment ago, it is said that the living body is born of the Dharma body.

Ikeda: We might explain this as follows: All practitioners of Buddhism strove to awaken to the Dharma (i.e., the Law, eternal life or the Thus Come One). But the moment they awakened to this, they understood that the self is none other than the child of the Thus Come One (i.e., a bodhisattva) born of the Dharma. I know this is somewhat confusing.

Endo: This development in thought seems to parallel the historic transition from Hinayana to Mahayana Buddhism. It is the change from Hinayana (or sectarian) Buddhism, which made the pursuit of the Dharma its object, to Mahayana Buddhism, which is a movement of bodhisattvas (or children of the Buddha).

The "Truth of the Mentor" Is Revealed in Response to the Earnest "Words of the Disciple"

Ikeda: To say this definitively would require more solid research. Some have said that Mahayana is a non-Buddhist doctrine with no relation to Shakyamuni, but this is definitely not the case. On the contrary, it is the result of an attempt to get at Shakyamuni's true intent.

Of course, regardless of who expounded a teaching, it should be judged on the basis of its own merits. The Lotus Sutra is not great because it was expounded by Shakyamuni; rather, Shakyamuni is the Buddha because he expounded the Lotus Sutra. No matter who the person is, one who expounds the Lotus Sutra is a Buddha. To say that a particular teaching is supreme because it was taught by Shakyamuni smacks of a kind of authoritarianism or elitism.

Suda: While Socrates is the protagonist of the enormous collection of dialogues left behind by his disciple Plato, the dialogues are not in fact a literal record of Socrates' conversations. However, we cannot on that basis dismiss the dialogues as lies or as representing a non-Socratic doctrine. I think they express the true intent of the mentor as grasped by the disciple Plato.

Ikeda: That's right. The Mahayana sutras were expounded by people committed to seeking Shakyamuni's true intent who exercised remarkable ingenuity in their effort to widely communicate that intent to others.

Endo: Mr. Jin says: "Finally I understood. This Mystic Law is what all the Mahayana sutras fundamentally are trying to express. The Mahayana sutras employ skillful expedient means in enhancing and explaining Buddhism so as to enable even the slow and unintelligent to understand and embrace it."

Saito: Certainly, the view that the Mahayana teachings are non-Buddhist is weak in that it accuses the compilers of the sutras of stooping to such shameful conduct as to attribute their own arbitrary ideas to Shakyamuni.

As indicated by the line "This is what I heard," which begins almost all sutras, it seems far more reasonable to assume that the people who set down these teachings in writing acted with the profound realization and genuine belief that they had "heard" these teachings from Shakyamuni.

Ikeda: In that case, when they say, "This is what I heard," from whom did they hear the teaching? It must have been from the eternal Buddha who is "always here, preaching the Law" (LSOC, 271).

They surely heard this teaching. The expression "This is what I heard" no doubt refers to a profound religious experience.

Suda: There are a number of scholars of Mahayana Buddhism who take such a position.

Ikeda: Naturally, it can also be conjectured that the sutras derived from teachings expounded by the historical Shakyamuni, which had been transmitted over time.

Endo: In practicing with the spirit of "single-mindedly desiring to see the Buddha" (LSOC, 271), it is not unusual for people to have profound religious experiences that defy all rational explanation. I imagine that such experiences certainly played a part.

Saito: Some scholars might dispute this, but someone who flatly denies the validity of such an experience of "seeing the Buddha" cannot possibly understand the history of Buddhism or for that matter the history of religion.

Endo: That would be like someone who has no knowledge of music whatsoever attempting to write a history of the subject.

Ikeda: The view that Mahayana is not the Buddha's teaching seems to be based on the major premise that there is no Buddha other than the historical person Shakyamuni. If that is true, however, then Shakyamuni's reason for expounding his teaching becomes obscure, because he expounded his teachings to awaken people to the fact that they, too, possess the same "state of immortality" he did. And there absolutely are people who have reached the same enlightenment as Shakyamuni.

Saito: Such people are also Buddhas—not in theory but in actuality.

Ikeda: Yes.

Suda: It must then follow that the people who compiled the Lotus Sutra were also Buddhas.

Ikeda: That is fair to say.

Endo: Why, then, does the sutra take the form of a teaching expounded by (the historical person) Shakyamuni at Eagle Peak?

Ikeda: This may have to do with Indian folklore. But more than that, it is probably because the compilers believed that this format represented Shakyamuni's true intent.

Suda: The Mahayana movement peaked over several centuries around the start of the Common Era; that would have put it about five hundred years after Shakyamuni's death. In terms of the doctrine of the "five five-hundred–year periods,"[9] it would roughly correspond to the period known as the age of meditation.

Saito: We can surmise that through the experience of meditation, practitioners of Buddhism could "see" the eternal Shakyamuni who is "always here, preaching the Law."

Endo: Recounting his enlightenment in prison, President Toda as well describes an experience in which he found himself present during the "assembly on Holy Eagle Peak which continues in solemn state and has not yet disbanded" (OTT, 135).

Ikeda: Our discussion today has centered on Buddhist history, but I think that in order for people of the modern age to grasp the essence of the Lotus Sutra, it is necessary to consider the teachings from this standpoint.

Endo: This conversation has solidified my understanding that the preaching of the Lotus Sutra, while not a statement of fact per se, nonetheless expresses the truth of life.

THE REVELATION THAT THE BUDDHA IS A HUMAN BEING

Ikeda: We're not done yet! If our readers find some parts too much to digest, it's perfectly fine to skip over them and continue on.

The history of Buddhism could broadly be summarized as follows: So-called early Buddhism put its energy into upholding the precepts that the living person Shakyamuni left behind for those who had renounced secular life. Because of its basically conservative nature, this teaching tended to lose sight of Shakyamuni's true intent—his desire to enable *everyone* to become a Buddha by revealing the cause of his own enlightenment.

Mahayana Buddhism, on the other hand, investigated the cause of Shakyamuni's enlightenment and pursued the eternal Buddha. Put another way, it was a reformist force. It expounded the existence of many Buddhas possessing extremely long spans of life, such as Amida, Vairochana and Mahavairochana of the Nembutsu and Shingon schools. From the standpoint of the Lotus Sutra, these teachings all explain different aspects of the Thus Come One inherently possessing the three bodies whose life is without beginning or end (i.e., the Nam-myoho-renge-kyo Thus Come One). But because of its exclusive pursuit of the eternal Buddha, the Mahayana teachings departed from the essential point of Shakyamuni the human being and even from the human being.

Suda: Amida is a Buddha said to dwell not in this *saha* world but in another land. And Mahavairochana is merely the Dharma body, possessing no physical form. Such beings are far removed from the human world. Rushana, likewise, is described as a great Buddha of beneficence, something completely separate from ordinary people.

Ikeda: Both Hinayana and Mahayana have such limitations. The Lotus Sutra integrates these two traditions, breaking down their limitations. That's because it reveals that the real identity of the person Shakyamuni is that of the Buddha who attained enlightenment in the remote past. It opens a path to the Buddha, who while eternal and awe-inspiring is at the same time familiar and accessible. It could be said that this constitutes returning to the essential point of Shakyamuni the human being.

Suda: In an earlier discussion you explained that the principle of "casting off the transient and revealing the true" signifies returning to Shakyamuni the human being.

Ikeda: The appeal to return to Shakyamuni the human being means to return to the true nature of humanity. It urges us to open our eyes to the dignity of human life.

Saito: The Lotus Sutra is then a sutra that integrates Hinayana and Mahayana.

Ikeda: That's right. Through the principle of casting off the transient and revealing the true, all Buddhas are unified as Buddhas instructed by Shakyamuni who attained enlightenment in the remote past. This is the Lotus Sutra's essential teaching. This unifies all Mahayana sutras.

The theoretical teaching (or first half) of the Lotus Sutra explains that the voice-hearers and cause-awakened ones, meaning those who uphold the Hinayana teachings, can attain Buddhahood. This is because it unifies all phenomena into a single truth called the true aspect.

The unification of all phenomena of the theoretical teaching and the unification of all Buddhas of the essential teaching are complementary. They are both integrated into the Mystic Law.

Saito: The Lotus Sutra is the summit of all Buddhist doctrine up to that point in the progress of Buddhist history. It is truly the king of sutras.

Ikeda: But this progress is not complete at this point. We have yet to touch on the Buddhism that is implicit in the Lotus Sutra.

Next time let's discuss the need for an implicit teaching. It is through the implicit teaching that the epochal and fundamental turning point in the history of Buddhism—the teaching that the common mortal is a true Buddha—first becomes a reality.

NOTES

1. *Budda no kotoba* (The Buddha's Words): *Sutta Nipata*, trans. Hajime Nakamura (Tokyo: Iwanami Bunko, 1994), p. 52. See *The Sutta-Nipata*, trans. H. Saddhatissa (Richmond Surrey: Curzon Press Ltd., 1994), p. 24.

2. *Budda no kotoba*, p. 138. See *The Sutta-Nipata*, p. 73.

3. *Budda no shinri no kotoba, kankyo no kotoba* (The Buddha's Words of Truth and Inspiration), trans. Hajime Nakamura (Tokyo:

Iwanami Bunko, 1994), p. 26. See *The Dhammapada: Sayings of Buddha*, trans. Thomas Clearly (New York: Bantam Books, 1994), p. 41.

4. *Budda no shinri no kotoba, kankyo no kotoba*, p. 41. See *The Dhammapada: Sayings of Buddha*, p. 77.

5. *Budda no shinri no kotoba, kankyo no kotoba*, p. 224. See Dharmatrata, comp., *The Tibetan Dhammapada Sayings of the Buddha: A translation of the Tibetan version of the Udanavarga*, trans. Gareth Sparham (London: Wisdom Publications, 1986), p. 109.

6. Fivefold comparison: Five successive levels of comparison set forth by Nichiren Daishonin in "The Opening of the Eyes" to demonstrate the superiority of Nam-myoho-renge-kyo over all other teachings. They are: (1) Buddhism is superior to non-Buddhist teachings; (2) Mahayana Buddhism is superior to Hinayana Buddhism; (3) true Mahayana is superior to provisional Mahayana; (4) the essential teaching of the Lotus Sutra is superior to the theoretical teaching; and (5) the Buddhism of sowing is superior to the Buddhism of the harvest.

7. Hajime Nakamura, *Gotama Buddha* (Los Angeles: Buddhist Books International, 1977), pp. 113–14.

8. This makes a reference to the passage in the "Life Span" chapter: "In their minds they will harbor a longing and will thirst to gaze upon the buddha, and then they will work to plant good roots" (LSOC, 268).

9. Five five-hundred–year periods: Five consecutive periods following Shakyamuni's death during which Buddhism is said to spread, prosper and eventually decline. The five periods are: (1) the age of attaining liberation, in which many people attain emancipation through practicing the Buddha's teachings; (2) the age of meditation, when meditation is widely practiced; (3) the age of reading, reciting and listening, in which studying and reciting the sutras and receiving lectures on them are the central practice; (4) the age of building temples and stupas, when many temples and stupas are built, but the spirit of seeking the Buddhist teachings declines; and (5) the age of quarrels and disputes, when strife occurs among the various rival schools and Shakyamuni's teachings become obscured and lost.

8 "Buddhism for the People"— The Implicit Teaching

As the light of the sun and moon
can banish all obscurity and gloom,
so this person as he advances through the world
can wipe out the darkness of living beings,
causing immeasurable numbers of bodhisattvas
in the end to dwell in the single vehicle.
Therefore a person of wisdom,
hearing how keen are the benefits to be gained,
after I have passed into extinction
should accept and uphold this sutra.
Such a person assuredly and without doubt
will attain the buddha way. (LSOC, 318)

Endo: I heard a woman from the Kansai area relate how, in 1957, a man was dozing off at a discussion meeting you were attending, President Ikeda. She said that her husband tried hard to rouse the man.

But you kindly said: "This man has come here after having worked hard all day, so he must be very tired. There's no need to wake him. Discussion of the Mystic Law cannot fail to enter a person's life—even if it has to be through the pores of the skin!" When you said this, the atmosphere at the meeting became relaxed and friendly.

Saito: I think there is an important lesson here. Those who make their best effort to attend meetings despite their busy schedules ought to be praised. Often people have to rush just to get there before the meeting ends. Certainly, no one has the right to take someone to task for arriving late at a meeting.

Endo: The same woman also described how, on another occasion, she reported something to you, President Ikeda, and was about to leave. To her surprise, you came over to see her off. Addressing her in the most courteous manner, you told her: "Thank you so much for your efforts. Please return home safely." She said that this gesture really moved her, and she thought to herself, "This is what it means to be a Soka Gakkai leader."

Ikeda: I'm surprised you would hear of such an account from so long ago!

Endo: It seems to me that the concept that religion exists for the sake of human beings ultimately comes down to people's conduct. That's all. The more I think about it, the more convinced I am of this.

Ikeda: How we behave as human beings is really the bottom line. Buddhism ultimately boils down to character. The purpose of Buddhism is to produce people of fine character.

People of excellent character are humble. They are not jealous. They are not self-absorbed but are concerned with everyone's happiness. For us, this means caring about kosen-rufu. People who do so are fair and compassionate. And because they have compassion, wisdom wells forth in their lives.

When any organization increases in size, it tends to become bureaucratic. But the SGI must never become this way. The SGI is a world of humanism.

It is the leaders who set the tone of an organization. The larger an organization grows, the more its leaders need to develop humility. It is the function of leaders in the SGI to treasure their fellow members. Where leaders genuinely make such thorough efforts, there is growth. Again, such efforts are what our Buddhist practice consists of. This is the Lotus Sutra.

Endo: I heard about another woman from Kansai who once consulted you regarding her recent appointment as a district women's leader. She was uncertain as to how to direct her efforts in that capacity. That was in the summer of 1959. You replied:

> There are no set guidelines dictating what you should do. It's as though the short staff you have been wielding until now has been switched to a long one. Because it is longer, you are not sure exactly how to manage it. But, the fact is, whether the staff you carry is short or long, the basic principle is the same; if you grab one end and swing it, the other end will move.
>
> The important thing is to earnestly chant daimoku and treat those around you with the utmost respect, just as you have done up to now. It's about really caring for one individual, about praying for the happiness of your friends and kindly and considerately encouraging them. Such determination will spread through the entire district. This is the principle of "they are endowed with both material and spiritual aspects"[1] (WND-I, 356).

It is a mistake to think that kosen-rufu will be accomplished if we fail to encourage people around us and share this practice with them.

Her insecurity vanished at once upon hearing this, like a mist that suddenly clears, and she felt great confidence that she would succeed.

Suda: While we tend to think that a leader has to engage in special activities, the reality is that the higher one's position in our organization, the more important it becomes to really focus on the basics of the practice.

WHERE DOES THE BUDDHA RESIDE?

Ikeda: At any rate, those who are working for kosen-rufu deserve the utmost respect. Ordinary people who honestly devote themselves to kosen-rufu are more noble—thousands, tens of thousands of times more noble—than any influential person.

It's not a matter of appearance, position or education. The strength of mind in which one is determined to help the suffering become happy and to accomplish kosen-rufu is most respectworthy. This is what it means to be at one with the Law.

The universe is also an entity of the Mystic Law; it is the great life of the Mystic Law itself. When we focus on the widespread propagation of the Mystic Law and devote our lives to realizing this goal, we become one with the Mystic Law in both body and mind. In a broad sense, we enter the path of "oneness of the Person and the Law."

Saito: Concretely speaking, the path of the Mystic Law is the path of kosen-rufu.

Ikeda: And more precisely, since the SGI is the only group striving for kosen-rufu, the path of the Mystic Law is actually found in SGI activities. Those who really exert themselves in the organization for kosen-rufu embark on the path of the oneness of the Person and the Law.

As was mentioned at the beginning of this discussion, while working long and hard in society, such people push themselves and take selfless action for the sake of the Law, society and others. They are truly noble. Though on the surface they may work at a company or take care of the home or what have you, their inner status is that of Bodhisattvas of the Earth. And a Bodhisattva of the Earth is a Buddha. While we may speak of the Buddha in various contexts, apart from people behaving in this way there simply aren't any Buddhas. This is a point that people really have a difficult time grasping.

Saito: Your remarks really get at the superb features of the Lotus Sutra's implicit teaching. One is that, as Nichiren says in *The Record of the Orally Transmitted Teachings,* "The Thus Come One refers to all living beings, as has already been explained in the section on the 'Life Span' chapter" (OTT, 167). This is the point that all living beings are Buddhas, which is nowhere explicitly stated in the text of the "Life Span" chapter. Another feature is that the implicit teaching, or the Buddhism of "from effect to cause," enables one to directly address the reality of the nine worlds on the basis of inherent Buddhahood.

Suda: All Buddhist teachings expounded before the Lotus Sutra encourage single-mindedly striving to attain Buddhahood. That is, they proceed from the nine worlds, or cause, to the world of Buddhahood, or effect. Because practicing those teachings means concentrating on one's own enlightenment first and foremost, they hardly bring forth the strength needed to change society.

Endo: I think that historically Buddhism on the whole has not been able to shake this static and passive tendency.

Ikeda: Simply put, viewing Buddhism as proceeding from the cause to the effect is like someone saying, "After I become wealthy, I will help others"; or "After I get my Ph.D., I will teach others what I know." But we never know whether these things will be accomplished. The view that Buddhism proceeds from the effect to the cause, on the other hand, provides others with supreme fortune and supreme wisdom right away.

Endo: This principle is contained in Nam-myoho-renge-kyo.

Ikeda: Yes, it's the "seed." Nichiren says, "The blessings and wisdom of the objective and subjective worlds are immeasurable. Nam-myoho-renge-kyo has these two elements of blessings and wisdom" (OTT, 218).

Suda: The teaching implicit in the Lotus Sutra is then completely different from all other Buddhist teachings.

Ikeda: Yes. We can discuss the differences from a variety of other perspectives, but the two points cited by Mr. Saito are the most important. They are two sides of the same coin.

REVEALING THE TRUE IN ACTUALITY AND PRINCIPLE

Saito: Regarding the idea that all living beings are the Buddha, let's first review the doctrine of "casting off the transient and revealing the true" that is written in the "Life Span" chapter. There, Shakyamuni refutes the view that he first attained enlightenment during his present lifetime and discloses that he has in fact been continuously expounding the Law in the *saha* world since the extremely remote time numberless major world system dust particle *kalpas* ago. This is sometimes called "revealing the true in actuality."

Ikeda: This is in contrast to "revealing the true in principle." This point is discussed in *The Record of the Orally Transmitted Teachings.*

Suda: Yes. Regarding the term *responding with joy,* which appears in the "Benefits of Responding With Joy" chapter, Nichiren says:

> "Respond" means to respond to and comply with actuality and principle. . . . By actuality is meant responding to and complying with the actual fact of Shakyamuni manifesting [in this life] his original state [of enlightenment] numberless major world system dust particle kalpas ago. By principle is meant responding to the principle of ordinary people being able to manifest their original state. In the end, then, responding means responding to and complying with the inner truth of the "Life Span" chapter. (OTT, 146)

Endo: In the section of *The Record of the Orally Transmitted Teachings* on the "Benefits of the Teacher of the Law" chapter, the Daishonin also refers to the "the principle and actual fact of manifesting the original state [of enlightenment] as revealed in the 'Life Span' chapter" (OTT, 150).

Ikeda: Since long ago, various arguments concerning revealing the true in actuality and in principle have been put forward by the Tendai and other schools. What exactly do these refer to?

Saito: In general, "actuality" indicates something that manifests as a phenomenon, while "principle" indicates an invisible law or truth that exists behind the phenomenon.

In the present case, "revealing the true in actuality" means the preaching of the "Life Span" chapter. As the Daishonin says, it points to "Shakyamuni manifesting [in this life] his original state [of enlightenment] numberless major world system dust particle *kalpas* ago" (OTT, 146). By contrast, "revealing the true in principle" refers to something that, while not explicitly stated in the text, is implicitly contained in the "revealing the true in actuality." I think it could be said to refer to revealing the true identity of the Buddha of absolute freedom since time without beginning.

Ikeda: That would probably be a fair conclusion. In the section of *The Record of the Orally Transmitted Teachings* that deals with the "Distinctions in Benefits" chapter, the Daishonin interprets "believe and understand" in the phrase "to believe and understand it even for a moment" [LSOC, 278], as follows: "This one word 'believe' means to believe in the principle of ordinary people being able to manifest their original state as revealed in the 'Life Span' chapter. And the word 'understand' means to understand the actual fact of the Buddha manifesting his original state" (OTT, 144). Since revealing the true in principle is not clearly articulated, it can only be grasped through belief. Therefore, this belief translates into an understanding of the core meaning of revealing the true in actuality.

Suda: In other words, when people heard the preaching of the "Life Span" chapter, that is, revealing the true in actuality, they grasped revealing the true in principle.

Ikeda: The term *revealing the true* sounds somewhat complicated, but in simpler terms it means to show one's full potential.

This principle is illustrated quite well by the popular Japanese historical drama of *Mito Komon* in which the former deputy shogun disguises himself as an ordinary citizen and travels throughout the country. At the end of each episode, Mito Komon discloses his real identity. In a way, this is an example of revealing the true.

Endo: Yes. Just when everyone thought him to be a retired grandfather, he turns out to be a very powerful man.

Suda: Then the villains shrink back in fear, and good people rejoice. This indicates the benefit that comes from revealing one's true identity.

Ikeda: Of course, this is only an analogy. In world literature, we could compare it with Alexandre Dumas's *The Count of Monte Cristo.* I am thinking of the scene where the true identity of the learned and wealthy count is revealed to be Edmond Dantès. Although it's a story about revenge, I think this is still a kind of revealing the true.

Saito: Those who had looked down on Mito Komon were certainly taken aback when they found out who he really was.

In the Lotus Sutra as well, great bodhisattvas like Manjushri are at first thought to be the disciples not of Shakyamuni but of other Buddhas. Therefore they view Shakyamuni as a new Buddha who has only just attained enlightenment. The revelation that Shakyamuni, in fact, has been the Buddha since the remote past refutes this illusion.

Endo: So, Mito Komon's sidekicks, Suke and Kaku, are comparable to bodhisattvas who attend a Buddha.

Ikeda: That means that just seeing these attendants inspires awe in those who know the true identity of their boss!

Saito: The relation between revealing the true in actuality and revealing the true in principle is similar to this. That is, those who are quick to grasp the meaning of Shakyamuni's "revealing the true in actuality" understand "revealing the true in principle."

Ikeda: On the Gohonzon, the Buddhas Shakyamuni and Many Treasures appear as attendants on either side of "Nam-myoho-renge-kyo Nichiren," which is written in large characters down the center. And flanking these two Buddhas are the four leaders of the Bodhisattvas of the Earth.

Revealing the true in actuality corresponds specifically to the attendant "Shakyamuni Thus Come One," who represents the true effect of the Buddha who attained enlightenment in the remote past. The benefits of this true effect are an extremely long life span and boundless wisdom and compassion to lead all beings to happiness.

Those listening to the preaching wonder what true cause gave rise to this great true effect, and what is the source of benefit of this true effect? To understand this is to grasp "revealing the true in principle."

Endo: With regard to the cause of his enlightenment in the remote past, in the "Life Span" chapter Shakyamuni says only, "Originally I practiced the bodhisattva way" (LSOC, 268). But the true cause of his enlightenment is implicit in these words. This is what we mean when we say that it is implicit in the sutra.

Suda: While the Tendai school does not have terminology to refer specifically to these two levels of "explicit" and "implicit" meaning, the school's interpretation of the sutra follows similar lines. They speak of "revealing the true in actuality and function" and "revealing the true in principle and entity." Also, there are other schools that call them "revealing the true in doctrine" and "revealing the true through mind-observing." Despite differences in terminology, the basic thrust of the approach to the sutra is the same.

Saito: Namely, that there is a revealing of the true that is not literally expressed in the sutra text.

Ikeda: Let's talk about that.

The preaching of the "Life Span" chapter is revealing the

true pertaining to the individual person, Shakyamuni. It could be said that the person Shakyamuni revealed the essence of his own life.

Though he completely revealed his true identity as an individual, revealing the true implicit in the sutra is another matter entirely; it is on a completely different level. It is a revelation of cosmic significance. It is revealing the true for all living beings of the Ten Worlds, from common mortals to the Buddha. The text of the sutra describes the eternal Buddha who has continued to expound the Law and instruct people from the remote past.

Suda: This is the idea of "Shakyamuni who attained enlightenment in the remote past."

Ikeda: While this Buddha might be thought of as eternal, in an absolute sense, he is not eternal. Although it was an extremely long time ago, there is still a specific time at which he attained enlightenment. This Buddha consequently cannot be identified with the Mystic Law that is one with the universe and without beginning or end. There is a gap. Therefore, the Buddha in the text of the sutra is presented as inferior and the Law as superior.

The true intent of the "Life Span" chapter in revealing this eternal Buddha is to hint at the existence of the perfectly eternal Buddha (the Buddha of absolute freedom from time without beginning). This Buddha is one with the Mystic Law that is without beginning or end and is identified with the great life of the universe itself, embodying the oneness of the Person and the Law.

Endo: That is to say that all living beings in the universe are perfectly eternal Buddhas, just as they are.

Ikeda: All living things are originally Buddhas. This is the central thesis of the "Life Span" chapter. The Lotus Sutra calls on us to open our eyes to this truth.

Saito: To recapitulate, revealing the true in the text of the sutra is revealing the true of the individual Shakyamuni. And revealing the true that is implicit in the sutra is revealing the true of all beings in the entire phenomenal world, that is, of the Ten Worlds.

Suda: In terms of both scale and profundity, they are completely different.

Ikeda: Yes, they are.

Only when we understand the implicit revelation of true identity do we grasp Nichiren's real meaning when he says that the essential teaching of the Lotus Sutra is as different from the theoretical teaching "as fire is from water or heaven from earth" (WND-1, 1112).

Endo: When the Daishonin says, "The Thus Come One refers to all living beings, as has already been explained in the section on the 'Life Span' chapter" (OTT, 167), he is speaking from the level of the implicit teaching.

THE IMPLICIT TEACHING COMPLETES BUDDHISM

Saito: Last time, we reviewed the history of Buddhism in terms of people's efforts to seek the cause of enlightenment. The conclusion is that the ultimate cause lies in the depths of the "Life Span" chapter. If this were not the case, Shakyamuni's desire to enable all living beings to become Buddhas would be incomplete.

Ikeda: Needless to say, the cause of Buddhahood implicit in the "Life Span" chapter is the Mystic Law that is without beginning or end, or Nam-myoho-renge-kyo. At the same time as this is the cause of enlightenment, it is also the effect of enlightenment. It is the inscrutable Law of the simultaneity of cause and effect. Those who listened to the preaching of the "Life Span" chapter realized this and attained enlightenment.

It is a mistake to read the "Life Span" chapter as a fantastic tale of a resplendent Buddha endowed with the thirty-two features suspended aloft in the Ceremony in the Air. If the point of the teaching were simply a matter of revering this august Buddha, it would ultimately be a teaching of looking outwards. Through the teaching of the Buddha's attaining enlightenment in the remote past, however, the participants at the Ceremony in the Air realize that they share the same origin as Shakyamuni.

It is as though by gazing upwards into the air they at last become aware of their feet on the ground. This is explained in Nichikan's *Commentary on the "Essence of the Lotus Sutra"* as "those at the highest stage of bodhisattva practice, or the stage of near-perfect enlightenment, changing into persons at the stage of initial aspiration and instantaneously attaining enlightenment."[2]

Suda: After proceeding through the bodhisattva stages step by step toward Buddhahood, as though climbing a staircase, in the end they return to their point of departure. This means that they perceive the life of the universe itself that gives rise to and sustains their very lives.

Endo: The Great Teacher Miao-lo of China expressed the same thing, saying that the fundamental cause of enlightenment is contained in the depths of the "Life Span" chapter and that those at the assembly of the Lotus Sutra could attain Buddhahood by virtue of their having discerned this original cause.

Saito: This original cause is Nam-myoho-renge-kyo. That is what they realized.

Ikeda: They understood the implicit teaching just by hearing the literal teaching. For beings with such high capacity, that's all it took.

But what about those unable to grasp this? This is why Shakyamuni entrusted Bodhisattva Superior Practices with propagating the teaching after his passing.

Superior Practices is a "bodhisattva-Buddha"—that is, a being whose life embodies the wonderful Law of simultaneity of cause and effect—who spreads that wonderful Law. Buddhism teaches in no uncertain terms that the Law and the person who expounds it are one.

Saito: Nichiren explains this idea when he quotes Tao-hsien: "The Law embodied therein is the Law that was realized countless kalpas in the past, and therefore it was entrusted to persons who had been the Buddha's disciples from countless kalpas in the past" (WND-1, 372).[3]

Ikeda: Nichiren Daishonin says, "Bodhisattva Superior Practices of the true cause is brought together with Shakyamuni of the true effect solely for the benefit of those in the Latter Day of the Law after the Buddha's passing" (GZ, 864).

To match the capacity of beings of the Latter Day, the Mystic Law of time without beginning, which is the original cause of Buddhahood, is expounded directly and clearly. That is the purpose of the transmission in the "Supernatural Powers of the Thus Come One" chapter.

Therefore, the meaning of "Thus Come One" in the chapter's title refers not exclusively to Shakyamuni but to all living beings. And "supernatural powers" means the power of life. The "Supernatural Powers" chapter reveals the true power of life of all living beings, and particularly of ordinary people. To indicate this, the Buddha's ten supernatural powers are expounded on a cosmic scale.

Endo: In other words, the magnificent Buddha endowed with the thirty-two features is simply a provisional Buddha serving to help people understand the truth.

"Becoming a Buddha Is Nothing Extraordinary"

Ikeda: The thirty-two features are a collection of ideal characteristics; perhaps these were qualities that the Indian people of that time revered. They were expounded initially to arouse in people a sense of respect and seeking toward the Buddha. The point is not whether Shakyamuni actually possessed these features. Their purpose is to lead ordinary people to the awareness that they themselves are Buddhas. Nichiren Daishonin refers to this principle in his writing "On the Ten Factors of Life." The Daishonin says: "These three factors [of appearance, nature and entity] constitute the Thus Come One of the three bodies. That these three factors represent the Thus Come One of the three bodies may seem to be an extraneous matter, but in fact it concerns these very lives of our own. One who understands this may be said to have grasped the meaning of the Lotus Sutra" (WND-2, 78).

The point is that after searching for happiness high and low, it turns out that it is found in your immediate surroundings, in your own home, as it were. Happiness does not lie way off in the distance; happiness means that your life is afire with the life force of your inherent Buddhahood, and that it is being expressed in a manner true to yourself. It means advancing continuously, no matter what happens, determined to fulfill your mission in this life. To have such faith is Buddhahood itself; it is eternal happiness.

Such things as learning, fame and social standing could be called the modern equivalents of the thirty-two features. In some instances, possessing these adornments might be useful in teaching others about the greatness of the Mystic Law. That's because there are people in whom those qualities inspire respect. But they are definitely not the goal.

As long as we cloak the self in such ornamentation, we cannot cultivate our true strength as human beings. We cannot understand the real meaning of faith, or of Buddhism. Such vanity is the spirit of Devadatta. In "Letter to Horen," Nichiren notes that Devadatta tried to adorn himself with the thirty-two features.

Suda: Yes. Devadatta is said to have possessed thirty of the thirty-two features, lacking only "the tuft of white hair" and "the markings of the thousand-spoke wheel." Thinking that this made him inferior to Shakyamuni and would cause people to look down on him, he contrived to collect the light of fireflies to smear in the middle of his forehead to achieve the effect of the tuft of white hair and to have a blacksmith brand the soles of his feet with the pattern of a chrysanthemum in place of the markings of the thousand-spoke wheel (see WND-1, 510).

Ikeda: But instead, his feet were severely burned! It's funny to think about, but it reveals Devadatta's true nature—his jealousy toward Shakyamuni and his vanity in seeking to embellish himself.

Many who have abandoned faith and turned against the SGI have displayed the same tendencies. There are also many people who, as Nichiren says, "if they have not given way in their practice, they have done so in their heart" (WND-1, 941).

Genuine practitioners of Buddhism do not put on airs; they act in a manner true to themselves. Things such as academic background have nothing to do with the world of faith; rather, to be obsessed with such extras is only an obstacle to one's faith.

True faith is selfless. It is not about looking out for one's own interests but actively challenging and seeking to overcome difficulties with a spirit of not begrudging one's life. To carry out the pure practice of the Buddhism of the true cause, which explains that the ordinary person is a Buddha, is to advance the great popular movement of the SGI. The fundamental spirit of the Lotus Sutra is found in Nichiren Buddhism, which teaches struggling against the personal affectations of power and authority.

Saito: Yes. The thirty-two features are characteristics that match people's worldly aspirations. They are taught "in accord with the understanding of others." This is one reason why Shakyamuni, while a Buddha of absolute freedom, is said to be the "Buddha who struggled to advance to the state of limitless joy through accumulated practice."[4]

Ikeda: Shakyamuni is a Buddha of absolute freedom, but on a scale completely different from that of the Buddha of absolute freedom of time without beginning. One is a Buddha who is enlightened as an individual, while the other is a Buddha embodying the entire universe.

Endo: I am reminded again of how wonderful is the teaching implicit in the sutra. If one were to compare various Buddhist teachings, this is truly the most advanced.

Ikeda: It is the great Buddhist teaching that can lead all people, whatever their capacity, to happiness. Nichiren says, "A slight ailment can be treated with ordinary medicine, but for grave illnesses, an elixir should be used" (WND-1, 414). And:

> Once the Latter Day of the Law has begun, however, with regard to the Hinayana sutras, the Mahayana sutras, and the Lotus Sutra that were entrusted to Mahakashyapa, Ananda, and others; to

the bodhisattvas Manjushri, Maitreya, and others; and to Medicine King, Perceiver of the World's Sounds, and others, though the words of these sutras will remain, they will no longer serve as medicine for the illnesses of living beings. That is to say, the illnesses will be grave, and the medicine, weak. At that time, Bodhisattva Superior Practices will make his appearance in the world and bestow the five characters of Myoho-renge-kyo upon all the living beings of Jambudvipa. (WND-1, 606)

This is the Mystic Law that is eternity itself. It is the original seed that has enabled all Buddhas throughout time and space to attain enlightenment. And the Daishonin says that if we embrace this original seed of enlightenment, "Becoming a Buddha is nothing extraordinary" (WND-1, 1030). This is a statement of no small significance.

When we truly have confidence in these words, we will never become deadlocked in life. We are Buddhas. We cannot possibly fail to be victorious. Buddhas never remain downcast. They are not defeated by hardship or hopelessness.

Whatever happens, it is vital that we muster our courage and continue advancing, reminding ourselves: "That's right! I have the Mystic Law! There is no difficulty that I can't overcome!" As long as we possess this fighting spirit, our lives will develop greatly in accord with the principle that earthly desires are enlightenment, in that our desires and sufferings work as fuel for our development.

A seed may be a tiny thing. But a single seed contains all the necessary elements to produce a towering tree more than a hundred feet tall. This is the mystery of the seed. When we plant the original seed of Buddhahood, Nam-myoho-renge-kyo, in our heart and cultivate it, we develop boundless good fortune and wisdom.

Giving a lecture on the Daishonin's teachings, President

Toda would often say, "If the benefit that each of you has received is the size of one's little finger, then the benefit I have received is large enough to fill this entire hall." My feelings are exactly the same.

THE HEART DETERMINES EVERYTHING

Saito: President Ikeda, you have received honorary doctorates and professorships from scores of universities around the world. In the ordinary course of affairs, for someone to receive so many accolades would be unimaginable.

Ikeda: I hope that people will view this as symbolizing the good fortune and benefit of all SGI members throughout the world.

I did not go to college. Instead, I dedicated my youth to President Toda. Because of the failure of President Toda's businesses, I changed my plans to attend college. I told him: "Please don't worry about anything. I will work; I will fix everything. So please rest assured." And I have done everything I said I would. I turned the Soka Gakkai, which had fallen upon the hardest of times, into a worldwide organization. I have made the greatness of President Toda and President Makiguchi known to the world.

I believed that to protect President Toda was to protect kosen-rufu and to protect Buddhism. There was no other way. I thoroughly devoted myself to the path of mentor and disciple.

I am confident that the cause I made to support President Toda rather than pursue my plans to attain an education has now come back to me in the form of these honorary degrees from universities across the globe. The law of cause and effect is unfailing.

Suda: This is truly a drama of actual proof of Buddhism that will be eternally remembered by generations to come.

Ikeda: The heart is key. Because of his spirit in making an offering of a mud pie to Shakyamuni, the boy Virtue Victorious was reborn as the great king Ashoka.

Endo: A little earlier we talked about not adorning the self. Everything depends on the state of one's heart, on whether one has genuine strength as a human being.

Ikeda: We should carefully consider the significance of Nichiren Daishonin's having been born into the lowest rung of the society of his day. If he were to have expounded a Buddhist teaching "according to the minds of others," he might have been better off born as a member of the nobility or of a powerful family.

But he was born as the "son of a commoner" (WND-1, 1006). The fact that he was not a member of a noble family helps explain why he encountered such a succession of incredible persecutions.

Endo: The Daishonin says of himself, "Nichiren . . . in this life was born poor and lowly to a chandala[5] family" (WND-1, 303).

Ikeda: To help people form a connection with Buddhism even through a reverse relationship, he boldly took on and endured great persecution. Forgetting this immense compassion, some treated the Daishonin with contempt. He says: "There are also those who appeared to believe in me, but began doubting when they saw me persecuted. They not only have forsaken the Lotus Sutra, but actually think themselves wise enough to instruct me" (WND-1, 306). This is deplorable. Without the path of mentor and disciple, there is no Buddhism.

Saito: The Daishonin describes how these arrogant people will meet great hardship: "The pitiful thing is that these perverse people must suffer in the Avichi hell even longer than the Nembutsu believers" (WND-I, 306). This is an unchanging principle, one that will apply as much in the future as it does today.

Ikeda: In any event, ordinary people understand the hearts of ordinary people. A citizen truly understands the feelings of other citizens. The Daishonin dared to be born as member of the most abused and reviled class, as the son of a *chandala*.

At the end of World War II, when the fighting moved to Okinawa, Japan's southernmost island, I heard that the locals there experienced severe discrimination at the hands of many Japanese officers and soldiers [who had in large part been mobilized from other parts of Japan]. The only soldiers who did not abuse them were those who were aboriginal Ainu from northernmost Hokkaido.

Saito: I, too, have heard unbelievable, sickening accounts of how the people of Okinawa were treated by the Japanese army. There are reports of soldiers murdering local citizens on suspicion of their being spies, simply because they were heard speaking in the Okinawan language, which to the soldiers was unintelligible.

Ikeda: But the soldiers of Ainu descent treated the locals differently. I think this was because they also had experienced discrimination as a minority. It seems that they were discriminated against and mistreated even by the army. That is probably why they treated the Okinawans kindly and saved the lives of many. They were truly noble.

Suda: That's very moving. To stand eternally on the side of the people, eternally on the side of those being mistreated—I think that is true humanity.

Zhou Enlai: "I Am Here Thanks to Everyone Else"

Ikeda: This kind of humanity is true Buddhism.

When a delegation of the Buraku[6] Liberation League of Japan visited China in 1962, Chinese premier Zhou Enlai met with them. The head of the delegation thanked him for taking time out of his busy schedule to meet with them, to which Zhou replied: "What are you saying? A premier who would not receive the most mistreated people in Japan on their visit to this country, the people who are suffering the greatest hardship, is no premier of China."[7]

At the time of the historic Long March, Zhou shared his personal rations with the troops. When his party advanced into the wetland region of Sichuan province, they had nothing to eat. For emergency rations, Zhou had a sack of beef that had been boiled and dried and a sack of barley flour. It was something that could be hydrated with cold or hot water and eaten anywhere.

The soldiers, who had no such provisions, at first resorted to eating rats, leaves and the roots of plants as they went along. As a result, they began to suffer from malnutrition. Seeing this, Zhou ordered that the beef be distributed to the soldiers and had his rations divided among everyone.

After a while, they again faced starvation. It was so bad that people who seemed healthy enough one evening would be found dead the following morning. Zhou immediately told his escort to distribute the barley flour. But the man did not ensure that everyone received a portion. When Zhou reproached him for failing to follow his directions, the man protested, "If I follow your orders, what will you have to eat, sir?"

Premier Zhou drew close and, gazing into the soldier's face, said: "I exist because you exist. The more of us who survive, even one more person, the more we can secure the justice of the revolution. I implore you to do it." Having no alternative, the escort divided the remaining rations among all the soldiers. Luckily the company finally reached a village four or five days later.

This is what it means to be a leader. This is what it means to truly treasure one's companions. The bonds of people united behind the same goal are more profound even than the bonds of parent and child or between siblings. These are bonds not of blood but of justice—of people fighting side by side for a common purpose. To cultivate and maintain such bonds is proof of one's humanity.

Leaders exist solely because of the people they lead. Genuine leaders are those who take the initiative and selflessly devote themselves to achieving a goal. There are, however, far too many "leaders" in the world who use the people to realize personal gain. The SGI exists to battle such evil tendencies. Without opposing the enemies of the people, one cannot attain Buddhahood. Without battling the "one great evil," without directly confronting the "enemy of Buddhism," kosen-rufu cannot be achieved. As Nichiren strictly states, "One must set aside all other affairs and devote one's attention to rebuking slander of the correct teaching" (WND-I, 126).

Saito: Among the many types of slander, the offense of slandering the votary of the Lotus Sutra is particularly grave. The Lotus Sutra says that slandering the sutra's votary in the age after Shakyamuni's passing is an even greater offense than continuously slandering the Buddha for an entire kalpa.

Slandering an ordinary person who is dedicated to the practice of the sutra is an even greater offense than slandering the Buddha who preaches the Law. This may seem odd on the surface, for it is impossible to grasp without realizing that it is common people in the Latter Day who directly propagate the Mystic Law, the ultimate source of enlightenment for all people.

Ikeda: That's it exactly. Of course, while the votary of the Lotus Sutra specifically refers to Nichiren Daishonin, we who follow the Daishonin are likewise votaries of the Lotus Sutra and are leading the most noble of lives.

President Toda said:

> I declare that those great champions of propagation who carry on the Daishonin's work will appear now without fail. . . . In time without beginning, these great champions of propagation are Buddhas of absolute freedom embodying the oneness of parent and child; in the intermediate term of the assembly at Eagle Peak, they stood beside Bodhisattva Superior Practices as his attendants; and in the near term, during the Daishonin's lifetime, they were without a doubt people who made a profound vow of mentor and disciple. I am firmly convinced that these people will put the Daishonin's prophecy into practice with their lives, will solidly vow to see to it that the original Buddha endowed with the three virtues of sovereign, teacher and parent does not become a Buddha whose prophecies are not fulfilled; and they will surely exert themselves in their practice with the spirit of not begrudging their lives.
>
> The fact that the Soka Gakkai has emerged at this time [seven hundred years after the time of the Daishonin] is cause for great joy!

As a human being, there is no more honorable way of life, no life of greater good.

The Age of the Bodhisattvas of the Earth Has Arrived!

Endo: As SGI members, each of us has been born with a tremendous mission. The "Supernatural Powers" chapter describes the activities of Bodhisattva Superior Practices as follows:

> *As the light of the sun and moon*
> *can banish all obscurity and gloom,*
> *so this person as he advances through the world*
> *can wipe out the darkness of living beings,*
> *causing immeasurable numbers of bodhisattvas*
> *in the end to dwell in the single vehicle.* (LSOC, 318)

Japan and the world are today cloaked in an impenetrable darkness. I think that for precisely this reason, our time has now arrived.

Ikeda: That's right. The deeper the darkness, the more brightly shines the Buddhism of the sun.

This is our chance to help countless people become truly happy. Kosen-rufu means enabling people "in the end to dwell in the single vehicle" (LSOC, 318) and to take faith in the Mystic Law. In *The Record of the Orally Transmitted Teachings*, Nichiren says, "The expression 'in the end' or 'ultimately' refers to widely declaring and propagating the teachings" (OTT, 170). For this reason, we were born in this world according to our own wishes. We need to live out our lives to the fullest as we work to fulfill our mission.

When our hearts blaze with the spirit to exert ourselves "bravely and vigorously" (LSOC, 56), ageless and immortal vitality wells forth. "Bravely and vigorously" means immense courage. "Exert" has two meanings: pure, in the sense of unsullied; and incessant, in the sense of continuous activity and unswerving advancement. Nichiren says, "Nam-myoho-renge-kyo is just such a 'diligent' practice" (OTT, 214).

We must never stop challenging ourselves; the "supernatural powers of the Thus Come One" are manifested through such faith. The Daishonin says, "If in a single moment of life we exhaust the pains and trials of millions of kalpas, then instant after instant there will arise in us the three Buddha bodies with which we are eternally endowed" (OTT, 214). It comes down to exhausting "the pains and trials of millions of kalpas"—not just one or two years' effort. This means wracking our brains and exerting ourselves wholeheartedly for kosen-rufu. This is what is meant by "as he advances through the world" (LSOC, 318). Those who take action in society are the Bodhisattvas of the Earth who have received the transmission of the "Supernatural Powers" chapter. They are people who, without putting on airs or adorning themselves, work tirelessly in the organization for kosen-rufu, that is, directly connected to Nichiren Daishonin.

Such people are more respectworthy than any dignitary or celebrity. They are the "emissaries of the Buddha" in the Latter Day of the Law. And they themselves are Buddhas.

NOTES

1. *Makashikan Bugyoden Guketsu* (Annotations on T'ien-t'ai's Maka Shikan [Profound Concentration and Insight]), vol. 5.

2. The true cause of enlightenment is Nam-myoho-renge-kyo Thus Come One. By awakening to this Mystic Law of time without beginning, bodhisattvas at the fifty-first stage of practice (according to T'ien-t'ai's doctrine of the fifty-two stages from bodhisattva to Buddha) return to the stage of initial aspiration, or that of ordinary people, and quickly jump over the intervening stages to reach the highest, the fifty-second, stage—that of enlightenment.

3. This statement appears in Miao-lo's supplement to the *Hokke mongu ki* (*Annotations on the Words and Phrases of the Lotus Sutra* by

the Great Teacher T'ien-t'ai of China) by the T'ien-t'ai scholar Tao-hsien of the T'ang period. Nichiren Daishonin cites this passage in "The Object of Devotion for Observing the Mind" and other writings.

4. "Through accumulated practice" refers to the process of transforming from the Buddha of the inferior manifested body expounded in Hinayana Buddhism, to the Buddha of the manifested body in Mahayana Buddhism, to the Buddha of beneficence in the teachings specifically targeted at bodhisattvas, and to the Buddha of absolute freedom in the essential teaching of the Lotus Sutra.

5. *Chandala*: A Sanskrit term designating the lowest social class, comprised of those professions required to kill living creatures. Nichiren Daishonin was born to the family of a fisherman.

6. *Buraku*: Originally referring to people living in a small village or hamlet, but came to mean the largest discriminated-against population in Japan. They are not a racial or a national minority, but a caste-like minority among the ethnic Japanese.

7. *Saichiro uesugi, jinken wa sekai o ugokasu* (Human Rights Move the World) (Osaka: Kaiho Shuppansha, 1991), pp. 127–28.

PART VI

"Entrustment" Chapter

9 Completing the Ceremony of Transmission

> *At that time Shakyamuni Buddha rose from his Dharma seat and, manifesting his great supernatural powers, with his right hand patted the heads of the immeasurable bodhisattvas mahasattva and spoke these words: "For immeasurable hundreds, thousands, ten thousands, millions of asamkhya kalpas I have practiced this hard-to-attain Law of supreme perfect enlightenment. Now I entrust it to you. You must single-mindedly propagate this Law abroad, causing its benefits to spread far and wide.". . .*
>
> *The multitude of bodhisattvas mahasattva repeated these words three times, raising their voices in unison and saying: "We will respectfully carry out all these things just as the world-honored one has commanded. Therefore we beg the world-honored one to have no concern on this account!"* (LSOC, 319–20)

Ikeda: The "Entrustment" chapter is a chapter of transmission. "Transmission" here indicates succession; and succession defines the relationship of mentor and disciple. The "Entrustment" chapter could therefore also be termed the "Succession" chapter or the "Mentor and Disciple" chapter. It is the "Mentor and Disciple of Kosen-rufu" chapter for accomplishing widespread propagation of the Law in the Latter Day. President Toda also felt this was a highly significant chapter.

Saito: The term *entrustment* in the chapter title comprises two

Chinese characters. The first means "to commit or leave something to someone with confidence."

The second means "something that is difficult or cumbersome." The Buddha is thus saying, in effect, "laborious though it may be, I leave the work of spreading the Law far and wide to you, my disciples."

Ikeda: From the standpoint of those who are entrusted, this is the chapter where disciples pledge to shoulder the hard work of propagating the Law. This defines the connection between mentor and disciple.

The mentor-disciple relationship is strict. Everything depends on how earnestly one can accept and act on even a single word of the mentor. A true disciple strives to actualize the mentor's vision—not by mimicking the mentor but by putting into action what the mentor has taught.

This is something of a digression, but once, when we were staying at the Hanazono Inn in Osaka, President Toda abruptly said: "I was just thinking, 'What if I were to die today?' and 'What if I were to become prime minister today?'" He was quite serious. I remember it was early in the morning.

At that time of day, people are usually thinking, "Is it time for breakfast yet?" or "I'd like to sleep just a little longer." But Mr. Toda was engaged in earnest contemplation. From that time forward, I took everything President Toda said as food for serious thought.

Saito: To think, "What if I were to die today," is to live with the spirit, "Now is the last moment of my life."

Ikeda: The point is to have such faith that we can declare with utmost conviction, "Even if I were to die right now, I would attain Buddhahood."

Of course, it is important that we live out our lives wholeheartedly, working for kosen-rufu and fulfilling our individual missions in this life. We should be confident that whenever we may die, even if at this very moment, we will have no regrets in our faith, we will know that we have really given it our best, and that our enlightenment is certain. Though we should not be arrogant, such pride and conviction in faith are vital. This is how I took President Toda's guidance.

Apart from faith, there is no way to attain Buddhahood in this present life; there is no way to experience the "greatest of all joys" (OTT, 212). This is something we can savor only when we really exert ourselves for kosen-rufu—regardless of who may be watching. It is important that we constantly keep watch over our own faith.

It is said that a person experiences 8,004,000 thoughts in a single day (see WND-2, 307). The mind is constantly in a state of flux; 8,004,000 a day is a phenomenal rate of change! During that time, how much are we thinking about kosen-rufu? About the Gohonzon? About the SGI or our fellow members? How much action did we take or not take?

The net balance of these determines our state of life. Faith is not a matter of formality. As Nichiren Daishonin writes, "It is the heart that is important" (WND 1, 1000).

Endo: So our faith should not be lukewarm or formalistic but steadfast—informed by the awareness that "now is the last moment."

Ikeda: As for Mr. Toda's other comment about becoming prime minister, as his disciple I believe he was talking about the importance of becoming trusted pillars in our own fields of endeavor and displaying freely our true strength and ability.

Buddhism is not a religion that exists for the sake of religion. It exists for the sake of society and real life. Faith is the source of energy that enables us to guide society and our lives in the direction of hope.

For that reason, Mr. Toda was saying we must take action

as leaders in all areas of society and show proof of our practice, causing people to say: "No wonder! That person practices Buddhism!" As leaders in the organization dedicated to kosen-rufu as well, we should become people appreciated for always lifting the spirits of others. In our broad struggle for kosen-rufu, it is important that we ask ourselves if we are becoming people who can say: "In this area, you can leave everything to me. Please rest assured."

In effect, President Toda was saying: "Develop and perfect yourselves thoroughly in the realms of faith and your chosen field." He was truly an insightful and wonderful teacher.

Saito: President Ikeda, I feel you have really lived these words of President Toda. The many meaningful dialogues with world leaders you have participated in as a private citizen are a source of inspiration to people of conscience everywhere.

Suda: The fact that you have received nearly sixty honorary doctorates and professorships from universities around the world is also remarkable.

Ikeda: My spirit is to always accept these honors on behalf of the first two Soka Gakkai presidents, Mr. Makiguchi and Mr. Toda. They were both educators who died fighting for kosen-rufu. Their good fortune flows to me and continues on; it passed from the first president to the second president and on to the third president. This is the oneness of mentor and disciple. This is humanity's ultimate principle.

It is my fervent desire to share that fortune. President Toda's spirit was the same.

THE GENERAL TRANSMISSION

Endo: To summarize the "Entrustment" chapter, after the "essential transmission" to Bodhisattva Superior Practices in the preceding "Supernatural Powers" chapter, Shakyamuni rises and exhibits his great supernatural powers. He stands up and pats the heads of the countless bodhisattvas present, saying: "For immeasurable hundreds, thousands, ten thousands, millions of asamkhya kalpas I have practiced this hard-to-attain Law of supreme perfect enlightenment. Now I entrust it to you. You must single-mindedly propagate this Law abroad, causing its benefits to spread far and wide" (LSOC, 319). This is repeated three times.

Saito: It's interesting that he touches their heads.

Suda: As this chapter is about entrustment, it may be that in doing so he is urging them to do their best despite the difficulty of the task.

Ikeda: That may well be.
   From his patting them on the head, we can also get a sense of someone encouraging a youngster, saying, "You're a good child, so please do your best."

Suda: Completely different from the transmission in the "Supernatural Powers" chapter, this is a gentle method of entrusting the teachings to the assembly, which now includes bodhisattvas of the theoretical teachings.

Endo: This is, after all, a general transmission to bodhisattvas of both the essential and theoretical teachings.

Saito: Shakyamuni must now accommodate the participants of even the lowest capacity.

Ikeda: Shakyamuni is strictest with the disciples whom he really trusts. He devotes himself wholeheartedly to their growth and leaves them everything.

President Toda said: "All those disciples with whom President Makiguchi was lenient gave up their faith and turned against him. Not once was I praised by Mr. Makiguchi. But I alone have remained and have carried on his teaching and succeeded him."

I, likewise, received training from President Toda more strictly than anyone else. Day in and day out he made demands on me that could only be described as unreasonable. There were those disciples who felt that they enjoyed President Toda's particular favor or received special treatment from him. That is all well and good, but the important thing is actualizing the mentor's intent.

People who merely try to imitate their mentor in terms of appearance or manner tend to go astray. This was true in President Toda's time, and it is true today. There is a unique path for each disciple, a path that lies solely in striving to actualize the mentor's vision.

Going a little deeper, in patting his disciples on the head three times, Shakyamuni is exhorting them to put his thoughts, words and deeds—the three categories of action—into practice.

Saito: The Record of the Orally Transmitted Teachings says, "The entrustment accompanied by the three pats symbolizes that the Buddha is entrusting to them the three categories of action, namely, actions of the body, mouth, and mind; the three truths; and the threefold contemplation [in a single mind, or realizing the three truths in one's mind]" (OTT, 171).

Ikeda: The disciples perceive the three kinds of wisdom in their hearts by practicing the teaching of the mentor through their thoughts, words and deeds. In other words, they awaken to the infinite world of Buddhahood existing in their own lives.

Suda: So it comes down to action.

Ikeda: It's a matter of propagation, of working for kosen-rufu. When we exert ourselves for kosen-rufu in thought, word and deed, then everything turns into great benefit without fail. If we simply act like we are working for kosen-rufu, however, while harboring negativity in our hearts, we will erode our good fortune through our own attitude.

Endo: In the Sanskrit text of the sutra, instead of patting the bodhisattvas on the head with his right hand, Shakyamuni holds their right hands in his. In other words, he shakes their hands. This is said to symbolize the idea that Shakyamuni, the mentor, does not have a closed fist; in other words, that he reveals all he knows without hiding anything.

Ikeda: Teachers of the Brahman caste derived their authority from "secret transmissions" or "secret teachings." I suppose that's what is meant by having a "closed fist." But Shakyamuni was different. Declaring, "At the start I took a vow, / hoping to make all persons / equal to me, without any distinction between us" (LSOC, 70), he taught his followers the highest secret teaching, the Mystic Law.

Saito: Buddhism is the first religion in human history to bring a universal message to all people. Before Buddhism, while religions might have communicated a secret teaching to a highly select group of people, there was never a teacher like Shakyamuni who sought to share his own enlightenment with all people.

Ikeda: Such teachings are indeed "closed-fisted."

Suda: The Nichiren Shoshu priesthood, too, frequently refers to "secret transmissions" and "lineage." In that sense, they sound like the Brahmans!

Fundamentally, there is no secret teaching more exalted than the Three Great Secret Laws. The transmission of the high priest ought to center on nothing other than the correct faith, practice and study of the Three Great Secret Laws.

Endo: To accomplish the widespread propagation of the Three Great Secret Laws is, after all, Nichiren Daishonin's will and testament. By rights, the high priest should take the lead in efforts for kosen-rufu, while bearing the brunt of attacks by the three powerful enemies. Nikko and Nichimoku, the second and third high priests, respectively, in fact did just that.

Just what kind of lineage is embodied by a high priest who not only fails to do this but who actively seeks to destroy the movement for kosen-rufu? Such a high priest is transmitting not a "secret Law" but a "false Law."

Saito: If he were to open his "clenched fist," we would find him empty-handed!

Suda: Come to think of it, there's a saying in India, "You cannot shake someone's hand with a fist." What it means is that peace can only be achieved through dialogue not brute force.

Ikeda: Shakyamuni did not conceal anything from his trusted disciples. The "Entrustment" chapter demonstrates this yet again, for here he unbegrudgingly leaves them everything.

Saito: That's true. It says: "The thus come one has great pity and compassion. He is in no way stingy or begrudging, nor has he any fear. He is able to bestow on living beings the wisdom of the Buddha, the wisdom of the thus come one, the wisdom that comes of itself. The thus come one is a great giver of gifts to all living beings" (LSOC, 319).

Ikeda: He is a "great giver of gifts." And he is generous. After all, there is no such thing as a stingy Buddha.

The Mystic Law is a cornucopia. It is the "wish-granting jewel" of the Buddha. It is the treasure of all treasures. And since the Buddha hands over this wonderful gift in its entirety, there is no greater generosity. Even so, he is hated, vilified and persecuted.

Suda: This is truly the evil age of the Latter Day.

Endo: I am reminded of the experience of Kiyomi Kumagai, who lived in the town of Ichinoseki, Iwate Prefecture. From the time she joined the Soka Gakkai in 1955, she enabled nearly 140 families to take faith in Nichiren Buddhism. What motivated her to carry out such earnest propagation is quite interesting.

She began practicing when told by a physician that she had only three years left to live because of stomach ulcers and heart disease. In just six months, she regained splendid health and left her sickbed for good. She then reportedly told a fellow member, "This faith is so wonderful, it's too good to share with anyone!"

The member then admonished her, saying: "What are you talking about? Do you mean to tell me that as long as you're OK, it doesn't matter what becomes of other people? Someone so lacking in compassion is no member of the Soka Gakkai!" Completely taken aback by these words, Ms. Kumagai determined to tell as many people about Nichiren Buddhism as possible.

Because of her absolute confidence in the Gohonzon and the care with which she looked after others, the people she introduced to the practice did not abandon their faith, and many in fact became leaders. There was just one person of whom she lost track, and to the end of her life, Ms. Kumagai remained concerned about what had become of the person. What a remarkable achievement!

Her children followed in her footsteps. Among them, they have helped nearly fifty families begin practicing Buddhism.

She died peacefully surrounded by many friends and well-wishers.

Ikeda: Ms. Kumagai is well-known; she worked earnestly for kosen-rufu. There are many such uncrowned kings and queens in the SGI. There is no world more noble than this.

THE BUDDHA FULLY REVEALS HIS "SECRET"

Suda: Nichiren Daishonin says that if Shakyamuni had not expounded the Lotus Sutra, he would have been guilty of the offense of begrudging people access to his true teaching (see WND-2, 232). In the Lotus Sutra, Shakyamuni reveals his "secret and his transcendental powers" (LSOC, 265) in their entirety.

Ikeda: Nichiren Daishonin describes this passage from the "Life Span" chapter as the "ultimate principle of the essential teaching." Its substance is the Law of Nam-myoho-renge-kyo contained in the sutra's depths. He says:

> The ultimate principle of the Lotus Sutra is Nam-myoho-renge-kyo. All beneficial doctrines, both Shakyamuni's practices and the virtues he consequently attained, the practices and effects of all Buddhas throughout time and space, the cumulative benefit of all the passages and phrases of the Lotus Sutra—all of this is contained in Nam-myoho-renge-kyo. In encapsulating this sutra, the *Words and Phrases of the Lotus Sutra* [chapter ten] says: "Speaking of the sutra as a whole, there are just four principles [name, function, entity and quality]. One grasps the crux of the matter and hands it on to others." The ultimate principle of the Lotus Sutra is none other than the daimoku that is entrusted to Bodhisattva Superior Practices. (GZ, 844)

We are spreading the fundamental cause that enables all beings in the universe over past, present and future to reveal their Buddha nature. This is exactly what is meant by "the secret of the Thus Come One."

Suda: The Lotus Sutra is generosity at its finest; it is the quintessence of free access to information!

Ikeda: It is a teaching of the highest compassion. President Toda used to say that someone who just practices without making any effort to advance kosen-rufu is like a person who stashes away some sweets in order to eat them later when no one is around. President Makiguchi also emphasized the importance of sharing Buddhism, saying, "Unless you carry out bodhisattva practice, you cannot become a Buddha." And he reprimanded the priesthood for having forgotten this spirit.

Saito: Distinguishing between "believers" and "practitioners," Mr. Makiguchi wrote:

> If you just believe and offer prayer, you will receive benefit without fail. But this alone does not amount to bodhisattva practice. There's no such thing as an egoistic Buddha who only seeks benefit for himself and does not endeavor to help others. Unless we carry out bodhisattva practice, we cannot become Buddhas. True faith, in other words, means spreading the teaching to others with the spirit of a parent toward his or her children. Those who do so are genuine practitioners.[1]

Ikeda: He says that we should spread the teaching with the compassion of a parent—that is *shakubuku*. This makes it very easy to understand. It's not a matter of increasing numbers or promoting our name, nor is it simply engaging in theoretical debate.

Always warmly, sometimes strictly, sometimes soothingly—this is how we should guide the other person. When sharing Buddhism with others, if we allow ourselves to be pulled into an emotional confrontation, then we are no longer behaving as an emissary of the Buddha. We need to firmly gird ourselves in the "armor of perseverance" (LSOC, 233). On the other hand, asking someone to "please just give it a try," as if begging, amounts to degrading the Law.

President Toda said, "*Shakubuku* means helping the other person overcome the evil in their minds, and enabling them to live according to the good in their minds." Parents cannot look on in silence and watch their children enter a mistaken path that will lead to misery. There are times when a parent is firm. Such compassion is *shakubuku*.

In short, it is an act of the greatest justice and courage. It is not easy for people to exhibit compassion. Many people who claim to have compassion are actually hypocrites. That is why *courage* is a more apt word than *compassion*. To courageously speak about what is right is tantamount to compassion. Courage and compassion are like two sides of the same coin.

Saito: This was expressed by the passage cited earlier from the "Entrustment" chapter that goes, "nor has he any fear" (LSOC, 319).

MR. MAKIGUCHI'S NOTES

Ikeda: The spirit to oppose the evils of the world is the *shakubuku* spirit. Likewise, we must not sit back and allow injustice to exist within the world of Buddhahood. The spirit of *shakubuku* applies in each of these realms.

During the war, the authorities went so far as to send special police to monitor Soka Gakkai discussion meetings. If the talk turned to the Shinto talisman, they would immediately yell, "Stop!" President Makiguchi would then turn to other topics for a while, but as soon as he mentioned the talisman again, the police would quickly yell, "Stop!" Those present wondered why President Makiguchi would repeatedly bring up this topic, fully knowing that he would be censured. No one understood President Makiguchi's profound intent. His spirit remained dauntless; it was as if he was trying to practice *shakubuku* even on the authorities.

By comparison, now is a time of great freedom. Therefore, to fail to fight for kosen-rufu now is to be a coward.

While exhibiting the courage of a lion king, President Makiguchi showed great care and affection for each person. Love for others is the most important condition in a person who leads. This is crucial.

Mr. Makiguchi taught with utmost sincerity and kindness those who had just begun practicing and were unfamiliar with Buddhism. When talking with someone, he would often take out some paper and make notes as the person spoke. He did this in order to remember the person's situation. Constantly referring to those notes, he would continue to encourage the person until he or she had overcome the problem.

He would also write down appropriate passages from the Daishonin's writings or some words of encouragement on pieces of paper and give them to people. As this was before the publication of the Daishonin's collected writings or any Soka Gakkai publications, members would carry these notes with them as they engaged in propagation activities.

Endo: In the "Entrustment" chapter, Shakyamuni entrusts all bodhisattvas, regardless of whether they are bodhisattvas of the theoretical or essential teaching, with the task of propagating the Law. Nichiren Daishonin describes this grand and solemn scene:

The essence of the "Entrustment" chapter of the Lotus Sutra is as follows: [Rising from his seat in the treasure tower,] the Buddha stood in open space and, in order to transfer the Lotus Sutra, patted no fewer than three times the heads of Bodhisattva Superior Practices and his followers, Manjushri and his followers, the great Brahma, Shakra, the gods of the sun and moon, the four heavenly kings, the dragon kings, the ten demon daughters, and others. They had clustered before the Buddha as thickly as dewdrops, crowding four hundred ten thousand million nayutas of worlds, like the grasses of Musashino Plain or the trees covering Mount Fuji. They knelt close to one another, bent their bodies so that their heads touched the ground, joined their palms together, and streamed sweat. Shakyamuni Buddha patted their heads just as a mother strokes the hair of her only child. Then Superior Practices, the gods of the sun and moon, and the others received the Buddha's auspicious command and pledged to propagate the Lotus Sutra in the latter age. (WND-1, 911)

Ikeda: The Daishonin describes this scene with allusions to the "grasses of Musashino" and the "trees covering Mount Fuji." He was a poet.

Suda: The bodhisattvas in this enormous gathering vow: "We will respectfully carry out all these things just as the world-honored one has commanded. Therefore we beg the world-honored one to have no concern on this account!" (LSOC, 319). They repeat this three times.

Ikeda: How bold! How refreshing! Their mentor must have been delighted. It's important not to cause the mentor to worry.

The mentor already has concern for the disciples beyond their imagination.

The "Entrustment" chapter further says that those who spread the teaching "will have repaid the debt of gratitude that [they] owe to the buddhas" (LSOC, 320). The sole prayer of the Buddha and the mentor is for kosen-rufu. That is why exerting oneself in spreading the teaching is what it means to truly repay one's debt of gratitude to the mentor.

To forget one's debt of gratitude is not Buddhism; in fact, it is not the true way of humanity. Buddhism teaches how to live as a human being. Buddhists must, therefore, be aware of and endeavor to repay their debt of gratitude.

Saito: I think it is vital that we never forget our debt of gratitude to the SGI, which has taught us about Nichiren Buddhism. Those who look down on the organization while themselves benefiting through their association with it are only bringing on their own downfall.

Suda: We need to "respectfully carry out all these things" (LSOC, 320) exactly as instructed by the mentor. This means putting the mentor's teaching into practice in its entirety without injecting personal bias. This is the path of a disciple.

Endo: People nevertheless tend to make excuses, saying things like, "My mentor says such and such, but because of my situation, I can't do exactly as he says," or "My mentor says one thing, but the reality is something else."

Ikeda: That's like cutting the power line between one's mentor and oneself. To do so is to stop the flow of electricity, thereby preventing the manifestation of true strength.

The bond of mentor and disciple comes down to the awareness of the disciple. It's not about formality. Meeting the mentor on numerous occasions, or spending time at the mentor's side, or being entrusted with a leadership position—these are all form [rather than essence]. Even if people are physically far from the mentor or have never spoken directly with the mentor, if they are aware of their role as disciples and strive to put the mentor's words into practice, then the mentor–disciple relationship is alive and intact.

How we define our relationship with the mentor is the foundation of everything. Organizational structures or positions are nothing but expedient means. Without this understanding, there will be grave consequences. It would be terrible if the world of mentor and disciple of Buddhism were destroyed, replaced by bureaucracy and formalism.

Even if your efforts go unnoticed or if you are exclusively working behind the scenes, if you are practicing just as the mentor instructs, a profound bond exists between you and the mentor. On the other hand, if you deviate from this path, then no matter how much you may be in the spotlight, your efforts will amount to nothing. Apart from the path of mentor and disciple, there is no Buddhism.

According to the Great Teacher T'ien-t'ai of China, one reason the Lotus Sutra is superior to other sutras is that it reveals that the original relationship of mentor and disciple is "far more profound in the essential teaching of the Lotus Sutra than that in the theoretical teaching of the Lotus Sutra and all pre-Lotus Sutra teachings." This is an extremely important doctrine.[2]

THE LOTUS SUTRA IS A GRAND "CEREMONY OF MENTOR AND DISCIPLE"

Endo: One gets the strong impression that the "Entrustment" chapter, in contrast to the "Supernatural Powers" chapter (where transmission is made to Superior Practices and the other Bodhisattvas of the Earth), is a transmission to the bodhisattvas of the theoretical teaching. But the transmission in "Entrustment" is in fact a general transmission to all bodhisattvas of both the theoretical and essential teachings.

Ikeda: That's right. And Superior Practices is the leader of the assembly in this chapter, too. While in a general sense it appears to be a transmission to the bodhisattvas of the theoretical teaching, on closer examination we find that Bodhisattva Superior Practices is the central figure. The true meaning of Shakyamuni patting them on the head three times is that of placing the "gem" of Nam-myoho-renge-kyo on their heads.

Suda: This brings to mind the parable of the priceless gem in the topknot of the king described in the "Peaceful Practices" chapter.

After a battle, the wheel-turning king rewards those who have fought with various treasures. But there is one object with which he will not part, a priceless gem that he wears hidden in his topknot. Finally he takes the gem from his hair and gives it to the soldier who has fought most valiantly. The priceless gem represents the Lotus Sutra, which is the priceless treasure that the Buddha imparts (see LSOC, 246).

Endo: In short, the "priceless gem" is the Gohonzon.

Saito: The true intent of the "Entrustment" chapter is to exhort people to spread the Gohonzon.

Ikeda: Yes. It predicts the appearance of Nichiren Daishonin.

Saito: The transmission to Superior Practices is referred to as the "transmission of the object of devotion" or the "transmission of the entity of the Law." There are two transmissions of the Lotus Sutra. One is the transmission of the scrolls of the sutra—the transmission of the twenty-eight–chapter sutra for the sake of the bodhisattvas of the provisional teaching. The other is the transmission of Nam-myoho-renge-kyo of time without beginning for the bodhisattvas of the essential teaching, the Bodhisattvas of the Earth. Nam-myoho-renge-kyo is the entity of the Law that is the object of devotion of all Buddhas, the entity of the Law found in the depths of the "Life Span" chapter.

Ikeda: Through the ceremony of transmission, the sutra identifies and praises most highly the person who will uphold this Gohonzon in the Latter Day of the Law. The Lotus Sutra is Shakyamuni's testament; he expounded it to explain who would lead humankind to enlightenment after his passing, and how they would accomplish this.

Specifically, this process begins in the "Teacher of the Law" chapter with Shakyamuni's appeals to the gathered bodhisattvas, and with the appearance of the huge treasure tower in the "Treasure Tower" chapter. Shakyamuni then raises the entire multitude into the air and calls out to them in a booming voice:

> "Who is capable of broadly preaching the Lotus Sutra of the Wonderful Law in this saha world? Now is the time to do so, for before long the thus come one will enter nirvana. The Buddha wishes to entrust this Lotus Sutra of the Wonderful Law to someone so that it might be preserved." (LSOC, 215)

Saito: The Ceremony in the Air continues from that point until its conclusion here in the "Entrustment" chapter.

Suda: Shakyamuni, having heard the reply of his disciples that he need not worry about the future, instructs all Buddhas who have gathered there from the worlds in the ten directions to return to the lands from which they came. He then brings the Ceremony in the Air to an end with the words, "The tower of

Many Treasures Buddha may also return to its former position" (LSOC, 320).

Endo: Seen in this light, it is clear that the reason for the Ceremony in the Air is transmission.

Ikeda: The Lotus Sutra in its entirety is a grand ceremony of mentor and disciple. To miss this point is to completely misunderstand the Lotus Sutra.

The Dynamism of "Three Assemblies in Two Places"

Endo: Incidentally, in extant Sanskrit texts of the Lotus Sutra, the chapter corresponding to "Entrustment" appears at the very end of the sutra.

Ikeda: We see the same in the Lotus Sutra of the Correct Law of Dharmaraksha,[3] another Chinese-language translation of the sutra.

Endo: Some suggest that this is the original format of the sutra.

Saito: I can see how the "Entrustment" chapter could logically conclude the sutra.

Ikeda: This topic requires some research.

Saito: People have debated the chapter order since ancient times.

Ikeda: While this is certainly a matter for further investigation, I think it is clear that the current position of the "Entrustment" chapter adds a dramatic touch to the sutra. This is because it establishes the dynamism of the "three assemblies in two places."

Suda: That's true. Before the Ceremony in the Air, the preaching takes place at the summit of Eagle Peak. After the Ceremony in the Air, the scene of preaching returns to Eagle Peak. Hence, we have three assemblies in two places. If the "Entrustment" chapter concluded the entire sutra, we would have the less interesting structure of "two assemblies in two places"!

Ikeda: As we discussed previously [in connection with the "Introduction" chapter], profound significance attaches to the three assemblies in two places. Through the overall framework of the Lotus Sutra, the move from the real world to the realm of eternal life (i.e., from Eagle Peak to the Ceremony in the Air), and then back to the real world (from the Ceremony in the Air to Eagle Peak) indicates the rhythm of human revolution.

Suda: We have a rhythm that alternates between two actions: that of "seeking the Way" and that of "guiding living beings."

Endo: This is analogous to the rhythm of our daily lives in which we go from the reality of life to the practice of gongyo and then back to the reality of life and society with renewed vigor.

Saito: The concept of dedicating one's life (as expressed by the Sanskrit term *namas*) to Myoho-renge-kyo includes the sense of both "returning to" and taking action "based on" the Mystic Law.

Ikeda: Both of these are indeed essential, for only when our practice incorporates these two aspects are we truly devoting ourselves to Nam-myoho-renge-kyo. To "return to" means to practice for oneself, while basing one's action on the Mystic Law means to practice for others.

When we fully integrate both the practice for ourselves and the practice for others, we get in sync with the rhythm of the universe. These two ways of practice are like the two planetary motions of rotation and revolution. The more we advance in the practice for oneself, the more our practice for others develops. And as our practice for others advances, our practice for oneself deepens.

President Toda often said with regard to propagation: "The key is to pray earnestly to the Gohonzon. There is no other way to spread this Buddhism!" We need to pray that the other person can sense our sincere desire for him or her to become happy. We have to pray: "Please enable me to fulfill my mission in this life as an emissary of the Buddha!"

Buddhism is a battle. President Toda was very strict when it came to winning or losing. During youth division athletic events, Mr. Toda would go to the team that was losing and give them some words of advice. Somehow, that team would often end up winning.

But regarding propagation, he once said: "Some people may have a hard time doing propagation, perhaps because they are awkward with words or simply too good-natured. And that's just fine, but they should practice joyfully nevertheless.

"There are those who will nevertheless tell them, 'You absolutely have to propagate this Buddhism!' But if someone just can't do it, scolding will not help in the least. If the person is appreciative for his or her practice to the Gohonzon, that is enough.

"The important thing is that people be encouraged so that they can truly understand faith. When they really grasp the greatness of the Gohonzon, they will naturally tell others about the practice. And that itself is propagation."[4]

Suda: That makes sense.

Ikeda: We need to enjoy our propagation efforts, keeping a generous spirit and an open mind. And we should do so smiling brightly with pride and appreciation, aware that there is no higher honor than telling others even a few words about the Mystic Law during this lifetime.

If people are instructed to introduce a specific number of people, on the other hand, they will only feel burdened. It will cause them suffering. Everyone will feel heavy, which will only hinder the kosen-rufu movement.

A leader's role is to enable everyone to enjoy their practice. But most leaders do just the opposite. We need to give people courage and hope. We need to applaud and encourage them with an open heart. It is of course important to set goals for ourselves. When we then pray for all members without exception to receive great benefit, our spirit will absolutely be conveyed.

To enable people to receive immense benefit, we must calmly discuss faith with them, saying, "Let's do our best together!" and "Let's enjoy vibrant health and live long lives!" When members encourage one another in this fashion, each person grows naturally, as does the entire organization.

Just praising the Mystic Law to others is itself splendid propagation. Whether others decide to take faith is a separate issue. By simply talking to people about the Mystic Law, we receive benefit without fail.

It is the same with sports or playing the piano in that by making continuous effort, one's ability develops in time. Likewise, in propagation, if we tell people about this Buddhism whenever the opportunity arises, our good fortune from doing so will protect our family and our descendants.

Those who tenaciously share Buddhism develop a foundation of good fortune as solid and strong as concrete. No devil can destroy it. Those who avoid propagation, however, no matter how high their organizational position, are as superficial as plated metal and at the crucial moment they will fall apart.

Suda: So the rhythm of the Lotus Sutra consists of both practice for oneself and practice for others.

Endo: I can really see now the significance of having the "Entrustment" chapter follow the "Supernatural Powers" chapter.

By Helping Others, We Help Ourselves

Ikeda: By helping other people become happy, we too become happy. This is also a tenet of psychology. How can those suffering in the depths of hell, who have lost the will to live, get back on their feet? Merely thinking about our own problems more often than not causes us to fall even deeper into despair. But, by going to someone who is also suffering and offering them a hand, we can regain the will to live. Taking action out of concern for others enables us to heal our own lives.

Saito: By helping others, we help ourselves. This indicates the inseparability of self and others. In that sense, when trying to introduce others to Buddhism, it is important that we humbly appreciate them.

Endo: It is impossible to know just how much the parents' will to live is influenced by anticipation of their children's growth and development.

Ikeda: These days, people seem to think that working for another's well-being is somehow a lost cause. We live in a world where even the mention of charity and compassion sometimes elicits cool derision. It is hard to imagine just how much suffering such arrogance is causing society.

An American missionary supposedly asked Mahatma Gandhi: "What religion do you practice and what form do you think religion will take in India in the future?" There happened to be two sick people in the room. Pointing in their direction, Gandhi replied simply: "My religion is serving and working for the people. I am not preoccupied with the future."[5]

For Gandhi, politics was also a matter of service, of helping the most destitute. It's all about action. Without bodhisattva practice, there is no religion. There is no Buddhism. Nor is there genuine politics or education.

Saito: Several years ago, a scholar offered an explanation for the stagnation of Japanese society. He noted that until Japan's defeat in 1945, the emperor system had served as a "religion," in that it provided social standards and a sense of national identity. After the war, in place of the emperor system, "Marxism and its intellectual progeny" fulfilled the role of religion. During rapid economic growth in the 1960s, he argued, Japan's sole desire to catch up with and surpass the advanced countries of the West became the country's new religion. That religion ended as Japan became an economic giant in the 1980s and '90s. He concluded that unless Japan finds another new religion, it will inevitably decline into a society devoid of all standards.[6]

Endo: Japan is certainly lacking in standards. It feels as if our society is coming apart at the seams and that anything could happen at any moment.

Ikeda: This is the tragedy of Japan, a country where people don't pay serious attention to religion. For this reason, we have a tremendous mission.

The Daishonin says, "More valuable than treasures in a storehouse are the treasures of the body, and the treasures of the heart are the most valuable of all" (WND-1, 851). To focus only on the "treasures of the storehouse"—the economy—will not improve the economic situation. Things may improve for a while, but this will ultimately not contribute to the welfare of society.

It is people, it is the heart, that matter most. The heart determines everything. Shakyamuni was the great giver of gifts, but propagation of the Mystic Law is to give people the ultimate treasures of the heart. When we possess treasures of the heart, when our lives overflow with good fortune and wisdom, we are naturally endowed with abundant treasures of the body and treasures of the storehouse.

Saito: I think this is the most important point to be aware of for the twenty-first century.

Ikeda: What is left when our lives end? It is the memories that we have engraved in our hearts and minds.

I met the Russian novelist Mikhail Sholokhov[7] when I visited Moscow in 1974. He told me: "The longer we live, the more difficult it becomes to remember the painful experiences. As time passes, the colors of the events in our lives fade and everything from the happiest times to the saddest starts to disappear from memory."

After taking in a breath, with a big smile he continued: "When you turn seventy, Mr. Ikeda, you will know that what I am saying is the truth." His words conveyed a wealth of feeling.

Everything passes. Both the soaring joys and crushing sorrows fade away like a dream. However, the memory of having lived one's life to the fullest never disappears. The memories of having worked wholeheartedly for kosen-rufu in particular are eternal.

"In my lifetime, how many people have I helped become happy? How many people can say that it is because of me that they know true happiness?" In the end, is this not all that remains?

The Daishonin says, "Single-mindedly chant Nam-myoho-renge-kyo and urge others to do the same; that will remain as the only memory of your present life in this human world" (WND-1, 64). I think this could be taken as the conclusion to President Toda's remark, "What if I were to die today?"

NOTES

1. *Makiguchi Tsunesaburo zenshu* (Collected Works of Tsunesaburo Makiguchi) (Tokyo: Daisan Bummeisha, 1987), vol. 10, p. 151.

2. This is the third of the three standards of comparison explained in the *Profound Meaning of the Lotus Sutra*. While the pre-Lotus Sutra teachings and the theoretical teaching (or first half) of the Lotus Sutra reveal only the mentor-disciple relationship with Shakyamuni who attained enlightenment during his present lifetime in India, the essential teaching (or second half) of the Lotus Sutra reveals the mentor-disciple relationship with Shakyamuni who attained enlightenment in the remote past.

3. (231–308?).

4. *Toda Josei zenshu* (Collected Writings of Josei Toda) (Tokyo: Seikyo Shimbunsha, 1984), vol. 4, p. 429.

5. Tatsuo Morimoto, *Ganji to Tagoru* (Gandhi and Tagore) (Tokyo: Daisan Bummeisha, 1995), pp. 116–17.

6. From an article by Takamitsu Sawa in the magazine *Sekai* (World), November 1995.

7. (1905–84).

Glossary

benefit (Jpn *kudoku*) *Ku* means to extinguish evil and *doku* means to bring forth good.

bodhisattva A being who aspires to attain Buddhahood and carries out altruistic practices to achieve that goal. Compassion predominates in bodhisattvas, who postpone their own entry into nirvana in order to lead others toward enlightenment.

Bodhisattvas of the Earth Those who chant and propagate Nam-myoho-renge-kyo. *Earth* indicates the enlightened nature of all people. The term describes the innumerable bodhisattvas who appear in the "Emerging from the Earth" chapter of the Lotus Sutra and are entrusted by Shakyamuni with the task of propagating the Law after his passing. In several of his writings, Nichiren Daishonin identifies his own role with that of their leader, Bodhisattva Superior Practices.

Buddhahood The state a Buddha has attained. The ultimate goal of Buddhist practice. The highest of the Ten Worlds. The word *enlightenment* is often interchangeable with Buddhahood.

casting off the transient and revealing the true The revealing of a Buddha's true status as a Buddha, and the setting aside of the Buddha's provisional or transient identity.

cause and effect (1) Buddhism expounds the law of cause and effect that operates in life, ranging over past, present and future existences. This causality underlies the doctrine of karma. From this viewpoint, causes formed in the past are manifested as effects in the present. Causes formed in the present will be manifested as effects in the future. (2) From the viewpoint of Buddhist practice, cause represents the bodhisattva practice for attaining Buddhahood, and effect represents the benefit of Buddhahood. (3) From the viewpoint that, among the Ten Worlds, cause represents the nine worlds and effect represents Buddhahood, Nichiren Daishonin refers to two kinds of teachings: those that view things from the standpoint of "cause to effect" and those that approach things from the standpoint of "effect to cause." The former indicates Shakyamuni's teaching, while the latter indicates Nichiren Daishonin's teaching.

daimoku   Literally, 'title.' (1) The title of a sutra, in particular the title of the Lotus Sutra, Myoho-renge-kyo. (2) The invocation of Nam-myoho-renge-kyo in Nichiren Buddhism.

Daishonin   Literally, 'great sage.' In particular, this honorific title is applied to Nichiren to show reverence for him as the Buddha who appears in the Latter Day of the Law to save all humankind.

dependent origination   Also, dependent causation or conditioned co-arising. A Buddhist doctrine expressing the interdependence of all things. It teaches that no being or phenomenon exists on its own, but exists or occurs because of its relationship with other beings or phenomena. Everything in the world comes into existence in response to causes and conditions. In other words, nothing can exist independent of other things or arise in isolation.

devil king of the sixth heaven   The king of devils, who dwells in the highest of the six heavens of the world of desire. He works to obstruct Buddhist practice and delights in sapping the life force of other beings. He is also regarded as the manifestation of the fundamental darkness inherent in life. Also called the heavenly devil.

dharma   A term fundamental to Buddhism that derives from a verbal root *dhri,* which means to preserve, maintain, keep, or uphold. *Dharma* has a wide variety of meanings, such as law, truth, doctrine, the Buddha's teaching, decree, observance, conduct, duty, virtue, morality, religion, justice, nature, quality, character, characteristic, essence, elements of existence, and phenomena. Some of the more common usages are: (1) (Often capitalized) The Law, or ultimate truth. For example, Kumarajiva translated *saddharma,* the Sanskrit word that literally means correct Law, as Wonderful

Law or Mystic Law, indicating the unfathomable truth or Law that governs all phenomena. (2) The teaching of the Buddha that reveals the Law. The *Dharma* of *abhidharma* means the Buddha's doctrine, or the sutras. (3) (Often plural) Manifestations of the Law, i.e., phenomena, things, facts, or existences. The word "phenomena" in "the true aspect of all phenomena" is the translation of *dharmas*. (4) The elements of existence, which, according to the Hinayana schools, are the most basic constituents of the individual and his or her reality. (5) Norms of conduct leading to the accumulation of good karma.

Eagle Peak   (Skt Gridhrakuta) Also, Vulture Peak. A mountain located to the northeast of Rajagriha, the capital of Magadha in ancient India, where Shakyamuni is said to have expounded the Lotus Sutra. Eagle Peak also symbolizes the Buddha land or the state of Buddhahood. In this sense, the 'pure land of Eagle Peak' is often used.

earthly desires   Also, illusions, defilements, impurities, earthly passions, or simply desires. A generic term for all the workings of life, including desires and illusions in the general sense, that cause one psychological and physical suffering and impede the quest for enlightenment.

earthly desires are enlightenment   Mahayana principle based on the view that earthly desires cannot exist independently on their own; therefore one can attain enlightenment without eliminating earthly desires. This is in contrast with the Hinayana view that extinguishing earthly desires is a prerequisite for enlightenment. Mahayana teachings reveal that earthly desires are one with and inseparable from enlightenment.

essential teaching   (1) The teaching expounded by Shakyamuni from the perspective of his true identity as the Buddha who attained enlightenment numberless major world system dust particle *kalpas* ago. T'ien-t'ai classifies the last fourteen chapters of the Lotus Sutra as the essential teaching. (2) The essential teaching of the Latter Day of the Law, that is, the teaching of Nam-myoho-renge-kyo.

expedient means   The methods adopted to instruct people and lead them to enlightenment. The concept of expedient means is highly regarded in Mahayana Buddhism, especially in the Lotus Sutra, as represented by its second chapter entitled "Expedient Means." This is because expedient means are skillfully devised and employed by Buddhas and bodhisattvas to lead the people to salvation.

five components Also, the five components of life and the five aggregates. The constituent elements of form, perception, conception, volition, and consciousness that unite temporarily to form an individual living being. The five components also constitute the first of the three realms of existence.

four sufferings The four universal sufferings of birth, old age, sickness and death. Shakyamuni's quest for enlightenment is said to have been motivated by a desire to find a solution to these four sufferings.

fundamental darkness Also, fundamental ignorance. The most deeply rooted illusion inherent in life, which gives rise to all other illusions and earthly desires.

Gohonzon *Go* means 'worthy of honor' and *honzon* means 'object of fundamental respect.' The object of devotion in Nichiren Buddhism and the embodiment of the Mystic Law permeating all phenomena. It takes the form of a mandala inscribed on paper or on wood with characters representing the Mystic Law as well as the Ten Worlds, including Buddhahood. Nichiren Daishonin's Buddhism holds that all people possess the Buddha nature and can attain Buddhahood through faith in the Gohonzon.

gongyo Literally, to 'exert [oneself in] practice.' In Nichiren Buddhism, it refers to chanting Nam-myoho-renge-kyo and reciting portions of the "Expedient Means" and "Life Span" chapters of the Lotus Sutra.

Gosho Literally, 'honored writings.' The individual and collected writings of Nichiren Daishonin.

Hinayana The teaching that aims at attaining the state of arhat. Hinayana, literally "lesser vehicle," was originally a pejorative term used by Mahayana Buddhists, who regarded the practitioners of these teachings as preoccupied solely with achieving personal emancipation and indifferent to the salvation of others. Hinayana teachings are represented by the doctrines of the four noble truths and the twelve-linked chain of causation. They regard earthly desires as the cause of suffering and assert that suffering is eliminated only by eradicating earthly desires.

human revolution   A concept coined by the Soka Gakkai's second president, Josei Toda, to indicate the self-reformation of an individual — the strengthening of life force and the establishment of Buddhahood — that is the goal of Buddhist practice.

inconspicuous benefit   Benefit that accumulates over a period of time and is not immediately recognizable.

Jataka   Also *Jataka Tales* or "Birth Stories." The stories of the previous lives of Shakyamuni Buddha. One of the traditional twelve divisions of the Buddhist canon. These stories depict the good acts carried out by Shakyamuni in previous lifetimes that enabled him to be reborn as the Buddha in India.

Jambudvipa   One of the four continents situated in the four directions around Mount Sumeru, according to the ancient Indian worldview. Jambudvipa is the southern continent.

kalpa   An extremely long period of time. Sutras and treatises differ in their definitions, but *kalpas* fall into two major categories, those of measurable and immeasurable duration. There are three kinds of measurable *kalpas*: small, medium and major. One explanation sets the length of a small *kalpa* at approximately sixteen million years. According to Buddhist cosmology, a world repeatedly undergoes four stages: formation, continuance, decline and disintegration. Each of these four stages lasts for twenty small *kalpas* and is equal to one medium *kalpa*. Finally, one complete cycle forms a major *kalpa*.

karma   Potential energies residing in the inner realm of life, which manifest themselves as various results in the future. In Buddhism, karma is interpreted as meaning mental, verbal and physical action, that is, thoughts, words and deeds.

kosen-rufu   Literally, to 'widely declare and spread [Buddhism].' Nichiren Daishonin defines Nam-myoho-renge-kyo of the Three

Great Secret Laws as the law to be widely declared and spread during the Latter Day. There are two aspects of kosen-rufu: the kosen-rufu of the entity of the Law, or the establishment of the Dai-Gohonzon, which is the basis of the Three Great Secret Laws; and the kosen-rufu of substantiation, the widespread acceptance of faith in the Dai-Gohonzon among the people.

ku   A fundamental Buddhist concept, variously translated as nonsubstantiality, emptiness, void, latency, relativity, etc. The concept that entities have no fixed or independent nature.

Latter Day of the Law   Also, the Latter Day. The last of the three periods following Shakyamuni Buddha's death when Buddhism falls into confusion and Shakyamuni's teachings lose the power to lead people to enlightenment. A time when the essence of the Lotus Sutra will be propagated to save all humankind.

Lotus Sutra   The highest teaching of Shakyamuni Buddha, it reveals that all people can attain enlightenment and declares that his former teachings should be regarded as preparatory.

Mahayana Buddhism   The teachings which expound the bodhisattva practice as the means toward the enlightenment of both oneself and others, in contrast to Hinayana Buddhism, or the teaching of the Agon period, which aims only at personal salvation. Mahayana literally means 'greater vehicle.'

mentor-and-disciple relationship   See *oneness of mentor and disciple*.

Miao-lo   The sixth patriarch in the lineage of the T'ien-t'ai school in China, counting from the Great Teacher T'ien-t'ai. Miao-lo reasserted the supremacy of the Lotus Sutra and wrote commentaries on T'ien-t'ai's three major works, thus bringing about a revival of interest in T'ien-t'ai Buddhism. He is revered as the restorer of the school.

Middle Day of the Law   Also, the period of the Counterfeit Law. The second of the three periods following a Buddha's death. During this time the Buddha's teaching gradually becomes formalized, the people's connection to it weakens, and progressively fewer people are able to gain enlightenment through its practice. Some sources define the Middle Day of the Law of Shakyamuni as lasting a thousand years, while others define it as five hundred years.

mutual possession of the Ten Worlds   The principle that each of the Ten Worlds contains all the other nine as potential within itself. This is taken to mean that an individual's state of life can be changed, and that all beings of the nine worlds possess the potential for Buddhahood. *See also* Ten Worlds.

Mystic Law   The ultimate law of life and the universe. The law of Nam-myoho-renge-kyo.

Nam-myoho-renge-kyo   The ultimate law of the true aspect of life permeating all phenomena in the universe. The invocation established by Nichiren Daishonin on April 28, 1253. Nichiren Daishonin teaches that this phrase encompasses all laws and teachings within itself, and that the benefit of chanting Nam-myoho-renge-kyo includes the benefit of conducting all virtuous practices. *Nam* means 'devotion to'; *myoho* means 'Mystic Law'; *renge* refers to the lotus flower, which simultaneously blooms and seeds, indicating the simultaneity of cause and effect; *kyo* means sutra, the teaching of a Buddha.

Nichiren Daishonin   The thirteenth-century Japanese Buddhist teacher and reformer who taught that all people have the potential for enlightenment. He defined the universal law as Nam-myoho-renge-kyo and established the Gohonzon as the object of devotion for all people to attain Buddhahood. Daishonin is an honorific title that means 'great sage.'

nonsubstantiality   One of the three truths. The truth of nonsubstantiality means that all phenomena are nonsubstantial and in a state transcending the concepts of existence and nonexistence.

oneness of body and mind   A principle explaining that the two seemingly distinct phenomena of body, or the physical aspect of life, and mind, or its spiritual aspect, are two integral phases of the same entity.

oneness of life and environment   The principle stating that the self and its environment are two integral phases of the same entity.

oneness of mentor and disciple   This is a philosophical as well as a practical concept. Disciples reach the same state of Buddhahood as their mentor by practicing the teachings of the latter. In Nichiren Daishonin's Buddhism, this is the direct way to enlightenment, that is, to believe in the Gohonzon and practice according to the Daishonin's teachings.

shakubuku   A method of propagating Buddhism by refuting another's attachment to heretical views and thus leading him or her to the correct Buddhist teaching.

Shakyamuni   Also, Siddhartha Gautama. Born in India (present-day southern Nepal) about three thousand years ago, he is the first recorded Buddha and founder of Buddhism. For fifty years, he expounded various sutras (teachings), culminating in the Lotus Sutra.

Soka   Literally, 'value creating.'

Ten Worlds   Ten life-conditions that a single entity of life manifests. Originally the Ten Worlds were viewed as distinct physical places, each with its own particular inhabitants. In light of the Lotus Sutra, they are interpreted as potential conditions of life inherent in each individual. The ten are: (1) Hell, (2) Hunger, (3) Animality, (4) Anger, (5) Humanity or Tranquillity, (6) Rapture, (7) Learning, (8) Realization, (9) Bodhisattva and (10) Buddhahood. *See also* mutual possession of the Ten Worlds.

theoretical teachings   The first fourteen chapters of the twenty-eight chapter Lotus Sutra, as classified by T'ien-t'ai. In contrast to the essential teaching—the latter fourteen chapters of the sutra, which represent preaching by Shakyamuni as the Buddha who attained enlightenment in the remote past, the theoretical teaching represents preaching by the historical Shakyamuni, who first attained enlightenment during his lifetime in India. The core of the theoretical teaching is the "Expedient Means" chapter, which teaches that all phenomena manifest the true aspect and that all phenomena are endowed with the ten factors.

three existences   Past, present and future. The dimension of time. The three aspects of the eternity of life, linked inseparably by the law of cause and effect. "Throughout the three existences" means throughout eternity.

Three Great Secret Laws The object of worship of Buddhism, the invocation or daimoku of Buddhism and the high sanctuary of Buddhism. These three constitute the core of Nichiren Buddhism.

three obstacles and four devils Various obstacles and hindrances to the practice of Buddhism. The three obstacles are: 1) the obstacle of earthly desires; 2) the obstacle of karma, which may also refer to opposition from one's spouse or children; and 3) the obstacle of retribution, also obstacles caused by one's superiors, such as rulers or parents. The four devils are: 1) the hindrance of the five components; 2) the hindrance of earthly desires; 3) the hindrance of death, because untimely death obstructs one's practice of Buddhism or because the premature death of another practitioner causes doubts; and 4) the hindrance of the devil king.

three poisons Greed, anger and foolishness. The fundamental evils inherent in life that give rise to human suffering.

three powerful enemies Also, the three types of enemies. Three types of people who persecute those who propagate the Lotus Sutra after the Buddha's passing, as described in the "Encouraging Devotion" chapter of the sutra. They are: (1) lay people ignorant of Buddhism who denounce the votaries of the Lotus Sutra and attack them with swords or staves; (2) arrogant and cunning priests who slander the votaries; and (3) priests respected by the general public who, fearing the loss of fame or profit, induce the secular authorities to persecute the sutra's votaries.

three thousand realms in a single moment of life A philosophical system set forth by T'ien-t'ai in his *Great Concentration and Insight*, clarifying the mutually inclusive relationship of the ultimate truth and the phenomenal world. This means that the life of Buddhahood is universally inherent in all beings, and the distinction between a common person and a Buddha is a phenomenal one.

Thus Come One One of the ten honorable titles for a Buddha, meaning one who has arrived from the world of truth. That is, the Buddha appears from the world of enlightenment and, as a person who embodies wisdom and compassion, leads other beings to enlightenment.

T'ien-t'ai   Also called Chih-i. The founder of the T'ien-t'ai school, commonly referred to as the Great Teacher T'ien-t'ai.

treasure tower   A tower adorned with treasures. A treasure tower often appears in Buddhist scriptures. In Nichiren Daishonin's writings, the treasure tower primarily indicates the tower of the Buddha Many Treasures that appears from beneath the earth in the "Treasure Tower" chapter of the Lotus Sutra. He also equated this with the Gohonzon and human life.

true cause   Also, the mystic principle of the true cause. One of the ten mystic principles of the essential teaching (latter half) of the Lotus Sutra formulated by T'ien-t'ai (538–597). It refers to the practice that Shakyamuni carried out countless *kalpas* in the past in order to attain his original enlightenment. *See also* true effect.

true effect   Also, the mystic principle of the true effect. The original enlightenment that Shakyamuni attained countless *kalpas* before his enlightenment in India. One of the ten mystic principles of the essential teaching (latter half) of the Lotus Sutra formulated by T'ien-t'ai (538–597). *See also* true cause.

Index

serious, 224; Nichiren Daishonin and, 72
immortality (*amata*), 184–86, 190–91
impatience, 67
inconspicuous efforts, recognizing 65–66
India, 96, 102; spirit of, 141
individual, treasuring a single, 93–94
initiative, 144
injustice, 244
inner fortitude, 44
insight, developing, 66–67, 69–70; Ikeda's, 64–65; power of, 63–66; Toda's, 64

Jataka (tales), 195
Jin Yong, 184–88
journalists, 176
joy, 43–44, Nichiren Daishonin and, 37; true, 50
Jung, Carl, 140–41

Kansai, 207, 209
karma, expiating negative, 106–07
Kegon Sutra, 166
Keller, Helen, 70–71
King, Martin Luther, 112
Kojima Akiko, 19–21
kosen-rufu, achieving, 116; advancing, 209; benefit of exerting oneself for, 23, 48, 62, 64, 83–84; benefit of working for, 158–59, 242; effects of advancing, 9; effects of pretending to work for, 242; expanding movement of, 51; importance of, SGI members working for, 210; means, 137–38, 231; movement, 32, 38, 148, 178, 247; purpose of the movement of, 141; process of, 77; Toda and, 30, 101, 248; way to exert ourselves for, 122,

127–28; world of, 150–51
kudoku (benefit), 5, 55. *See also* benefit(s)
Kumagai, Kiyomi, earnest propagation activities of, 245
Kumarajiva, 93; in Chinese, 92
kuon ganjo (time without beginning), 168
Kyoto Chapter, 41–42

Lankavatara Sutra, 186
Latter Day of the Law, 96, 160, 176, 246; *amrita* (elixir of immortality) in the, 193; declaration of, 190; start of the, 16
lawyers, 176
leader(s), conduct expected of a Soka Gakkai, 208; function of a Soka Gakkai, 208–10; genuine, 229, qualities for a Buddhist, 83, 95; role of the SGI, 257; in society, 95; Toda's expectation for SGI, 239–40
learn, spirit to, 189
"leave off," Shakyamuni's expression of, 190–91
"lessening one's karmic retribution," 19
"Letter to Horen" (Nichiren), 221
Leviathan, 111
Li Lou, 73
life, 44; alternate name for, 165; eternity of, 22; importance of human, 139; polished, 22; ultimate path in, 83; way to build a lofty state of, 121
life force, 60–61, 99
"Life Span" chapter (Lotus Sutra), 121–22, 126, 131, 135, 191, 211, 214; appearance of the Buddha of the, 195; basic paradigm of the, 191; benefit of believing in the, 5, 9, 10, 13, 22; central theme of the, 215;

Min-On Concert Association, 68
Mito Komon (Japanese historical
   drama), 214–15
Mitobe, Kikutaro, 183
Murao, Koichi, 184
music, power of, 76; melancholy, 74
myo (mystic), 193
Mystic Law, 8, 15, 121, 123, 153–54,
   171, 191–92, 198, 216–17, 226,
   244; benefit of believing in the,
   70–71, 83; benefit of practicing
   the, 17, 47–48, 114, 126, 159, 185,
   224–25; benefit of propagating
   the, 50, 167; benefits of helping
   others to practice the, 48, 242,
   257–58; Nichiren Daishonin
   and, 23, 159, 171, 210, 220, 224;
   effects of slandering ordinary
   person who practices the, 228;
   embodies, 43; entity of the, 16;
   one with the, 210; power of the,
   18, 22, 33–35; teaching of the, 9;
   transient manifestation of the,
   153

Nagarjuna, 197
namaste, 97
Napoleon, 70
NASA (National Aeronautics and
   Space Administration), 15
nationalism, 39, 105, 139; Makiguchi's struggle against, 111, 114;
   religion of, 106–08, 138; Toda's
   struggle against, 111, 114
Nazism, rise of, 138
Nembutsu, school, 201; Nichiren
   Daishonin condemns chanting
   of, 73
Never Disparaging Bodhisattva,
   behavior of the, 93–103, 105,
   110, 112; Nichiren Daishonin
   and, 100–01; effects of slandering the, 100; practice of the,
   103–04; Shakyamuni with

regard to, 103; SGI members
   and, 103–04; spirit of the, 111–13
Nichijun, 31, 47
Nichikan, 17, 153; Commentary on
   the 'Essence of the Lotus Sutra,'
   216
Nichimoku, 244
Nichiren, means, 128
Nichiren Daishonin, 4–5, 9, 12, 17,
   128, 154, 172, 177, 223; behavior
   of, 113; Buddhism of, 60, 178;
   daimoku and, 153; effects of
   slandering, 224; five practices
   in the Buddhism of, 62–63; importance of studying Buddhism
   of, 103; mission of, 167; power
   of insight of, 66; significance of
   the birth of, 226; state of life of,
   44–45; will of, 243
Nichiren Shoshu, behavior of the
   priesthood of, 244; priesthood
   of, 32, 111, 125, 243; teachings
   being transmitted within the
   priesthood of, 243
Nietzsche, Friedrich, 140
Nikko Shonin, 244
nine worlds, 150, 154
Nirvana Sutra, 19
nonregression, attaining state
   of, 22

obedience, in Buddhism, 45–46
object of worship, after Shakyamuni's death, 46
"Observe the Patient," 72
obstacles, Nichiren Daishonin
   and, 11
Ohashi, Yukie, 40–43
Okinawa, 224
Okinawa Training Center, 66
omens, Nichiren Daishonin and,
   138
"On the Ten Factors of Life"
   (Nichiren), 218

"One Hundred and Six Comparisons, The" (Nichiren), 167
one's present form, attaining Buddhahood in, 69
oneness of good and evil, 113
oneness of Person and Law, 46
optimism, Buddhist, 23
original cause, 220
Osaka Incident, 124

"Peaceful Practices" chapter (Lotus Sutra), parable in the, 248–49
people, good, 111; illustrating the power of the ordinary, 177–78, 180–82; ordinary, 218
philosophy, 6
physically challenged people, 71
physicians, T'ien-t'ai and, 72
Plato, 200
Poison-drum relationship, 113
politicians, 176
power, 112; corrupt nature of, 142; cruelty of, 107; negative potential of, 39
practice, two ways of, 257, 259
practitioners, distinguishing between believers and, 248
praise, 257–58
Prajnaparamita Sutra, 186
prayer, 122, 155–57; earnest, 68–69
pre-Lotus Sutra, reason for the superiority of the Lotus Sutra to the, 248; teaching of, 211
present, importance of the, 165
priesthood, 243. See also Nichiren Shoshu
priests, 56; exist, 174; place of, 136–37
Profound Meaning of the Lotus Sutra (T'ien-t'ai), 73
propagation, 29–30, 32–33; benefit of Buddhist, 23, 35, 104; benefit of praising those who practice, 51; effect of avoiding, 254;

essence of, 50; joyful, 257; Makiguchi and, 243; practice of, 5; SGI members and, 55–58; soul of, 40; Toda and, 55–56, 98, 257; true meaning of, 18; widespread, 31. See also shakubuku

"Real Aspect of the Gohonzon, The" (Nichiren), 64
"Record of the Orally Transmitted Teachings" (Nichiren), 4, 8, 56, 97, 112, 126, 211–13; 231; significance of three pats according to the, 242
religion(s), 95; genuine, 107–08; role of a, 177; strife in, 96; view of, 136
renge (lotus flower), 187
respect, 92, 114
"revealing the true," meaning of, 212
"revealing the true in actuality," 210–16
"revealing the true in principle," 210–15
Russian Buddha, 204

sacred. See sage
sadness, overcoming, 43
Sado Island, 103; exile in contemporary terms, 44
sage, Chinese character for, 73
saha (world of suffering), 132–34, 149
Sapporo Convention, 180
science, advances of, 64; tendency of, 65
seed, potential of a single, 222
Seikyo Shimbun, 80
Sekino, Chii, propagation activities of, 57–60
self, greater, 141–42
self-improvement, ways to seek, 169

self-interest, 132
sense organs, purifying the, 62–63, 75, 82
SGI. *See* Soka Gakkai International
shakubuku (spreading the teaching), prayer for doing, 257; spirit of, 244; Toda with regard to, 243–44; ways of doing, 243. *See also* propagation
Shakyamuni Buddha, 15, 46, 114, 128–33, 137, 149, 173–74, 190–91, 198, 198, 219–20, 226; bodhisattva practice and, 134; bodhisattva's view of, 216; cause of enlightenment of, 216–17; communicating his enlightenment, 192; compassion of, 237, 244; enlightenment of, 122, 134–35, 157, 161–62, 190–91; entrustment of the Mystic Law by, 236–37; funeral instructions to his followers, 194; as a human being, 204; last wish of, 192; mentor of, 123; prayer of, 122; purifying the eye and, 66; reason for the appearance of, 92; reason for expounding his teaching by, 200; significance of holding right hands of disciples by, 243; significance of patting his disciples by, 238, 248; revolutionary, 177; tales describing the past lives of, 193; theories concerning the nature of the body of, 195; true intent of, 201; true nature of, 163; upholding as their mentor after the death of, 123; will of, 122
Shariputra, 35
Shih K'uang, 73
Shiiji Shiro, 73
Shingon school, 204
Shimizu, Masao, 60

Shinto talisman, Makiguchi's refusal of the, 110
Shirai, Toku, propagation efforts of, 36–37
Sholokhov, Mikhail, 261
sight, benefits of purifying the sense of, 77; sense of, 74
six sense organs, 4; purifying the, 68
slander, Nichiren Daishonin and 226
smell, 73, 76; benefit of purifying the sense of, 77
society, 144; achieving prosperity in, 39; action in, 229; creating a true democratic, 39; source that guide, 239; stagnation of Japanese, 255
Socrates, 8, 198
Soka Gakkai, 68; benefit of protecting the, 18; development of the, 91–92; Ikeda's poem for the seventieth anniversary of the, 103–04; reason for the appearance of the, 96; Toda and, 227
Soka Gakkai International, 30, 103, 159, 206; activities of the, 43, 51, 121, 194, 208; conduct of the leaders of the, 114–15; existence of the, 93; mission of the, 31–32, 173; propagation efforts of members of the, 36–40; reason for the existence of the, 226
Soka Gakkai International members, benefit of working for the welfare of, 173; effect of disparaging, 114–15; effect of forgetting the debt of gratitude to, 250–51; effect of using, for personal gain, 173; identity of, 208–09; importance of praying for fellow, 207; mission of the, 227–29; modern tales of, 194; protecting, 83